Illicit Drugs
Use and control

Adrian Barton

Routledge
Taylor & Francis Group

LONDON AND NEW YORK

First published 2003
by RoutledgeFalmer
11 New Fetter Lane, London EC4P 4EE

Simultaneously published in the USA and Canada
by RoutledgeFalmer
29 West 35th Street, New York, NY 10001

Reprinted 2004

Routledge is an imprint of the Taylor & Francis Group

Typeset in Garamond by BC Typesetting, Bristol
Printed and bound in Great Britain by
The Cromwell Press, Trowbridge, Wiltshire

British Library Cataloguing in Publication Data
A catalogue record for this book is available from the British Library

Library of Congress Cataloging in Publication Data
Barton, Adrian.
    Illicit drugs: use and control/Adrian Barton.
        p.   cm.
Includes bibliographical references and index.
        1. Drug abuse–Great Britain. 2. Drug traffic–Great Britain.
3. Narcotics, Control of–Great Britain.   I. Title.
    HV5840.G7 B34 2003
    362.29′0941–dc21   2002151948

ISBN 0–415–28171–7 (hbk)
ISBN 0–415–28172–5 (pbk)

Contents

Figures and tables

Figures

Tables

1 Introduction

As Dorian hurried up its three rickety steps, the heavy odour of opium met him. He heaved a deep breath, and his nostrils quivered with pleasure. . . . Dorian winced, and looked around at the grotesque things that lay in such fantastic postures on the ragged mattresses. The twisted limbs, the gaping mouths, the strange lustreless eyes, fascinated him. He knew in what strange heavens they were suffering, and what dull hells were teaching them the secrets of some new joy.[1]

'This is a sex-crazing drug menace . . . a gloomy monster of destruction.'[2]

Compare the two quotations above: the first is fiction and relates to Dorian Gray's visit to an opium den in the East End of London at the turn of the nineteenth century; the other is journalistic, part of a series of headlines taken from American newspapers of the 1930s and relates to cannabis use. The point of using them in this introduction is their timelessness: they could have been culled from today's fiction or newspaper headlines, because they seem to reflect the same concerns and issues that we have about illicit drugs at the start of the twenty-first century. Their inclusion demonstrates that our fascination, horror and concern with illicit drug use, often demonstrated in equal measure, is not new, nor are the facets of drug use that fuel those concerns a new phenomenon.

At first glance, this work simply falls into the same pattern: it talks about illicit drug use in terms of 'problems' and 'solutions', both of which are normative statements representing a value system that sees the recreational use of certain stimulants as wrong and in need of control. What marks it out is the fact that, ultimately, it questions the nature of the 'problem' and makes a concerted effort to explore a range of factors relating to illicit drug use. This is timely as illicit drug use is a prime area of concern and one that is generating a considerable degree of debate in Britain and beyond. In Britain, for example, among other things, we are in the throes of a process that is reclassifying cannabis, effectively decriminalizing possession. Further afield, it is coming to be recognized that the overthrow of the Taliban in Afghanistan is being viewed in that region as a green light for renewed and increased cultivation of the opium poppy, almost invariably leading to an increase in the amount of heroin available in Britain and the rest of Europe. Domestically and globally, illicit drugs are one of the key issues and problem areas for governments and society, leading to pressure on governments to solve the problem.

These problems fall into a number of discrete but connected areas. For example, in terms of the responsible organization, is illicit drug use a medical or law and order problem? Philosophically, how can we prohibit some mind-altering substances yet openly promote others, and even, as with wine during communion, use them as an integral part of some Christian ceremonies? Strategically, should we seek to stop illicit drugs at the point of production, point of entry into the country, at the point of distribution or the point of consumption? Economically, are we prepared to subsidize replacement crops in developing nations in order to prevent production of opium or coca? Educationally, do we aim for zero use or promote a harm minimization approach? Tactically, do we fight a 'war on drugs' or negotiate an 'honourable peace'? So it goes on.

Obviously, in targeting the drugs issue we are dealing with a subject that encompasses a range of academic disciplines and thus provides myriad oppor-tunities to analyse quite specific aspects of the illicit drug scene. For instance, illicit drugs can be and have been examined under the rubric of history, sociology, criminology, economics, medical science, politics, philosophy and policy studies. There are also elements of geography and anthropology evident in some works. It is even possible to use literary criticism to analyse illicit drug use! The result can be a bewildering amalgam of facts and directions, each with an important part to play, but somewhat confusing when viewed as separate entities.

The aim of this book is to draw together some of those disparate threads and provide the reader with a broad overview of the history, development and contemporary state of the British drug scene. Inevitably, such an approach occasionally sacrifices detail to grasp the wider picture. The conten-tion here is that specific detail surrounding, say, the link between drugs and crime can be found in specialist publications. It is the aim of this book to locate specific aspects of illicit drug use, such as drugs and crime, within a broad framework of interrelated events and circumstances, allowing the reader to gauge the complexities involved in defining and solving the 'drug problem'.

With that broader framework in mind, the book is divided into three sections. The first section, Chapter 2 to 4, introduces and locates illicit drug use and associated policy responses within a British context. In detail, Chapter 2 offers an historical overview of drug use from the early 1800s to the 1960s. Chapter 3 builds on the conclusion of the previous chapter, namely the apparent rise in the misuse of illicit drugs during the past four decades. It takes as its core the problems we have in measuring drug misuse. It compares and contrasts two types of measurement: official statistics compiled by treatment providers and the criminal justice system; and self-report data compiled by non-practice organizations and academics. It then reviews the methodological weaknesses of each approach and highlights the difficulties in measuring a hidden population such as drug users. The chapter concludes by employing the available data to draw a picture of contemporary drug misuse in Britain.

Chapter 4 sets out to explore the official responses to drug misuse in Britain. It examines the two key approaches to illicit drug use in Britain: the medico-socio treatment model and the criminal justice based punishment model. It begins by arguing that policing in the context of drug misusers is based around notions of control, control that can be exerted via either the medical or criminal justice systems, and it reviews the content of the Misuse of Drugs Act 1971. It examines the manner in which the medical profession polices drug misusers through treatment regimes and prescription policies. The chapter concludes with a discussion of the dual nature of the British approach to policing the same 'problem'.

The second section of the book traces the life of some of the illicit drugs available in Britain, moving from cultivation and synthesis, through market based exchanges, the sources and problems of funding which drug markets create for users and the state, to a review of the consequences of drug misuse. It begins with Chapter 5, which marks a watershed in the work. Up to this point drug misuse has been discussed in a somewhat narrow and parochial manner. The purpose of Chapter 5 is to alert the reader to the fact that drug misuse in Britain is, in fact, part of a much wider global phenomenon. Following this, the chapter provides a geographical breakdown of the main drug growing nations and their outputs. The chapter then focuses on the impact the growth and production of drugs has for the economies of some of the drug producing nations. The chapter finally moves to explore the production of synthetic drugs in Europe.

Chapter 6 builds upon the foundation laid above. It suggests that given the economic impact of drug production it may aid understanding to view illicit drugs as tradable commodities above all else. To support this view, the chapter begins by reviewing some basic economic theory concerning the relationship between supply and demand and their combined effect on prices. It moves away from economic theory and outlines the nature of the drug market in Britain, identifying key players and their respective roles in each stage of the retailing of illicit drugs. The chapter concludes with a review of the potential which the application of economic theory has as a controlling mechanism for dealing with drug misuse.

Chapter 7 looks at the cost of drug use in a number of terms. Having identified and clarified the economic aspects of drug misuse, this chapter turns its attention towards the problems drug misuse pose for the user and society both in terms of paying for the goods and in health and social welfare related costs. The chapter begins by exploring the links between drugs and crime. It then offers a typology of drug criminals and identifies and discusses three distinct, but not mutually exclusive, groups. It then broadens the definition of cost and asks the reader to view costs not solely in economic terms but also in terms of health and social welfare.

The third section begins with an examination of the current policies adopted by Britain in its attempt to combat illicit drug use. It then moves to explore the normalization thesis. Following this it compares the development of policies in Britain with those adopted elsewhere, specifically the Netherlands and Sweden. Here, the links between socio-economic, cultural and political systems and drug control strategies are explored.

Chapter 8 looks specifically at the demand for drugs in terms of the normalization thesis and its links with youth sub-cultures. Chapter 9 takes as its focus contemporary developments in drug policy, locating them in wider developments elsewhere in social policy, namely the growth of the partnership approach. This is used to explain the growth in the concept of harm reduction, and comment is made on the transition from harm reduction as a strategy based around individual need to its more recent application to encompass individual and societal harm. The chapter also reviews key legislative and policy developments since 1990, in particular *Tackling Drugs Together* (1995) and *Tackling Drugs to Build a Better Britain* (1998).

The work concludes by comparing Britain's drug policy with that of two of its near neighbours. Outlining the usefulness of comparative work, it also seeks to alert readers to the need to consider a number of socio-cultural, political and economic factors when making comparisons. The chapter then reviews the drug policies of two nations. The Netherlands has a well-known policy of tolerance, but the socio-cultural influence is noted as a key to the Dutch approach. Sweden on the other hand has one of the continent's hard-line approaches towards drugs. Again, a variety of factors is examined to cover the reasons behind this. The work closes by offering a review of the impact the British state and society have had on our own approach to drug misuse.

Before embarking on the first substantive part of the book it is important to clarify one point. Throughout the book, the terms 'drug', 'illicit drug' and 'substance' will be used interchangeably, although the preferred option is 'illicit drug'. These terms relate to all substances covered under the 1971 Misuse of Drugs Act and nothing else, except where specifically stated. The work does not, nor is it meant to, cover licit substances used by persons under the legal age of consumption, neither does it refer to the misuse of substances such as aerosols, lighter fluid, correction fluids and the like. Equally, it does not refer to the misuse, either through zealous or uncontrolled prescription, or misappropriation, of prescription drugs. This is not to say that I do not recognize the potential harm these substances pose, it is simply that this book takes as its focus drugs that are outlawed for all and sundry.

Finally, although I am the sole author of this book and take full responsibility for its content, it is important to note that a work such as this always involves other people, a number of whom need to be mentioned and thanked.

Much gratitude goes to David Smith, recently retired from the University of Glamorgan, for his initial enthusiasm about this project. Had he not provided me with the opportunity and encouragement to develop this wide-ranging approach to teaching and researching illicit drug use, I would never have embarked on this book. Thanks must also be extended to my colleagues at the University of Plymouth who have provided solid support and even managed to continue to look interested when I have droned on and on about this work. Mari Shullaw and James McNally at Routledge have always been on hand to offer advice about any queries I may have had. Once again, Sally and her American computer came to the rescue in the end. Finally, I should like to acknowledge my debt to three people who, in all probability, will never know of this work's existence yet who could not have been more instrumental in its inception all those years ago: Dave, Keith and Andrea. I can honestly say that without them this book would never have been started.

Notes

1 Wilde, Oscar (1986) *A Picture of Dorian Gray*. London: Marshall Cavendish.
2 Goode, E. and Ben-Yehuda, N. (1994) *Moral Panics*. Oxford: Blackwell.

2 An historical overview of the social construction of the British 'drug problem'

Introduction

This opening chapter provides an historical overview of the manner in which many of those substances now categorized as illicit drugs came to be so. It is important to begin in this manner for two reasons. Firstly, it sets the scene for the rest of the work, inasmuch as it alerts the reader to the fact that the book sees the 'drug problem' as essentially a social, political and economic construct. Secondly, it provides an historical framework that is central to developing an understanding of contemporary British drug policy. As Berridge (1989: 34) notes, 'history can indicate . . . the need for an awareness of the determinants, attitudes and policies, and an indication of the nature and consequences of options'. In this way, history encourages the reader to view substance use through a variety of lenses so that the British experience may come to be seen as a consequence of a number of interrelated historical and contemporary events, some of which are totally outside the control of British policy makers.

In order to achieve this, the chapter focuses on six eras in which events relating to substance use have collectively shaped the current approach to the control of some substances. The chapter begins by examining the period from 1800 to 1850, a period when the use of, and market in, substances such as opium went largely unchecked by the British state. The second era looks at the period from 1850 to 1900. These five decades saw the beginnings of public concern and debate around the unrestricted use of opium in Britain, and a questioning of continued British involvement with the opium trade. Key in this change was the influence of both morality and medicine in the early construction of the 'drug problem'.

From there, the chapter moves on to detail events in the period 1900 to 1926. This is an important era as it marks the beginnings of a dual approach to substance use within British policy, as well as charting the growing influence of international treaties on domestic policy. The discussion then moves across time from 1927 to 1964, noting that this period was one of relative inactivity as far as substance use was concerned. However, the final two eras, 1964 to 1979 and 1980 until the present are characterized as periods of intense activity as the British state seemingly struggles to cope with a burgeoning 'drug problem'.

1800 to 1850: the era of *laissez-faire* in substance control

There are any number of starting points that could have been chosen in a history of substance use in Britain. For example, reference could have been made to the Viking warriors' use of the mushroom *Aminita musicara* to induce feelings of aggression, or to the fact that in medieval times plants such as mandrake, henbane and belladonna were used by some to stimulate visions and a sense of flying (Grilly 1998: 2). However, I have chosen 1800 as a start date in order to align the work with the beginnings of modern Britain, a period which Fraser (1984) sees as the genesis of our contemporary approach to civil society and social policy.

One of the immediate features of the period between 1800 and 1850 is the relative lack of anxiety exhibited by society over substances that today cause us considerable concern. In our contemporary language, substance use in the early 1800s was 'normalized', and for the majority of the nineteenth century supply was unrestricted (Berridge 1989). Indeed, while most histories of Britain acknowledge that alcohol has always had a widespread appeal and usage (Stearn 1975), few give space to the fact that 'Opium has been consumed wholesale, largely with equanimity, in Britain for centuries' (Harding 1998: 1). As an example, Berridge (1989: 24) estimates that home consumption of opium in the period 1800 to 1850 was around 2–3 lb per thousand of the population. Nor was it only opium: morphine, cannabis and latterly cocaine were all freely available and unrestricted, although it appears that opium was by far the most used by the general public (Berridge 1989; Mott and Bean 1998).

As an indication of normalization of opium use, Berridge (1989: 23) cites an inquest held in Hull during 1854 where the coroner noted that a baby was poisoned due to an overdose of laudanum (a liquid opiate consisting of raw opium, distilled water and alcohol). The child was given the laudanum as a result of it being mistaken for syrup of rhubarb. Berridge further remarks that the original sale was to a child messenger of six or seven years old. It appears that the grocer kept opium-based products on a shelf alongside 'other bottles of the same shape and size'. Why, then, was there so little concern over the use of what are now seen as dangerous drugs?

There are two significant sets of reasons. Firstly, at the beginning of the eighteenth century the medical profession was only just starting to capitalize on the advances set in train both by the Enlightenment (Gamble 1981) and the industrial revolution (Hobsbawm 1969). As a result, medicine was often far from 'scientific'. For example, doctors were not always well trained, held in high esteem, or easily accessible for large sections of the population (Coleman 1985). Such was the mistrust of the motives of the medical profession that Fraser (1984: 59) notes Britain saw many anti-medical riots during this period, especially around the 1832 cholera outbreak (Lawrence 1994: 49). Thus, at the start of the 1800s the medical profession was only just beginning to establish itself in the form we know today, and certainly did not have the professional or political power, or widespread public support to 'own' the control of opium or other drugs.

As a consequence, for many people the locus of medical attention was the family. Treatment and cures were often dependent upon folk remedies and recourse to tried and tested methods. The lack of trust, accessibility and affordability of doctors experienced by large tracts of the population meant that self-medication was widespread and often the only option. Within this framework, opium and opium derivatives had a long-established position as a 'cure-all'. This is apparent in the literature of the time: in *The Trumpet Major* (1880), Thomas Hardy depicts Bob Loveday falling into a state of unconsciousness due to the over-use of poppy head tea; a point endorsed by London *et al.* (1990) who note the prevalence of poppy head tea drinking during this period. Moreover, the absence of a professional body to oversee the dispensing of substances such as opium meant that there was a variety of outlets. As we have seen, grocers and hawkers vied with pharmacists in the supply of all manner of substances (Berridge 1978: 438).

The key point to recognize here is that opium use, especially among the working classes, was confined to a 'culturally sanctioned practice restricted largely to self-medication' (Harding 1998: 3). Among the working class in some areas of Britain, most notably the Fens, regular and sustained opiate use had reached endemic proportions (Berridge 1989: 24). The result was that opiate use was not the object of moral opprobrium, due, in the main, to its associations with medical and not 'luxurious' use (Edwards 1981).

That is not to say that there was a lack of recreational use of opiates. De Quincey (1821) charted its non-medical use in *Confessions of an Opium Eater*, but as Berridge (1989) remarks, public reaction was muted, never rising far above mild curiosity. Moreover, as Robson (1994: 127) notes, recreational use was seen to be the domain of 'creative types' such as authors like Barratt-Browning, Coleridge, Collins and Dickens. Similarly, there were some fears expressed over the recreational use of opium by Chinese in and around London's docklands, but it is arguable this had more to do with issues of race, especially 'otherness' and concern over 'foreigners', than worries around opium use (Berridge and Edwards 1981; Robson 1994).

Therefore, one of the primary reasons that opiate use was seen as unproblematic at the beginning of the nineteenth century was widespread social acceptance, and use, of opiates. The result of this was a lack of moral condemnation and an acceptance of use. In addition, the fact that there was an absence of a professional body able either to claim expertise or to establish the power to exercise control over the use and supply of opium and other substances must also be taken into consideration. The second set of reasons why opiate use was not considered problematic during this period is explained in the position of the British government, especially in relation to the global trade in opium and, more specifically, to the smuggling of opium, grown in British colonial India, into China.

At its most extreme, Hooker (1996) argues that

> By the 1830s, the English had become the major drug-trafficking criminal organization in the world; very few drug cartels of the twentieth century can even touch the England of the early nineteenth century in sheer size of criminality. This trade [in opium] had produced, quite literally, a country filled with drug addicts, as opium parlours proliferated all throughout China in the early part of the nineteenth century. . . .

Certainly, Britain was heavily involved in the illegal importation of opium into China. Chesneaux *et al*. (1976: 54) chart the growth of the trade during the period from 1820 to 1835. They state that in 1820 the number of crates of opium being smuggled into China stood at 9,708, which rose to 35,445 crates by 1835.[1] The effect of this trade was devastating to Chinese society. Chesneaux *et al*. (1976: 55) note that

> Around 1835, senior officials and generals assumed that 90 per cent of their staff were opium smokers. Estimates of the total number in the population were various and imprecise: Lin Ze-xu reckoned that there were 4 million opium smokers in China, while a British doctor in Canton set the figure at 12 million. Because of opium, business slowed down, the standard of living fell, and public services no longer worked smoothly.

The motives behind the British state's entry into drug smuggling are complex, and a detailed examination is beyond the remit and scope of this work. However, it is important to point out that the move was a calculated one, designed to balance British trade with China, which, at the time, had a closed-door policy to foreign goods. A desire to force China to accept imports from Britain and British colonial India, coupled with an unwillingness by the British state to continue to pay for Chinese goods in silver, led directly to the British government sanctioning the breaking of Chinese laws relating to the use of opium. Some would add that it was a calculated move to destabilize China and precipitate a conflict in order to 'improve' trading relations between the nations. If this was the case, British strategy succeeded when in 1839 Britain declared war on China following a series of arrests and confiscations of opium in and around the Canton area. The ensuing conflict brought a comfortable victory for the British, and led to the signing of the Treaty of Nanking in 1842, which opened up parts of China to western merchants (Chesneaux *et al*. 1976: ch. 3).

Thus, the second set of reasons behind the relaxed attitude to opium in the first half of the 1800s can be seen to revolve around the role of the British state. Clearly, it would have been difficult for a nation to go to war to protect the trade in opium while at the same time striving for control or prohibition at home. However, this situation did not last, and by the time the century ended there was a discernible feeling among both the public and professionals that certain substances were problematic and in need of strict control, added to which, as we shall see, there was growing international pressure, notably from the USA.

1850 to 1900: merging morality and medicine; changing definitions and perceptions

Domestically, two social groups were instrumental in the development and growth of this change of attitude towards opium and other substances: the medical and pharmaceutical professions were keen to cement their newly won public acclaim triggered by improvements in public health (South 1997); and the increasingly influential moral philanthropists, many of whom were inspired by religious zeal (Thane 1996). In many respects, the concerns of these two groups were intertwined, and across the last part of the nineteenth century their respective claims became mutually reinforcing. In turn, their growing confidence, alongside increasing public support, enabled pressure to be exerted upon the British government to tighten the controls governing domestic use of substances, and to desist from participating in the global opium trade.

Although the widespread use of opiates continued unabated post-1850, the situation was giving rise to increasing public concern, especially in relation to the use of opium-based products as 'quieteners' for infants, and the rising numbers of accidental poisonings this practice generated (Edwards 1981). This coincided with more specific worries about the state of children, stimulated by public outrage over the issue of 'baby-farming' and the systematic infanticide of young children who were fostered to unscrupulous professional child minders (Burke 1996). Moreover, as medical knowledge increased in the 1800s there was a re-evaluation of opium and its long-term effects on those users who had increased habitual use.

Harding (1998) provides an interesting analysis of this period, examining developments through a Foucaultian perspective. He argues that prior to 1850, habitual use of opium was recognized, but seen as an effect of the drug itself or as result of the social condition of the user. Hence, at that time there was an absence of moral condemnation of the user, due to the fact that the addictive properties of opium were seen as the problem rather than any moral laxity on the part of the user. However, by the middle of the 1800s there was a growing chorus of voices linking opium use to morality: Harding (1998: 3) cites a Dr Thompson, writing in 1840, who suggested that opium use by women 'affected all that was good and virtuous . . .'.

Equally, the developing medical professions, firmly rooted in middle-class ideology, were keen to establish control over the use and supply of opium.

Self-medication and widespread availability ran counter to their aspirations for increasing professionalization of medical and pharmaceutical practice and knowledge (Duin and Sutcliffe 1992). Added to this, the medical professions were beginning to gain some form of public recognition and, as Lawrence (1994) notes, were keen to cement the advances they had made in public confidence following their work in the cholera epidemics of 1853 to 1854. Lawrence (1994: 29) also notes the impact of one other factor on the growth of confidence in the medical profession, the use of medicine as a form of social policing

> A rationally organized society, so the texts on the medical police said, would be based on knowledge of how men's minds, and thus their morals, were produced from the social and physical environment in which they lived. Who better to study this and prescribe for change, the texts went on, than a single body of professional medical men?

This concept, according to Harding (1998), led to an increasing concern on the part of the medical profession with the behaviour of the working class. This was especially the case in respect of their use and abuse of certain substances, with very real concern being voiced over the use of opium as a cheap alternative to alcohol, itself seen as a corrupting influence on the 'deserving poor' (Midwinter 1994).

By 1850, the medical profession's growing confidence, increasing public and political support and acknowledged scientific knowledge afforded it a firm base from which to begin to make inroads into all manner of social practices, as well as to start to take control and ownership of previously society-wide practices in, for instance, public health (Hobsbawm 1969). An example more germane to this book can be seen in the 1868 Pharmacy Act, which Berridge (1978) views as a result of the confluence of a number of factors, including increasing medical concern over the effects of opium, the general concerns over the need to control poisons, and worries over the morality of the working class. The resultant 1868 Act started to regulate the sale of opium, allowing only registered pharmacists to sell it. Interestingly, however, patent medicines, many of which were opium-based, were exempted from the restrictions of the Act, thus allowing the general sale of opium-based products to continue.

Another manifestation of this growth in medical power was a reformulation of the habitual use of opium, a process that entailed a move away from a perspective which saw addiction as a property of the drug, and towards a view that the addict was an 'irresponsible individual wilfully adopting a course of self-destruction' (Harding 1998: 4), to be blamed for their addiction and then visited upon with moral indignation and medical treatment. It is at this stage that the growing power and influence of the medical profession became intertwined with the burgeoning late-Victorian moral philanthropic movement, and particularly in the case of opium, with the Society for the Suppression of the Opium Trade (SSOT). Like many of their peers, these particular moral philanthropists were bent on promoting temperance, thrift and rational recreation for the respectable upper working classes.

Formed in 1874, the Society for the Suppression of the Opium Trade quickly became 'the most prominent organization in the Victorian anti-opium movement' (Harding 1998: 5). The SSOT was part of a general moral crusade undertaken by members of the religious group, the Society of Friends, or Quakers, as they are more commonly known. Paralleling the influence of the Calvinist movement on the development of capitalism (Weber 1976), it was the Quaker movement's approach to life that enabled Quaker-inspired groups such as the SSOT to exert such a profound influence on British society.

Harding (1998: 6–10) argues that a number of factors combined to provide the Quakers with the discursive power needed to impact upon public perceptions of opiate use. Firstly, Quakers have a unique view on the influence of the corporeal world on the soul. Essentially, the path to righteousness needs a combination of prayer and a dynamic pursuit of activities that feed the soul's morality, as well as an avoidance of factors that adversely affect the soul. Thus, pride, extravagance, self-indulgence, extreme behaviour and luxurious living are to be avoided. Harding (1998: 7) suggests that Quakers were able to implicate the non-medical use of opium as damaging to morality. In addition, the Quakers possessed a formidable organizational structure that spawned some of the most influential philanthropic reformist movements of the Victorian period, including the National Temperance Society and the Anti-Slave Society.

These organizations gained the necessary gravitas thanks to an overt commitment by Quakers to their beliefs, allied with a knowledge base derived from hands-on information gathered by Quakers working within poor communities. This information was then disseminated across the whole Quaker organization via regular 'business meetings' where data on the physical and moral condition of Britain's poor was shared and discussed. Harding (1998: 7) notes that 'The Quakers' organizational structure functioned as an apparatus for surveillance of society's moral order'. In this way, the Quaker movement acquired social prestige and a reputation for providing the 'truth', in terms of social commentaries.

Concomitant with the formation of the SSOT, and its overtly moralistic stance on opiate use, came the growth of concerns within the medical profession about substance misuse generally, and inebriation specifically. This led to the foundation of the Society for the Study of Inebriety in 1884, headed by a medical doctor, Dr Kerr. Kerr, and like-minded physicians on both sides of the Atlantic, began to reformulate notions and definitions of addiction. It will be recalled that prior to this period opium addiction was seen as a result of the properties of the drug and not of any failing on the part of the user. This changed dramatically, to the point where

What emerged by the end of the [nineteenth] century was the hybrid 'disease of the will' concept, in which the eugenic bias of scientific thinking emphasized the importance of race and constitutional inheritance in predisposition to addiction. It was a form of 'moral insanity' or 'moral bankruptcy'.

(Berridge 1978: 458)

This allowed the moral imperative of the SSOT to mesh with the growing professionalization of the doctors and their desire to own and control the right to prescribe certain substances, and, as some of a more radical persuasion would argue, act as moral police to the working classes (Doyal and Pennell 1979). Berridge (1978: 459) expands this point, arguing that there was significant cross-fertilization between both groups. The powerful combination of medical 'expertise' and moral high ground influenced 'educated public opinion', and began to transform opium use into a deviant activity, in need of more strict state control. This groundswell of public opinion brought calls for a tightening of legislation, as can be witnessed in the increase in legislation aimed at controlling the negative effects of opium use. For example, the medical profession attempted, but failed, to include opium addiction in the 1888 Inebriates Act, which allowed for the voluntary detention of habitual drunkards. Undaunted, the medical profession were able to utilize their diagnostic powers to control opium addicts two years later following the passing of the 1890 Lunacy Act (South 1997).

The British state still maintained and supported the opium trade, fighting a second opium war with China between 1856 and 1860 (Chesneaux *et al.* 1976). Nevertheless, at the very end of the century the government responded to growing public concern over the opium trade by setting up a Royal Commission on Opium. Berridge and Edwards (1981) note that the ensuing report, published in 1895, is generally seen as a whitewash, finding in favour of a continuation of the trade. Moreover, the British state seemed uninterested in the problems of addiction, and was reluctant to make it part of government policy (Berridge 1978). Importantly, however, a number of authors point out that the opium trade was diminishing in economic importance by the end of the 1800s (Edwards 1981; South 1997; Mott and Bean 1998), as was the domestic consumption of opiate-based products. Equally, there was growing international concern about the use of opium and other substances. By the end of the 1800s opium use in British society still remained 'something quite normal . . . everyone has laudanum at home' (Robertson 1975; in Berridge 1978), but the dawning of a new century would see a sustained and successful challenge to this situation.

1900 to 1926: the birth of the 'British system'

The period 1900 to 1926 marks the birth of our present system of control and also represents the era in which substance use and misuse came to be recognized by the state as a serious social, political and economic problem. It is important to note that, as Berridge (1978: 461) remarks, '. . . the attitudes which underlay control . . . were already formed. Developments in the 1900s brought into play the complex motivations which had marked responses to opiate use in the nineteenth century.' Those attitudes can be best understood as a continuum along which substance misuse is seen as a medical problem in need of treatment at one extreme, and substance misuse as a vice in need of control via law and order is at the other.

Still the British state was reluctant to become involved in any policy initiative relating to the use and control of substances, beyond a general concern over poisons. This can be evidenced in the Poisons and Pharmacy Act 1908, which amended the 1868 Pharmacy Act but made no changes to the controls put in place in 1868. That apart, the British state exhibited little or no visible interest in substance control. This may be partially due to the apparent decline of opiate use, and the misuse of other substances, including alcohol, in the early part of the 1900s (Edwards 1981: 7), due to improvements in social conditions wrought by the 'Great Liberal Reform Period', the years from 1906 to 1914. It may also be the case that social attitudes towards opium and other substances had shifted from the concerns of the late 1800s and moved towards a 'more relaxed co-existence with the opiates' (Edwards 1981: 7).

However, the seventeen years from 1909 to 1926 witnessed a massive shift from this *laissez-faire* approach to a situation which saw the stringent control of a number of substances. This section explores some of the factors responsible for that change and details the legislation that helped to produce the 'British system'. Essentially, there are two significant forces of change: first, the advent of international concern forcing Britain to take action to control certain substances; and, second, the developments of moral panics concerning the use of substances, especially during the First World War.

Once again, Britain's involvement in supplying opium to China plays an important part in influencing policy developments. Mott and Bean (1998: 32) refer to the fact that in order for the United States of America (USA) to control the opium problem on the newly acquired Philippines, the USA decided gradually to prohibit the sale of opium over a three-year period starting in 1904. This would have proven difficult if the flow of opium into China from European nations had remained constant. Hence, to facilitate the implementation and success of their policy for the Philippines, the USA arranged an international convention, inviting major European trading nations as well as representatives from the producing nations of Turkey and Persia to attend.

At first Britain was reluctant to participate, seeing little point in the process since in 1907 Britain had negotiated the Anglo–Chinese agreement with China to reduce shipments of opium by 10 per cent per year up until 1916 when the trade would cease, thus marking the end of its economic importance. Eventually Britain became one of thirteen attendees at the

1909 Shanghai Commission. At the request of Britain and the Netherlands, the findings of the Commission were only recommendations with no binding force on the signatories. Nevertheless, as Mott and Bean (1998) point out, the Shanghai Commission marked the starting point for the international control of substances.

Three years later, again following agitation from the USA, the Hague Convention was signed and circulated for ratification as international law. The 1912 Hague Convention had four main provisions:

1   the production and distribution, including import and export, of raw opium to be controlled by national legislation;
2   opium smoking to be gradually and effectively repressed;
3   the manufacture, sale and consumption of morphine and cocaine and their salts to be limited by national legislation to medical and legitimate purposes, and to be controlled by a system of licensing;
4   statistics relating to the drug trade, and information about national laws and administrative arrangements, to be exchanged through the Netherlands government.

Following a further two conferences at The Hague in 1913 and 1914, Britain ratified the Convention in 1914 (Walker 1991), although somewhat reluctantly. Robson (1994: 131) cites Britain's continued economic interest in the drug trade as a reason for this tardiness, arguing that Britain's role as the major morphine producer was a significant barrier to ratification. Interestingly, and demonstrating a lack of state concern over substance misuse up to this point, there was no government department responsible for substance control, and none willing to assume the mantle. Subsequently, early British substance misuse control became the responsibility of the Privy Council Office (Mott and Bean 1998).

Such a reluctance to take on new work is understandable at a time when Britain and the rest of the world were plunged into a war that was to wreak havoc across mainland Europe. In a more parochial context the First World War was also to have an influence on the control of substances in Britain, and it is to this aspect of the conflict that this chapter now turns its attention.

Central here is the Defence of the Realm Act (DORA). Thurlow (1994: 48) provides a clear description of DORA, stating that 'DORA, and its attendant regulations for the period 1914 to 1920, meant that a watered down form of martial law was superimposed on the workings of the common law and civil jurisdiction'. Citing DORA allowed wartime leaders to intervene in all manner of areas of state and social life. For instance, Taylor (1992) provides an example where DORA regulations were imposed to censor news reports in the early war years. Similarly, he notes that Lloyd George, the then Chancellor of the Exchequer, was prepared to invoke DORA to ensure unskilled and female labour were allowed to work in the munitions factories, despite the protests of skilled engineers.

How did such far-reaching powers, clearly central to Britain winning the war, come to be applied to substance use? Mott and Bean (1998) suggest that DORA's ambit was extended to substances following a series of moral panics over the use and abuse of cocaine and opiates by British and Canadian troops, allied to wider concerns that substance consumption by munitions workers hampered their ability to work at capacity. It appears that troops on leave from or preparing to go to the trenches were in the habit of visiting prostitutes and taking all manner of substances, possibly as a reaction to being sent into the trenches, where 'Kitchener's army found its graveyard' (Taylor 1992: 61).

The government had pre-empted this situation to a degree, making the sale or gift of intoxicants to a member of the armed forces, with the intent to make him drunk or incapable, an offence under the initial DORA (1914) legislation. However, there were no such controls over civilians. Robson (1994: 131) comments that legislation pre-1916 was weak and that there was a 'roaring' black market in cocaine and other drugs as soldiers were 'keen to get hold of drugs which might make life in the trenches a bit more acceptable'. He notes that it was possible to buy morphine and cocaine kits, complete with syringe and spare needles in Harrods. These kits were labelled 'A Useful Present for Friends at the Front'.

This state of affairs was causing concern for the Army commanders who, in May 1916, banned the non-medical sale or supply of cocaine to armed forces personnel. However, this had very little impact upon the sale and use of cocaine among the troops, leading, in July 1916, to DORA 40B coming into force. It is here, as a result of moral panics over the use of substances by its troops, that the British state made its first big inroads into defining and controlling 'harmful' substances. DORA 40B restricted those who could possess cocaine to authorized persons, including doctors and retail pharmacists. Transactions in cocaine were to be recorded in order that they could be inspected by the Secretary of State. These regulations were further amended in December 1916 when licences were issued for the manufacture of cocaine, making it an offence to issue a prescription for cocaine, other than in accordance with the legislation. Importantly, the ability to check records on the use and supply of cocaine was extended to police officers of the rank of inspector and above (Mott and Bean 1998). Robson (1994: 131) adds that DORA 40B placed some restrictions on opium use at the same time.

As South (1997: 937) notes, 'a significant step had been taken', because implementation of DORA 40B meant that unauthorized supply and all unauthorized possession had been criminalized. In turn, this moved the Home Office to centre stage in terms of government policy on substance use and misuse. At this point it might be worthwhile to note the absence of a Ministry for Health; such a ministry did not emerge until 1919 (Leathard

2000). Thus, even if it had wanted to, the wartime government may have felt uneasy entrusting the policing of substances to a medical service whose 'administration . . . had been found inadequate' (Leathard 2000: 12). Further domestic legislation followed renewed international pressure at the end of the First World War. The Treaty of Versailles, which marked the end of hostilities, contained a clause which required all signatories to introduce domestic legislation to deal with their respective drug 'problems' as a condition of accession (Lowes 1966; Bruun *et al.* 1975). In Britain this led to the Dangerous Drugs Act 1920.

Edwards (1981) suggests that the passing of this legislation marked the birth of our contemporary system. It could also be added that the 1920 Act set in train a still unresolved dilemma as to which arm of the state should 'own' the drug problem: in short, is drug misuse a medical or criminal justice issue? This will be explored in depth in a later chapter. For now, it is important to note that from 1920 onwards possession of all opiate and cocaine-based products without the necessary authorization or medical prescription became proscribed, with heavy legal penalties and social disapproval for those infringing the regulations.

It will be of little surprise, considering that the state department with responsibility was the Home Office, that the state response to the 1920 Dangerous Drugs Act was decidedly penal in nature (Berridge 1989). There are two points worthy of consideration here. Firstly, and this will be discussed in more detail below, the Home Office was particularly keen to emulate developments in the USA, where the passing of the Harrison Act in 1914 had practically outlawed the medical prescribing of opiates and thus created a very minor role for the medical profession in the 'ownership' of the drug problem. Thus, according to South (1997) non-medical use, possession and supply came to be perceived as criminal matters.

Moreover, and due in some measure to the above point, the public's reaction to drug use had shifted considerably in the century between its 'mild interest' in De Quincey's revelations of opium eating in 1820 and the death of actress Billie Carleton in 1919 and dance instructor Freda Kempton in 1922. There was a high degree of concern over drug use, and, again paralleling developments in the previous century, the media emphasized the involvement of 'outsiders' and 'foreigners' in the supply of these newly dangerous substances. Mott and Bean (1998: 40), for example, point to extensive media coverage of the trails of Edgar Manning, a Jamaican, and Brilliant Chang, a Chinese, for their involvement in trafficking cocaine.

Such levels of public unrest had an impact upon the government and 1923 saw the Dangerous Drug Amendment Act enter the statute books. Berridge (1989) notes that this new Act provided a significant impetus to the penal approach to substance control. Although this initial raft of substance control legislation gravitated towards a punitive and legalistic approach, it should not be assumed that the medical profession, so instrumental during the previous century in bringing substance misuse to the public's attention, was ready to relinquish its claim of ownership of substance policy.

Kidd and Sykes (1999: 17) draw on the content of the Act to comment that a doctor was allowed to dispense opiates only 'so far as may be necessary for the exercise of his profession'. They argue that such phrasing provided the Act, and doctors wishing to prescribe opiates, with a vagueness that allowed the medical profession a great deal of leeway. The problem at this time was a lack of clarity, and the ever-present threat of prosecution, which led to some pharmacists and physicians refusing even to prescribe or dispense cocaine or opiates. As a result, the newly formed Ministry of Health set up a committee to investigate opiate prescribing and to clarify what constituted legitimate prescribing practice. Headed by Sir Humphrey Rolleston, the Committee's report, published in 1926, was instrumental in shaping British drug policy for at least the next sixty years.

As noted above, the Home Office was keen to own and control the policing of substance misuse and apply the US model to Britain. However, leading physicians, such as Dr Dixon, a reader in pharmacology at the University of Cambridge, were adamant that the control of opiate addiction would remain in the hands of the medical profession and not become a police matter. In support, it was claimed that physicians needed to be able to use their professional discretion by retaining the ability to diagnose 'addiction' and thus be able to prescribe maintenance doses. Berridge (1989: 32–3) is clear as to the importance of this point to the medical profession:

> . . . the profession's function of control and of definition was important. Doctors were not willing to act simply as licensed distributors of drugs, but had to be satisfied that those who obtained drugs from them were playing the correct sick role.

Unsurprisingly for a committee comprised entirely of delegates holding medical qualifications (BMA 1997), Rolleston found in favour of the retention of significant medical input into the 'problem' of substance misuse. Key among their findings was the argument that the prescribing of opiates should be seen as a legitimate medical treatment and therefore that the threat of prosecution should be lifted from doctors prescribing maintenance doses. By acknowledging the right to prescribe, Rolleston established that addiction and substance misuse became a medical problem, capable of being addressed by doctors and not police officers.

Rolleston defended this stance by claiming that

> There are two groups of persons suffering from addiction to which the administration of morphine or heroin may be regarded as legitimate medical treatment, namely:
> (a) Those who are undergoing treatment for cure of the addiction by the gradual withdrawal method;

(b) Persons for whom, after every effort has been made for the cure of addiction, the drug cannot be completely withdrawn. . . .

By virtue of the committee's findings, Rolleston created a 'British system' whereby addicts who were prepared to play the 'sick role' could receive a regular supply of heroin or morphine in order to maintain or gradually reduce their use. Doctors were able to diagnose and prescribe with immunity from prosecution, creating a situation diametrically opposite from that prevailing in the USA.

There are a number of reasons for the difference in the British and US approaches to substance regulation. Firstly, the medical profession was keen to defend its position in relation to the state. As Berridge (1989) notes, issues such as the ownership of the definition of addiction were seen as direct challenges to the autonomy of doctors, and the medical profession was prepared to go to great lengths to resist such challenges. Secondly, the use of opiates was declining even as the Rolleston Committee sat. Rolleston estimated that there were only in the region of five hundred addicts in the whole of Britain and they were to be pitied not persecuted. Moreover, there was a distinct class element to Rolleston's deliberations: he saw opiate addicts as middle aged, middle-class and drawn mostly from the medical profession (South 1997).

The legacy of Rolleston was to create a dual approach to substance use and misuse. On the one hand the police retained the power to prosecute unauthorized use, supply and possession, thus criminalizing drug users not authorized by the medical profession. On the other hand, the medical profession retained the right to diagnose, define and treat addiction. In this way a dual approach developed, with substance misusers being defined as either criminal or sick depending on the arm of the British system with which they came into contact.

1926 to 1964: inactivity and apathy

It would be easy simply to leave a space in the manuscript here. Edwards (1981: 9) encapsulates this period as one during which he claims that 'Britain's drug problem was of interest exactly and only because of its trivial size'. South (1997) notes that medical and recreational use were in decline, due to law enforcement efforts, leading to scarcity of substances and related expense. Most addicts were elderly and, because of the British system, were able to receive maintenance doses from their doctor. It appears that recreational use elsewhere was small and restricted to the 'fast set'. Kohn (1992) claims that there was still the occasional lurid media reporting of drug misuse, but overall substance use had all but disappeared.

As an example, the first Brain Committee, an interdepartmental group set up in 1961 to investigate the use of illicit drugs, stated that the British drug problem was of little concern. In 1958 there were only 58 known addicts, with none under the age of twenty. Britain's only involvement in substance policy during this period was ratifying international treaties. Initially, following the Hague Convention of 1912, the League of Nations was the international body with responsibility for drug policy; from 1964 responsibility was transferred to the United Nations. Mott and Bean (1998: 39) list Britain's substance control legislation from 1923 to 1964, noting that each Act was implemented as a response to international treaties, not domestic problems. They were:

1   The 1925 Dangerous Drugs Act, as a response to the Geneva Convention;
2   The 1932 Dangerous Drugs Act, in response to the 1931 Limitation Convention;
3   The 1964 Dangerous Drugs Act, in response to the 1961 Single Convention.

Key developments in these Acts were the extended control of alkaloids of opium and cocaine as well as the creation of offences in relation to cannabis.

This was the situation at the beginning of the 1960s, a decade seen by many as the catalyst for a number of society's current problems (James and Raine 1998). The inactivity, complacency and apathy regarding Britain's drug problem shown by the first Brain Committee in 1961 were about to disappear as a combination of changing culture, expansion of travel and communication routes and increasing wealth brought a rapid return to the 'luxurious' use of substances.

1964 to 1979: increased use and increasing legislation

The next two sections will only provide brief summaries: detailed analysis of these periods will be provided in subsequent chapters. The purpose here is rather to provide a feel for the pace of change since 1964. By the time the second Brain Committee sat in 1965 the pattern and prevalence of substance misuse in Britain were undergoing a significant change. Bean (1994) provides a number of pieces of evidence for this. For example, the number of known addicts stood at 470 in 1961; by 1965 this figure had almost doubled, to 927. Equally the demographics of addicts was changing: in 1961 the 'non-therapeutic' total was 153; in 1965 it stood at 580. Addicts were also getting younger. In 1961 addicts aged 50 plus comprised the largest group; by 1965 addicts aged from 15 to 34 had become the largest group. This increase in substance misuse related workloads was not restricted to the medical profession: the number of prosecutions/convictions under the Dangerous Drugs Acts also rose in the period 1961 to 1965, from 365 in the former year, to 767 in the latter. Socially, the profile of substance misusers was also changing. As Bean (1994: 105) notes, by the mid-1960s users were: 'the antithesis of their pre-war counterparts'; in short substance misuse was becoming increasingly a pastime of working- and middle-class youth.

The rise in 'problematic' drug use among younger people from the working class was mirrored by an increase in 'recreational' substance use. Shapiro (1999: 20–3) notes that during the 1960s, as a result of a burgeoning youth culture, substance use became more prevalent among musicians and their fans. Initially, the substance of choice for recreational use was amphetamine, but increased consumption of LSD and a more wide-ranging use of cannabis rapidly followed. The growth in recreational use was restricted mainly to young people, as South and Teeman (1999: 73) comment: 'Use of illegal drugs is largely confined to the young . . . relatively few being over thirty five. . . .' The reasons behind this phenomenon will be explored in Chapter 8; the concern here is to chart the state's response to the growth in substance misuse.

What we witness in Britain during the 1960s and 1970s is not only the growth of recreational use of prohibited substances among young people, but also a growth in the variety of substances being used. In terms of policy, this created a number of problems as the old control regimes struggled to come to terms with the rapid developments in substance use culture and practice. As a result, the period from 1964 until the present can be seen as one where the state has been forced constantly to re-assess both the policy and practice of controlling substance use. What is interesting in the period 1964 to 1979 is that there were two distinct sets of problems taxing policy makers: old problems and new developments.

Looking first at the old problems – addiction to opiates, opiate derivatives and cocaine – at one level the 'British system' was seemingly struggling to cope with the rapid increase in use. Much of this appears to centre round the ability of doctors to prescribe 'maintenance doses' with impunity. There was clearly over-prescribing taking place, leading to pharmaceutical heroin being diverted on to the illegal market. Evidence for this can be seen in a number of instances. For example, Leech (1991: 35–6) reports that one doctor prescribed 6 kilos of heroin in 1962 alone. Much of this began to filter out into the 'street' market. Stimson (1987: 39–40) states that until the start of the 1970s there was little or no smuggled heroin in Britain: almost all illegally used heroin was diverted from medical sources. Customs and Excise did not make their first major seizure until 1971.

At the same time, new problems were emerging: young people were using other substances, hitherto seen as unproblematic, for 'luxurious' purposes. Shapiro (1999) points out that most of the amphetamine used by Mods in the 1960s was diverted from licit sources. LSD was increasingly being taken by young people, and, up until 1966 use, supply and possession of LSD were not against the law (Robson 1994). Cannabis, initially seen by the state as a problem restricted to the (*sic*) 'coloured population' (Bean 1994), was beginning to find its way into white youth culture.

As a result of this relatively sudden upsurge in drug misuse, the government reconvened the Brain Committee which issued its second report in 1965. What followed was a 'battery of legislation' (Kidd and Sykes

1999: 19). The details of these pieces of legislation will be explored in Chapter 4; this chapter will simply outline the legislation and provide a brief overview of its content. However, it is important to recognize one point: the dichotomy between treatment and punishment introduced by the Rolleston Committee in 1926 was neither compromised nor, indeed, challenged. The resulting legislation still contained the essential paradox of the British system: namely, the use of criminal law to achieve public health gains (Pearson 1999: 16), with its inherent tensions between the needs of health and those of law and order. Stimson puts this rather more forcibly, claiming that since substance control legislation was first introduced Britain has always had a 'vigorous legal and penal approach to drugs . . . set within a criminal system that penalized non-medically authorized possession. . . .'

The first piece of legislation was the Dangerous Drugs Act 1967. This allowed prescription to continue but with more stringent controls on general practitioners and a requirement to notify the Home Office of new addicts. Moreover, specialist Drug Dependence Units were opened in 1968, mainly around the London area, where 'experts' in addiction monopolized the prescription of heroin and cocaine. The 1967 Act was quickly followed by the 1971 Misuse of Drugs Act.

This Act established the standing Advisory Council on the Misuse of Drugs (ACMD), a committee whose remit is continually to monitor and review the misuse of drugs within the UK. Other features of this Act were recognition of the distinction between possession offences and supply offences as well as of the difference between soft and hard drugs. This was achieved by introducing the controlled status to the manufacture, supply and use of drugs. Substances were divided into classes A, B and C, with sanctions and penalties graded according to harmfulness if the substance were misused (Kidd and Sykes 1999). The next piece of legislation was the Misuse of Drugs (Notification and Supply to Addicts) Regulations (1973). This required doctors treating a patient whom they believed to be addicted to drugs to notify the Chief Medical Officer; it also further restricted the ability of GPs to prescribe substitute substances such as diamorphine and dipipanone.

Stimson (1987: 37) sees much of the thrust of this legislation as an attempt by the state to 'make the major task [of the medical profession] the social control of drug distribution' in order to 'keep the Mafia out'. If this was indeed the intention of policy in the period 1964 to 1979, it failed somewhat spectacularly. By all available measures problematic substance misuse kept on rising: levels of addiction, levels of recreational use, levels of prosecutions and levels of seizures (Bean 1994; Pearson 1999; Stimson 1987). The drug 'problem' had reached a level beyond which the Brain Committee (1965) inspired legislation could cope. By the end of the 1970s society was changing just as rapidly as it had in the early 1960s. Old certainties were being questioned and a 'new social order' was developing (Gladstone 1995). The penultimate section of this chapter will now outline how this affected substance misuse policy.

1979 to present day: changing patterns of use and changing responses

The beginnings of the 1980s saw a different type of Britain, with a different type of political leader, prepared to 'think the unthinkable' in almost every form of public service provision. In 1979 Margaret Thatcher came to power as an unrepentantly right-wing Prime Minister armed with a mission to introduce a 'radical programme in economic and social policy' (Gladstone 1995). The initial impact this had is well documented elsewhere (Gamble 1986; Harrison 1985), but suffice to say Britain witnessed record levels of unemployment, crime, urban decay and social dislocation.

For our purposes, we need to see Thatcher as a confrontational politician willing and fully prepared to declare 'war', both rhetorically and actually, on any number of 'enemies', whether other nation states, as in the case of the Falklands, the trade union movement, dubbed the 'enemy within' (Johnson 1991), or, in this case, substance misuse, proclaiming a 'war on drugs'. There can be little doubt that the culture of substance misuse and the state's reaction to it changed during the 1980s and 1990s.

There are a number of reasons for this change. Firstly, problematic drug use has continued to rise despite repeated and consistent attempts by the state, both domestically and internationally, to control it. Both strands of the British system, the health service and the criminal justice system, are now dealing with record numbers of people. Secondly, the early 1980s saw a growth in the rise of heroin use, and especially intravenous use, which created a public health concern over the transmission of HIV and AIDS. Linked to this, the tightening of controls over the medical profession's ability to prescribe (Kidd and Sykes 1999), coupled with increases in poverty created by structural unemployment (Fuller 1990), led to a rise in drug-related crime. Thirdly, the early 1980s saw the beginnings of an increasing use of recreational drugs by large numbers of young people, fuelled in some part by the rise in popularity of dance music. This phenomenon has led some academics to claim that drug use has now become 'normalized' for the majority of young people (Parker *et al.* 1998), allowing some social groups to return to a situation similar to that of Britain in the 1800s where substance use is without moral condemnation.

A further contributory element is that the drug culture itself changed with the advent of recreational polydrug users, who, according to Gilman (1999), are knowledgeable about pharmacology and how to maximize the effects of their drug of choice and who use different substances for different occasions. In this case, drug users of the past two decades see drug use as an integral part of a number of cultures: terrace culture, club culture and so on. In fact, many parts of youth culture are openly associated with substance use. In effect, and in support of the normalization thesis, drug use has moved away from the margins of society and into the mainstream.

Changes in the political landscape, including the introduction of the 'mixed economy' (Gladstone 1995) to health and social care provision, allow greater scope for a number of specialist voluntary and community groups to enter into the substance use arena as providers of treatment and advice (Howard *et al.* 1993). Allied to this, wider changes to the delivery of services based upon the multi-agency approach (Colebatch 1998), saw substance misuse policy change from unilateral, isolationist approaches to one where joint working has become paramount. Finally, the 'drug problem' has come to be identified by politicians, the media and numerous social commentators as a serious social ill in need of almost constant attention. In turn, this has fostered the politicization of substance misuse on an unprecedented level. At present, there remains a political consensus over the nature and direction of policy (South 1997), although, as will be explored in a later chapter, this consensus may well evaporate in the near future.

These wider issues are evident in policy developments over the past two decades. Initially, and reflecting the tough rhetoric used by the Thatcher administrations of the 1980s, substance policy adopted a hard-line, enforcement-based approach. South (1997: 940) notes that the government was able to 'make provision for the recovery of the profits of crime; jettison its liberal recommendations relating to sentencing and introduce . . . the Drug Trafficking Offences Act (1986)'. However, the compromise between strict enforcement and treatment remained. This can be seen in the government's key strategy document *Tackling Drug Misuse* (HMSO 1985). This raised the issue of the need to incorporate joint working, and gave five fronts for action, grouped around enforcement, but also recognizing the widespread and seemingly entrenched use of substances in certain social groups; the document also allowed for treatment and prevention initiatives.

Politicization of substance use has required politicians to provide a constant stream of responses and ideas. Latterly, as further acknowledgement of the 'normalization' of substance use, the concept of harm reduction and prevention has become important, but again within a framework that retains the right to punish those non-medically approved users. The importance of prevention can be seen in the inclusion of substance use education into the National Curriculum (Barton 2001). Equally, in terms of enforcement, the rise in drug-related crime has brought a realization that reducing problematic substance use may require the offender to be forced into obtaining treatment; for, if successful, such treatment can benefit individual users and the communities in which they reside. In short, contemporary approaches have sought to merge both arms of the British system.

Subsequent policy documents have all incorporated this trend. Barton (1999: 465) identifies *Across the Divide* (Howard *et al.* 1993); *Tackling Drugs Together* (Department of Health 1995) and *Tackling Drugs to Build a*

Better Britain (Cabinet Office 1998) as all contributing to the merger of health and justice. The same author argues that there has been a broadening of approach, culminating in our current position where policy makers have

> realiz[ed] that the provision of an efficient system [for dealing with sub-stance misuse] . . . addresses the needs of the user and the needs of the community and depends on some form of union between the health (treatment) and criminal justice (enforcement) approaches.

Arguably, the apotheosis of this approach are the Drug Treatment and Test-ing Orders (DTTOs), which came 'on-line' in 2001. These use orders of the court to coerce drug-misusing offenders into a treatment programme (Barton and Quinn 2001).

Conclusion

Clearly, substance use has changed out of all recognition over the last two hundred years. It has become, arguably, one of the three major social problems in contemporary Britain and receives considerable state and public attention. Advances in medical science and shifts in morality have been significant contributors in the move from widespread use and acceptance of use in the 1800s to today's controls. However, do we really know the extent of drug use in Britain today? Often, some of the statements made are based on noth-ing more than supposition and personal opinion. Does the actual prevalence of drug use in contemporary Britain match the level of investment in policing it? These questions form the basis of the next chapter, which examines the extent of drug use in modern Britain, and the problems we have in measuring use.

Note

1 These figures are approximations. Each crate weighed somewhere in the region of 60 to 72 kg.

3 Measuring the 'problem'

Drug use in contemporary Britain

Introduction

In the introductory chapter it was stated that to fully understand the nature of the 'drug problem' in contemporary Britain, it was necessary to draw from a number of academic disciplines. Chapter 2 used history as its base to provide a broad overview of the previous two centuries, looking at the use of, and state response to, drug use. This chapter employs social science research methods as its foundation, questioning as it does the capacity to generate accurate figures on the extent of illicit drug use in Britain.

The ability to provide detailed and exact measurement of illicit drug use is important, not least because the apparent increase in the use and misuse of drugs over the past two decades has generated a great deal of public and state concern. Accordingly, successive governments have had to respond to clarion calls by the media, by opposition politicians, by community leaders and by the Churches for 'something to be done', leading to a whole raft of initiatives and policy documents. However, in order to 'do something' in an effective manner, there is a need to be clear as to the extent of the problem – in short, in order to produce and implement effective policy, it needs to be known exactly, or as exactly as possible, how many, who, what, where, when, how and, if possible, why people take drugs. Although this may appear axiomatic, the practice of supplying such information is fraught with difficulties. As the Institute for the Study of Drug Dependency (ISDD) (1995) noted: 'Estimating just how many people use illicit drugs in Britain is like trying to do a jigsaw puzzle with many of the pieces missing'.

The chapter will not, and cannot, for reasons that will become clearer as the work progresses, complete that jigsaw. Instead, it takes as its core the problems we have in measuring drug misuse. It begins with a review of the methodological weaknesses of each approach to measuring drug misuse and highlights the difficulties of measuring a population involved in illicit activities, such as drug users. It then compares and contrasts two types of measurement: official statistics compiled by the treatment providers and the law enforcement agencies, with self-report studies compiled by government agencies and academics. The chapter concludes by employing the available data to draw a rough sketch of drug use in contemporary Britain, noting the division between 'heavy-end' drug users, who are most likely to come to the attention of the state system, and recreational users who do not, yet appear to represent the majority of drug users in Britain. The chapter relies heavily on two sources of data, the British Crime Survey (BCS) and the work of Goddard and Higgins (1999 a and b) for the reason that both are easily accessible to students.

Before discussing those points, it is perhaps germane to close this section with a brief explanation as to why accurate measurement is important. At present, the lack of a definitive figure, based on solid research, allows any number of speculative assertions about the prevalence of drug misuse in Britain. For example, George Howarth MP (1999: 11; original emphasis) writing as a government spokesperson stated that 'Drug misuse *is* a serious problem'. In the same vein, Strang *et al.* (1992) talked about a 'major heroin epidemic'. The media often take up this message where headlines such as 'Mothers March To Clean Up Needle City' (Kahn 2001) abound.

Several authors (Sutton and Maynard 1993; Hay 1998) question the veracity of such statements and raise issues about the data on which they are based. Indeed, the former authors argue that statements like those above are 'unquantified assertions based on opinion rather than measurement' (Sutton and Maynard 1993: 455). Such imprecision should, in theory, make it difficult for policy makers to: (a) allocate funds, (b) target policy and (c) measure outcomes. However, that is patently not the case as central government spends ever-increasing sums of money tackling the 'drug problem'; a problem whose true nature and extent are somewhat opaque, making definitive statements about its prevalence difficult. Citing Sutton and Maynard once more (1993: 456), it is difficult to argue with them when they claim that

> . . . policy design and execution in this area is conducted in an almost data free environment where, because of ignorance, it is impossible to set sensible policy targets, let alone measure the success of spending hundreds of millions of pounds across the Whitehall Departments. One wonders, for example, how targets for drug use, such as those for alcohol and tobacco in the *Health of the Nation* can be set and monitored.

For now, it is important to remember that failure accurately to measure the prevalence of illicit substance use creates problems in terms of deciding what to input, where and when to make that input and how to measure 'success'. Accurate figures that provide information on all aspects of substance misuse are important, but difficult to provide. The next section turns its attention to the methodological weaknesses of our current measurement instruments.

Measuring the 'problem': conflicting messages

It is important to be clear from the outset that although this chapter will offer a critique of a variety of organizations and the manner in which they measure illicit drug use, none of the agencies claims the capacity to provide the definitive picture of drug use in Britain. Instead, each offers a very varied picture of drug use related to its own particular field of interest, whether organizational or academic. In short, each measurement sector produces data relative to its own concerns and based on the contacts it has with drug users in that particular organizational context.

Sutton and Maynard (1993: 455) identify four existing sources of information relating to illicit drug use in Britain: 'indirect measures provided by the seizure and intelligence arms of enforcement agencies, surveys of drug use attitudes, knowledge and experience, surveys of known users and surveys of hidden users'. The ISDD (1995) narrows this down somewhat and suggests that, essentially, there are two forms of data available:

> . . . regularly collected official statistics on drugs or drug misusers who are known to the authorities, which have the benefit of a degree of continuity; and (usually one-off) surveys conducted according to no standard methodology and therefore difficult to use as trend or national indicators.

For our purposes, we can classify these two as official statistics, which relate to data collected by state agencies during the course of their work, and general household surveys, which relate to data derived from self-report questionnaires. Recognition is given to the fact that other forms of data collection may take place, but these two methods are most instrumental in informing official policy, thus fit the general concerns of this work. With that caveat in mind, the next section reviews each of these methodological approaches, searching for weaknesses that may impact on the validity of the data, thus reducing the capacity accurately to measure the extent of substance misuse in Britain.

Data collection and the problem of hidden populations

Many people who use certain forms of illicit drugs are reluctant to be identified, either by the state, their employers or, in some instances, their families for fear of negative reactions. Therefore, they become part of a hidden population that is not readily available for accurate measurement. Everyone working within the substance misuse field recognizes this as the key weakness in methods designed to measure the 'drug problem'. For example, the Advisory Council on the Misuse of Drugs is clear about the nature of the methodological problems faced by research and practice:

. . . it can be difficult to define adequately cases or categories of use. The illicit nature of drug taking makes the task of establishing its prevalence very complicated. Self-report data can be unreliable. There are sampling difficulties . . . [this] should be borne in mind when trying to draw conclusions from questionnaire research.

ACMD (1995: 32)

Essentially, much of our data relating to drug misuse is derived from two basic sources: those collected from official sources and those which emanate from general population surveys where randomly selected members of house-holds and/or schools are asked to complete self-report questionnaires. While each has its strengths, each has a corresponding degree of weakness and it is to these the chapter now turns its attention. Before starting, it should be made clear that no attempt is being made here comprehensively to review the methodological pros and cons of each approach. More accurately, the intent is to provide a broad overview of the general problems and pitfalls of each methodology.

Official statistics

May (1997: 65) provides a succinct working definition of official statistics as 'data collected by the state and its agencies', making drug-related data derived from medical and criminal justice sources part of a whole range of information collected and disseminated by the state. However, just because these 'facts' are released by the state does not automatically mean that they should be accepted at face value and taken as some form of ultimate truth. Rather, as a number of social scientists have noted (Cicourel 1964; Turk 1969), official statistics need to be seen as a 'social construction', whereby they do not reflect any social reality but merely 'actions of persons in the social system which define, record and classify certain behaviour . . .' (Cicourel and Kitsuse 1963). Thus, official statistics can be seen to reflect the concerns, working practices and interests of the compiling organization, as opposed to any definitive measurement.

In more detail, and focusing on the construction of crime statistics, it is possible to see that far from being accurate indicators of crime, these figures simply represent the criminal justice system's ability to detect, define and process certain, but not all, criminal actions. May (1997: ch. 4) provides an informative review of this process. Essentially, May argues that it is important to remember, as Quinney (1970: 104) reminds us, that 'Full enforcement of the criminal law . . . is not a realistic expectation'. Wasik *et al.* (1999) expand this point and argue that police discretion as to which laws to enforce, and when to enforce them, is a key determinant of 'policing' any crime.

For example, Ian Miller, writing in the *Daily Mirror* (31 May 2001), provides details of how Customs and Excise officials decided to let 'two drug smugglers walk free after being caught with a £100,000 haul of cannabis'.

Miller reports that customs officers were 'too busy' after being 'swamped' by people trying to smuggle cocaine into the country. The pair of smugglers were held for three hours and then released without even being interviewed. Although that example is extreme, it demonstrates that the processes between the act of breaking the law, even when the crime is as serious as that cited, and being convicted, then sentenced for that act, are highly complex and dependent upon the discretion of a number of officials and the manner in which those officials define the actions and demeanour of the offender.

Equally important is the fact that the public, in the guise of either victim or offender, may choose not to report the crime to the police. For the offender, the motivation not to report is axiomatic. However, victims often choose not to report for a variety of reasons, including fear of the offender, thinking the police will dismiss the crime as insignificant, or a general mistrust of the police. This leads to the creation of a 'dark figure of crime'. Barclay *et al.* (1995) suggest that incomplete recording by the police and reporting by the public mean that only somewhere between 27 and 39 per cent of crimes end up as 'official statistics'. As Mayhew (2000: 104) notes, drug possession is a classic exemplar of the type of crime that is very often not reported to the police.

The crime being detected or reported and a suspect being identified and subsequently arrested are simply the start of the process. Following arrest and charge, the police pass details of the case to the Crown Prosecution Service, which then makes a decision as to whether to prosecute based on the joint criteria of evidential sufficiency and public interest (Ashworth 1998: 176–88). Finally, the prosecution need to prove satisfactorily to a magistrate or jury that the accused is guilty, prior to punishment being meted out. Thus, instead of being a measure of all illicit activity related to drug use, Home Office and Customs and Excise figures can be seen simply to represent those crimes the criminal justice system knows about and, importantly, decides to act upon. Moreover, changes in policy or policing agency practice can lead to alterations in rates and patterns of recorded crime, a point noted by Corkery (2001) in relation to the impact the Lawrence Inquiry seems to have had on stops and searches in London, with a concomitant effect on drug related offences.

A similar critique can be made of medical data. Not all those presenting to doctors and specialist drug agencies will be automatically classified as in need of help, or registered as 'addicted'. Indeed, some academics argue that many patients, including heavy-end drug users, who present to doctors will not receive the treatment they may need due to their reluctance to comply with the 'sick role' (Navarro 1979). Bean (1994: 91) provides evidence of this, citing the *British Medical Journal* 'Any questions?' section as an indicator that if heavy-end drug users are co-operative they will be treated, if not they run the risk of being labelled 'difficult' and may not receive the treatment they need.

Equally, just as in the crime statistics, there is a large unreported 'dark figure' of medical problems. Jones (1994: 11–12) cautions against assuming that medical data provide an accurate indicator of the health of the nation. Rather, Jones (1994: 11) suggests medical statistics are seen as unreliable indicators of illness because: (a) some people do not present to the doctor for treatment and thus go unrecorded and (b) not all those who present across the country to different doctors will be treated or recorded in the same way. In this manner, far from being definitive figures, official medical records, and official classification of illness, are 'influenced by individual circumstances and the different methods of recording and reporting sickness across the country'.

Self-report data

Clearly, therefore, many drug users remain hidden from the gaze of official statistics. In order to combat the recognized discrepancy between 'actual' figures and 'official' figures in areas such as crime and ill health, many researchers have turned to self-report surveys, issued to households identified either from the Electoral Register (ER) or Small Users Post Code Address File (PAF) (Mayhew 2000). A prime example of this type of work is the British Crime Survey (BCS), which looks at people's experience of being victims of crime, and, since 1992, has included questions on illicit drug use. The BCS uses a sample of 40,000 people aged between 16 and 59 from England and Wales selected at random via the ER or PAF. Scotland has its own version of the BCS.

The BCS only provides data on adults and thus fails to provide data on younger children. Some surveys are exclusively aimed at school children aged 11 to 15, such as that conducted for the Office of National Statistics (Goddard and Higgins 1999a and b). Work of this type provides, among other things, an indication of drug use among school children. The sample size here was 5,000 English children and 3,500 Scottish children. Other notable surveys of this type include the work of Balding (1999).

There are, however, problems with this methodological approach, something articulated by Mayhew (2000: 104–5) who has comprehensive experience of this type of work, being a key figure in previous BCS research. Commenting directly on the BCS, she notes five problem areas, which can be broadened to cover all self-report, general household surveys.

Mayhew suggests that:

1 household surveys of this type do not measure each and every incident for a variety of reasons;
2 no matter what sampling frame is used, surveys of this type will not be representative of the population. Hard to reach groups such as the homeless, those living in non-household environments, such as prisoners, and

others with chaotic lifestyles, will not be included. Ironically, being a victim of crime and being involved in illicit drug use is often highest amongst these hard to reach groups;

3   there are sampling errors that may be imported. For example, Mayhew notes that for rare crimes, even a survey as large as the BCS fails to sample adequately. The same may be said of drug addiction, itself apparently a relatively rare occurrence among the general population;

4   respondents often undercount incidents for a variety of reasons;

5   people have trouble in remembering and locating incidents within a time frame. For example, Mayhew (2000) claims that people are prone to pulling forward in time serious events and not remembering repetitive incidents.

Clearly, each of the primary measuring instruments has its flaws and is unable to reach adequately the hidden population of drug users. That being the case, data derived from official statistics and general household surveys should be treated with caution. However, that is not to say that they lack merit: they do and, when taken together, can begin to provide an overview of the extent of illicit drug use in Britain, as well as giving us an indication of trends over time.

Remembering the caveat that each set of figures is compiled for particular reasons, and not with the purpose of providing a definitive picture of drug misuse in Britain, comparisons of the different findings offer a fascinating picture of the manner in which the sectors of the British system define and deal with the 'drug problem'.

Medical data: patients and clients

The first set of figures to be examined originates from within the medical sector. These data are derived from the Regional Drug Misuse Database (RDMD), a relatively recent measurement tool, which was set up in 1989 following recommendations from ACMD (Department of Health 2000). Prior to 1989, medical-based figures were collected in a significantly different form, and by an agency not readily associated with the medical profession: the Home Office. It is interesting to trace the development of this situation, which reflects the inherent tensions between the health and law arms of the British system.

Mott (1994) provides a comprehensive account of this train of events. She notes that the Brain Committee (1965), echoing a suggestion (subsequently omitted from the final report) of the Rolleston Committee (1926), recommended that doctors notify a central authority about the addicts they were treating. Brain justified this move by reference to various Public Health Acts under which doctors have a duty to notify a central authority about patients 'who are suffering from an infectious disease' (Mott 1994: 272). Brain argued that drug addiction is an infectious disease, thus ensuring the medical profession retained 'epidemiological assessment and control' of the drug problem. In a move further designed to protect doctors, the Brain Committee suggested that any physician failing to notify should be dealt with by the General Medical Council, and not the criminal courts.

The Chief Medical Officer at the Home Office was subsequently named as the central authority to be informed by doctors, placing that central authority within the Home Office. This provoked reactions from doctors, again reflecting the on-going struggle for 'ownership' of the drug problem. Mott (1994: 273) points to an article that appeared in the *British Medical Journal* (1965) that was supportive of the idea of notification on the grounds that it would allow the creation of treatment centres for addicts. However, Mott further reports that in the same year another author, contributing to the *Lancet*, made the point that 'On the one hand the Home Office has done well for a long time overseeing this exceedingly difficult problem; on the other, it does use policemen for the purpose.'

The requirement to notify re-addicts first came into force under the Dangerous Drugs Act 1967. This was subsequently modified under the Misuse of Drugs Act 1971 and the (Notification and Supply to Addicts) Regulations of 1973. Under these regulations doctors were required to notify the Home Office of the name, age, sex, address, National Health Service number, date of attendance and type of drug used of all people addicted to one or more of fourteen Class A drugs, including heroin and cocaine. Absent from the list of notifiable substances were amphetamines, barbiturates and benzodiazepines. Data from notifications were published annually by the Home Office as the *Home Office Statistical Bulletin: Statistics of drug addicts notified to the Home Office, United Kingdom* series.

However, the information produced by the Addicts Index was limited and did not provide the type of detail required by the Department of Health (DoH), which was trying to respond to changing patterns of drug use. In 1982 the ACMD called for local drug teams to be set up to collect more detailed information on the patterns and methods of use, as well as types of drug used (it is worth remembering that this was around the time of serious worries as to the effects of HIV and AIDS and thus can be seen to reflect wider social and medical concerns). This subsequently happened, and by 1989 all Regional Health Authorities (RHAs) had in place a regional monitoring system. The Department of Health funded the (then) Regional Health Authorities to create anonymous databases relating to drug misusers who were attending specialist services. The RDMDs return data to the DoH on a six-monthly basis and the findings from the RDMDs are used to inform medical policy and responses to the 'drug problem'.

This approach was modified again in 1996 and from 1 April 1996 the health regions have been required to submit data on 'people presenting to services with problem drug misuse for the first time, or for the first time in six months or more' (DoH 2000). These data include information on the following: 'age, sex, and other personal information; details of up to five

drugs misused, information regarding injecting/sharing equipment behaviour, treatment profiles, together with the type of agency attended and the
Health Authority (HA) of treatment' (DoH 2000). It is important to note also
that the scope and range of substances recorded broadened considerably and
now includes 'any drug of misuse, including solvents and tranquillizers but
excluding tobacco'; there is also a provision to include alcohol, but only as
a subsidiary drug (DoH 2000).

Clearly, the RDMDs provide a fuller picture of those people who turn to
the medical profession for help with their drug problems than did the old
Home Office Index. The RDMDs supply some interesting information regarding drug misuse in relation to the medical profession. Using the latest figures
available at time of writing (June 2001) it is possible to examine the situation
in England[1] for March 2000:

- About 31,800 users were reported as presenting to drug misuse agencies;
  this is an estimated increase of 8 per cent over the previous six month
  period.
- Of those, 51 per cent were in their twenties, with 14 per cent being under
  20.
- The ratio of males to females stood at 3:1.
- Heroin was still the most frequently reported main drug of use, accounting for over half the users. The next most frequently reported main drugs
  of misuse were cannabis (10%), methadone (9%) cocaine (6%) and
  amphetamines (4%).

(DoH 2001)

Thus, it is possible to argue that for today's medical profession, drug
misuse is a serious and growing problem, but one that involves a relatively
small number of patients. Moreover, one drug – heroin – is clearly the
most problematic. If, however, these data are flawed, in as much that they
cannot provide an accurate picture of current levels of use, do they have
any value for the policy community? The answer lies in their ability to
allow us to compare trends over time.

Comparison of data over the last thirty years demonstrates that Britain has
witnessed a paradigmatic shift in the characteristics and numbers of those presenting to health agencies, yet the drug of problem for the medical profession
has remained the same. Even given the methodological problems inevitable in
using different sets of data, it is possible to see that heavy-end substance use
has increased, and that users have become younger, with a recognizable
growth in the number of under-twenties presenting for treatment. In the
six months up to March 2000, of the 31,800 people presenting to health
agencies in England and Wales, about 4,340 were aged 20 or below (DoH
2000). This can be compared (tentatively) with the 1964 figures, where,
from a total of 753 known addicts on the Home Office Index, only 40 were
aged 20 or below (Bean 1994: 98 Tables VI and VII). However, the drug

that creates most problems for addicts, heroin, has remained the main problem drug across all age ranges in both 2000 (DoH 2000) and 1964 (Bean 1994: 99, Table VIII).

Criminal justice data: offenders and offences

There are three main agencies from which these data are derived: HM Customs and Excise, the National Crime Squad (NCS) and from the various police forces across Britain. Seizures and arrests made by the first two agencies generally 'reflect levels or drugs types at, or soon after, the point of importation' (Corkery 2001: 2), whereas police seizures may give an indication of the distribution patterns for 'home produced' drugs or those diverted from medical sources. The police, NCS and HM Customs and Excise deal with offences that contravene the 1971 Misuse of Drugs Act and the Drug Trafficking Act 1994. The data relating to this are available from the Home Office and are published in the *Drug Seizure and Offender Statistics* series.

Based on the most recent figures at the time of writing, it is possible to examine the extent of drug misuse as recorded by the law and order arm of the British system. The Home Office provides data relating to drug seizures and drug offenders (Corkery 2001). Turning attention to the former, the number of drug seizures reported to the Home Office in 1999 stood at 132,200, a 13 per cent fall on the previous year's figure. These raw data can be broken down into their component parts in order to provide a picture of which agencies seized what drug, as well as the types of drug being seized. All of the following data are derived from Corkery (2001).

As will be seen in Chapter 4, the 'policing' of drugs by the law and order arm of the British system operates a distinct division of labour, which is visible in seizure figures. Essentially HM Customs and Excise and the NCS tend to make fewer seizures, but of larger amounts, than their police force counterparts. Table 3.1 gives figures for drug seizures by type, organization and number for 1999.

However, when these figures are compared in respect of numbers and quantity of drugs seized, it becomes clear that Customs and Excise seize larger amounts. For the sake of illustration, Table 3.2 provides data concentrating only on the cannabis and heroin seizures that took place in 1999.

What of the general picture concerning drug seizures? Based on the Home Office data it is possible to see that, in 1999,

- heroin remained the most commonly seized Class A drug with 15,100 seizures netting 2,342 kg;
- cocaine and crack was the next most seized Class A drug with 8,000 seizures netting 2,970 kg;
- there were 465 seizures of LSD, providing 67,400 doses;
- there were 6,400 seizures of ecstasy type drugs netting 6,323,500 doses;

Table 3.1 Class of drug, seizing organization and number for 1990

Class of drug and organization seized by	Number of seizures
Class A drugs	
HM Customs and Excise	1,315
Police forces including Transport Police	28,717
Class B drugs	
HM Customs and Excise	4,298
Police forces including Transport Police	102,819
Class C drugs	
HM Customs and Excise	34
Police forces including Transport Police	2,469
All drugs (Classes A, B, C)	
HM Customs and Excise	5,647
Police forces including Transport Police	134,005
Total	139,652

Source: Corkery 2001

- of the Class B drugs, there were 102,000 cannabis seizures providing 68.9 tonnes;
- there were 13,200 amphetamine seizures grossing 2,017 kg.

Looking at drug offenders, 1999 saw 79,200 cases dealt with by the courts and/or other means of sentencing, such as cautions by the police, fines (in Scotland), or compounding (an administrative sanction issued by HM Customs and Excise), in Britain, leading to 120,000 persons being found guilty of drug offences. Just as with the medical data there was a gender divide, with only 11 per cent of offenders being female. In terms of age, 33 per cent of offenders were under 21, with an average age of just over 25.

In terms of drug offences, the vast majority were for unlawful possession: 90 per cent of all drug offenders being found guilty or cautioned for possession, either alone or with other offences. Of the rest, 14 per cent were dealt

Table 3.2 Cannabis and heroin seizures, 1999

Organization	Type of drug	No. of seizures	Weight in kgs
HM Customs & Excise	Heroin	158	848.0
Police	Heroin	14,950	1493.7
HM Customs and Excise	Cannabis	4,211	56,721.4
Police	Cannabis	97,795	69,314

Source: Corkery 2001

with under trafficking offences, which include unlawful production, supply, intent to supply, export and import. Of offenders, 68 per cent were dealt with for cannabis related offences, making it far and away the drug most dealt with by the criminal justice system. Finally, in this section, the focus falls on the action taken against offenders. There are essentially two options: a non-custodial penalty (probation or community sentence order, a fine, a caution) or immediate custody. In 1999 only 9 per cent of drug offenders were sentenced to immediate custody, the remainder receiving some form of non-custodial penalty.

However, these bold data alter dramatically when the nature and type of offence are taken into consideration. For example, possession, which concerns 90 per cent of all offences, most often led to a non-custodial penalty with 'few . . . sentenced to immediate custody' (Corkery 2001: 34). Of those charged with unlawful production, 14 per cent received a custodial sentence. Moving along, in terms of seriousness of offence, unlawful supply drew a more severe sentence, with 51 per cent of those found guilty being given a prison sentence. The treatment of those found guilty of unlawful import or export is similar with 52 per cent receiving a prison sentence (Corkery 2001: 32–43).

At this stage we can begin to construct some tentative comparisons. Clearly, the law and order arm of the British system deals with more people than the medical arm. It also has a different main 'problem' drug, in as much that, as Runciman (1999) forcefully comments, 'cannabis is the drug most likely to bring people into contact with the criminal justice system'. Evidence for this is provided by the manner in which people charged with cannabis offences dominate the prosecution figures and also in the way cannabis features heavily in seizure statistics. It may be, however, that this pattern will change dramatically given the recent shift in government policy, with its current emphasis on Class A drugs.

However, a close inspection of the medical and legal data might legitimately beg the question whether somewhere in the region of 160,00 people, known by the state agencies to be involved in the use and/or supply of illicit drugs, out of a total population of about 60 million people, really constitute the 'serious problem' claimed by politicians and the media. If we add the fact that some of those receiving medical help for their drug problem will have been simultaneously processed by the criminal justice system, the actual 'official' number of 'problem' users can seem insignificant and raises questions relating to the millions of pounds being spent on substance misuse programmes. The final set of figures paints a somewhat different picture, and perhaps offers a rationale for our current concerns over substance use.

Self-report data: the bigger picture?

Thus far, concentration has focused on those people who, for one reason or another, have come to the attention of the state agencies in relation to drug use. One way to conceive of this group is to see them as 'problematic drug users', either by virtue of the fact of the extent and nature of their use, making them a medical problem, or because of the social danger their drug use poses in terms of law and order, making them a criminal justice problem.

However, this problematic group remains relatively small, even allowing for under-counting; so small, in fact, that they cannot possibly be representative of the true extent of drug use. Arguably, this becomes clearer if greater attention is paid to the level of drug seizures. Stimson (1987: 50) claims that 'no law enforcement agency anywhere in the world credibly claims more than a 10 per cent interception rate'. Thus, even if the law enforcement agencies were achieving that maximum target, it can be estimated that at least 23,420 kilo of heroin, or in excess of 60 million doses of ecstasy type drugs were circulating in Britain during 1999. There are two conclusions that can be drawn from these figures: (a) either the known drug users are consuming vast quantities of drugs or (b) there is a substantial 'hidden population', who, for the most part, use drugs without registering a drug problem.

The next data sets examined seem to indicate that the latter scenario is a more accurate picture, pointing to a very large population of drug users, unknown to the state agencies. Data that attempt to gauge this are derived from self-report questionnaires, many of which are part of larger government-sponsored projects such as the British Crime Survey (BCS), which has included questions on personal drug use since the 1992 survey (Mott and Mirrlees-Black 1993). Other information emanates from agencies such as the Health Education Authority (Heuston *et al.* 1996) and the Schools Health Education Unit (Balding 1999). There is also the work of academics such as Parker *et al.* (1998) and Aldridge *et al.* (1999) whose longitudinal work on drug use has been extremely enlightening. There is a remarkable similarity across all of these surveys, and collectively they paint a picture very different from the two previous sources of information.

Space precludes a detailed examination of each and every survey, so the intention in this section is to combine sets of data to provide a broad picture of the results. Essentially, the concern of academic researchers and government departments over the past ten years seems to be: (a) to examine the extent of use, (b) to search for differential patterns of use across time and age groups, (c) to identify 'drugs of preference' and, latterly, (d) to gauge public attitudes toward different types of drug.

Extent of use

The concern here is to try to gauge how many people use illicit drugs and whether there have been any changes over time. It would appear that there is a rise in use across the 1990s. For example, Mott and Mirlees-Black (1993), working with data from the 1992 BCS, found that 17 per cent of their sample admitted to taking an illicit drug. This rose in subsequent BCS findings, from 28 per cent in 1994 (Ramsay and Percy 1996), to 29 per cent in 1996 (Ramsay and Spiller 1997) to nearly 32 per cent in 1998 (Ramsay and Partridge 1999).

Goddard and Higgins (1999a and b) found that overall 13 per cent of English and 18 per cent of Scottish children aged between 11 and 16 reported ever having taken drugs. However, both sets of figures represent lifetime use and are guilty of aggregating data from very broad age ranges. They do not tell us very much about current use or differential patterns of use between age groups.

Differential patterns of use across time and age groups

Once the time and age variables are factored in to the findings, the bold data, outlined above, begin to assume a different pattern and paint a clearer picture of where drug use is most commonly located in contemporary society. Concentrating first on school children, it is possible to view significant differences in use both across time and age groups. For example, in England and Scotland:

- about 3 per cent of 11 to 12 year olds admitted to ever having used drugs;
- this rose to 13 per cent and 19 per cent of 13 to 14 year olds in England and Scotland respectively;
- it was among the older children (15 years old) where prevalence of use was highest, with 31 per cent of English children and 39 per cent of Scottish children admitting to ever having used a drug.

(Goddard and Higgins 1999a and b)

What is equally interesting, and in contrast to the medical and criminal justice figures, is that although boys admit to using substance more than girls, the difference is slight, with only a 2 per cent difference across all age ranges (DoH 2000).

This pattern of age difference in illicit drug use is repeated across the adult population. Working with data drawn from the BCS, the DoH and Drug-Scope (DoH 2000; DrugScope 2000) note that in 1998, 32 per cent of those aged 16 to 59 admit to having ever used a drug, compared to 28 per cent in 1994. However, if that wide age band is broken down into sub-groups, it appears that drug use is more prevalent among younger people:

- Of 16 to 29 year olds, 49 per cent admit to ever having tried a drug compared with 25 per cent of 30 to 59 year olds.
- This difference becomes further marked among the group aged 20 to 24 where 55 per cent admit to some use, making this age group the highest lifetime users.
- Again, although across all age groups, males were likely to have used drugs more than females, the difference does not reflect the medical or

criminal justice data. Recent work by Aldridge *et al.* (1999) suggests that gender differences in drug use are no longer a significant variable on life-time drug use.

However, while this information can tell us about lifetime use (that is, ever having used an illicit drug) as DrugScope (2000: 57) remarks, 'lifetime use does not accurately reflect the proportion currently using drugs on an occasional or regular basis'. In order to assess current practice it is necessary to examine more recent use. According to the 1998 BCS (Ramsey and Partridge 1999):

- Just under 30 per cent of those aged 16 to 24 used illicit drugs in the last year, with this falling to just under 20 per cent claiming usage in the last month.

This can be compared with other age groups:

- Of those aged 25 to 34, 8 per cent admitted to using drugs in the last month.
- Of those aged 35 to 44, 3 per cent admitted to using drugs in the last month.
- Of those aged 45 to 54, 2 per cent admitted to using drugs in the last month.
- Of those aged 55 to 59, 1 per cent admitted to doing so.

There is also a gender element present here with more males across all ages admitting to recent illicit drug use. For example, across the whole BCS population women were about 50 per cent less likely to admit to using drugs in the last month than males. Examining the data for children aged 11 to 15, 6.7 per cent of children in England admitted to using illicit drugs in the past month compared to 10 per cent of 12 to 15 year olds in Scotland (Goddard and Higgins 1999a and b).

Drug of preference

Most of this information stems from the BCS data. Cannabis is the most widely used drug in both the adult and child populations. For example, the BCS (Ramsay and Partridge 1999) states that 25.1 per cent of all adults aged 16 to 59 admit to ever having used cannabis. This figure rises to 44 per cent of those aged 16 to 24. However, in terms of recent use, only 5 per cent of all adults admitted to using cannabis in the last month. Again, there is a marked difference between age groups with 17 per cent of the youngest group (aged 16 to 24) claiming use in the last month compared to 0.2 per cent of the oldest (55 to 59).

Looking at children aged 11 to 16, 11.8 per cent of children in England and 16 per cent of children in Scotland admit to ever having used cannabis. This percentages rises over time with 1.7 and 3 per cent of 11 to 12 year olds in England and Scotland respectively claiming use, compared to 29.6 and 38 per cent of 15 to 16 year olds. This pattern is repeated in more recent use, with 0.4 and 1 per cent of children aged 11 to 12 admitting use in the last month compared to 15.7 and 23 per cent of 15 to 16 year olds in England and Scotland respectively (Goddard and Higgins 1999a and b).

The other most commonly reported drugs used by BCS respondents were hallucinogens (LSD, magic mushrooms and amyl-nitrate) cocaine, ecstasy and amphetamines. Figure 3.1 provides the details. Again, the pattern established with cannabis use repeats itself, with use among the younger groups being more prevalent than among the older age group. However, and again mirroring the cannabis experience, those figures fall when respondents are questioned about last month use. For example, less than 0.5 per cent of those aged over 35 reported use of any of those four drugs in the last month. Even among the younger age groups, where use is more prevalent, there were falls in recent use, compared to lifetime use. In the group aged 16 to 24, 5.1 per cent admitted to using amphetamines, 2.8 per cent hallucinogens, 2 per cent ecstasy and 0.9 per cent cocaine in the last month.

Turning our attention to children, DrugScope (2000: 32) provides details of use of hallucinogens, amphetamines, cocaine and ecstasy among children aged 15 to 16 in England and Scotland. Table 3.3 gives the percentage figures for consumptionn of these drugs by this group.

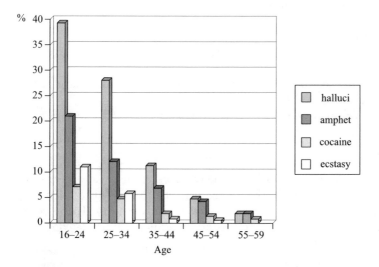

Figure 3.1 Percentage use of drugs other than cannabis by age cohort (Source: British Crime Survey 1999)

Table 3.3 Use of hallucinogens, amphetamines, cocaine and ecstasy among children aged 15 to 16 in England and Scotland

Time period	Cocaine, %	Amphetamine, %	Ecstasy, %	Hallucinogens, %
Lifetime:				
England	2.8	7.6	2.5	6.1
Scotland	1.0	12.0	4.0	10.0
Last month:				
	1.0	2.0	0.7	1.8
	0.0	4.0	1.0	3.0

Source: DrugScope 2000

Public attitudes towards illicit drugs

Information for this section comes from the work of Leitner *et al.* (1993) and a MORI poll commissioned by the *Independent on Sunday*. The former survey concentrated on the views of people aged 16 and above, whereas the latter included the views of school children aged 11 to 16. Much of this is covered in the Runciman Report (1999: ch. 2). In summary, Runciman suggests that

- Across all ages, heroin, cocaine, ecstasy and amphetamines are judged as harmful or very harmful by 90 per cent of the population.
- Across all ages, only one third (33 per cent) judged cannabis to be harmful or very harmful.
- Across ages 16 to 59, 66 per cent wanted strong and effective drug laws.
- Nearly 50 per cent of all adults wanted a change in the drug laws so that the use of cannabis was no longer illegal.
- Less than one half of 1 per cent saw cannabis users as a police priority.

The changing nature of drug use in Britain

By now it should be clear that it is beyond the scope of this, or any other study for that matter, to make definitive claims as to the true extent of illicit drug misuse in Britain at the beginning of the twenty-first century. That explains why any text, when discussing numbers or figures in any way related to drug misuse, is littered with caveats:

> *Best guess* at nos. of problem users who need treatment . . .
>
> (Edmunds *et al.* 1999; emphasis added)

Because of the absence of reliable prevalence data . . . questions relating to prevalence of drug misuse in the adult population *cannot be answered with certainty*.

(Welsh Drug and Alcohol Unit 1998: 11; emphasis added)

Anyone working with use and misuse of drugs issues is immediately confronted with the difficulty of obtaining good information.

(Davidson and Sturgeon-Adams 1997)

However, it is possible to offer some tentative conclusions based on the available data. Official statistics drawn from medical and legal data show that for some people using illicit drugs creates problems. These problems can be medical, social or legal, and a problematic user can experience all of these problems simultaneously. Medical and legal data also show that drug use is mainly the preserve of the young, with few people aged over 30 coming to the state's attention. Where there are problems, especially medical problems, the drug that causes most concern seems to be heroin. Over the last thirty years there have been marked rises in the numbers of people coming to the attention of both the medical and legal arms of the British system. Equally, we know through seizure data that there are relatively large amounts of illicit drugs circulating in Britain. Care needs to be taken in basing conclusions on these figures alone as there are serious methodological weaknesses with these data and it is generally recognized that official statistics do not cover all aspects of drug use, be that 'problematic' or 'recreational'.

Household surveys provide a fuller picture, although, again, the data they produce are self-acknowledged as lacking accuracy. Based on work such as the BCS, it is possible to suggest that recreational or experimental drug use has risen in Britain across the 1990s. At present, a significant minority, somewhere in the region of a third of the British population, has used an illicit drug at some time in their life. It is impossible to be categoric about this, as our research cannot provide definitive information. The BCS seems to show that use is sporadic and/or experimental and appears to be confined to those in their teens and early twenties, with use reducing considerably by middle age. Equally, those who use drugs recreationally or experimentally seem to favour one in particular – cannabis. However, it is highly likely that drug use is underreported and that people are more likely to report soft drug use rather than the harder drugs.

Nevertheless, it is arguable that cannabis use is the most prevalent form of illicit drug taking, leading to a situation where it is not seen as a problem in the way in which drugs such as heroin or cocaine are. In turn, this creates a situation where public attitudes to that particular drug are at odds with those of the state. Where the public and state do seem to agree is on the problems posed by 'harder' drugs such as heroin and cocaine.

However, no one can say for sure that this amalgam of data provides the definitive picture. Social scientists, government researchers and those working for state agencies dealing with illicit drug use have yet to devise a method that counts and measures hidden populations with any degree of accuracy. The most any camp can do is to offer 'best-guess' figures, and it is on these, plus anecdotal evidence, plus the 'knowledge' of those working in the drug scene, that much policy is based. It is a measure of the seriousness with which the British state treats the 'drug problem' that sums of money as large as £6 billion are spent, especially when based on such evidence. The next chapter focuses on two aspects of state reactions to drug use by examining the manner in which the use of illicit drugs is 'policed' by both arms of the British system.

Note

1 The combined figure for England, Scotland and Wales was 37,681 in September 1999 (Drugscope 2000).

4 The British state's legal and medical responses to illicit drug use

Introduction

Chapter 3 identified the fact that measuring the extent of illicit drug use in Britain was fraught with difficulties, leading to a lack of clarity over the true extent and nature of illicit use. Despite this, the British state exhibits numerous signs of concern over the 'drug problem' in Britain. Such concern has spawned a number of policy initiatives, all aimed at dealing with various aspects of substance use. In terms of the British state, these responses emanate chiefly from two sources: the medical profession and the legislature, thereby both reflecting and cementing the dual approach of the British system.

The purpose of this chapter is to explore the manner in which drug use is 'policed' in Britain. In order to achieve this the chapter will provide an overview of the broad policy approaches and the main statutory instruments that dictate the responses of the criminal justice agencies and the medical profession. These two bodies together, and very often independently from each other, 'police' drug use in Britain. The rationale in including this discussion is to establish the parameters of 'policing' and alert the reader to the *general* direction of British drug policy. No specific policy initiatives will be explored at this stage in the book, contemporary policy developments being covered, in detail, in Chapter 9. Rather, this chapter will demonstrate that the British state's policing of drugs is based on the control of certain types of drug, via the manner in which, and by whom, they are supplied and used, or by ensuring that drug use is carried out safely within medically defined parameters. Additionally, the chapter will emphasize the importance of realizing that 'policing' drug use can be affected either through the law or medicine, or, in many cases, combinations of both.

The chapter begins with a brief discussion of the meaning of policing as employed in the context of this work. From there, it continues by outlining the international context from which most of Britain's drug laws emerge and are based. This mixture of internal political pressure to 'do something' in relation to drugs, coupled with external requirements to ratify international treaties, gave rise to the 1971 Misuse of Drugs Act (hereafter

MDA) which at present is the key British legal control relating to drugs. From this base, the chapter moves to review the content of the MDA.

Following this, the chapter turns its attention to the other main form of policing, the control of drugs by the medical profession. It outlines the importance that the concept of prevention holds for the medical profession, before moving to review *Drug Misuse and Dependence: Guidelines on Clinical Management* (DoH 1999). In particular, it notes the manner in which the DoH suggests that problematic drug users are policed via a mixture of prescription, increased compliance, withdrawal and dependence management. The chapter concludes with a brief discussion of the general nature of drug policy, noting the tension between the various ways in which the arms of the British system deal with what is, essentially, the same problem.

'Policing' drugs: a broad definition

For a number of readers, a discussion around a definition of 'policing' may seem slightly superfluous: policing is surely what the police do. Policing revolves around the images television programmes such as *The Bill* provide on an almost daily basis. For those of that persuasion, the notion that the medical profession can be engaged in 'policing' may be seen as (a) a novel idea or (b) stupid. However, neither is the case: consider this quotation from Reiner:

> It is important to distinguish between the ideas of 'police' and 'policing'. 'Police' refers to a particular form of social institution, while 'policing' implies a set of processes with specific social functions.
>
> (Reiner 2000: 1)

He continues, noting that 'policing' is, in fact, a set of activities that attempt to maintain a particular form of social order. That order may result from a society wide consensus, or it may be the result of latent conflict between differently placed social groups. Whatever the case, the function of 'policing' is to ensure that a particular form of social order is encouraged, maintained and upheld.

In turn, social order is dependent upon two related concepts: that of creating and encouraging conformity and that of maintaining control over populations. However, as Reiner (2000: 2–3) points out, there is a problem in linking 'policing' to general social control. Policing is, according to Reiner, a specific aspect of the overall social control process. Policing excludes concepts such as punishment, socialization, family structure and religious beliefs, all of which have different functions within the totality that has become known as social control. Policing is one of many sub-sets in the whole social control process. Reiner provides a definition that neatly summarizes the approach to policing taken in this book. For our purposes then, policing should be seen as

... systems of surveillance coupled with the threat of sanctions for dis-
covered deviance – either immediately or in terms of the initiation of
penal processes or both.

(Reiner 2000: 3)

As will be argued below, this definition can encompass the work not only of
the police and the other law enforcement agencies such as Customs and
Excise, but can also be seen to cover much of the work of what are defined
as 'welfarist' agencies, such as social workers, and, of course, the medical profession. Using this definition allows us to conceive of policing as a continuum.
At the 'hard-end' of the continuum are the law and order agencies, employing
legislation, which is often a blunt instrument, to achieve control and conformity. At the other, 'soft-end', are the 'social' agencies, which often employ
less overt, more subtle means, but nevertheless use the twin tools of surveillance and threat of sanctions as a means of controlling populations, allowing
these agencies to be seen by some of a radical persuasion as being 'iron fists in
velvet gloves' (George and Wilding 1992).

This difference in approach between the two ends of the continuum is a key
concept to grasp. While the manner in which the law enforcement agencies
operate within our particular definition of policing may be axiomatic, the
involvement of the medical profession in policing may need to be explained
further. Viewing medicine as a sub-set of social control may go some way
to endorsing a few of the points made in Chapter 2, concerning the medical
profession's early interest in, and links with, late Victorian moral philanthropists. It also allows us to look beyond medical involvement with problematic drug users from the simplistic 'treatment model' perspective, and ask
questions about the social, moral and political functions performed by doctors
in 'treating' (perhaps policing?) drug dependent users. This becomes important because control of the work of both the hard-end and soft-end agencies
emanates from the state and, as previously stated, it is a contention of this
book that the 'drug problem' in Britain is at least in part a political construct.

In that respect policing the drug problem by hard- and soft-end agencies
clearly has functions beyond arresting and/or treating drug users; it also
becomes part of wider social control by promoting and cementing conformity
to a certain set of practices. That said, the chapter moves on to its main task,
that of exploring and examining the central documents that shape Britain's
general policy approach to policing drugs. The immediate section will provide a brief contextual overview of the genesis of the key British legal policy
document, the 1971 Misuse of Drugs Act.

The 1971 Misuse of Drugs Act: a brief contextual note

As Chapter 2 explained, the genesis of much British drug policy lies in
various international treaties. By creating laws such as the MDA, Britain is
able to meet its international obligations, although as Runciman (1999)

notes, the MDA goes beyond the scope of many of the United Nations (UN) conventions. The MDA is able to do so because, although the United Nations conventions oblige signatories to meet certain broad demands, including the creation of criminal offences for contravening the conventions, the day-to-day minutiae of the law enforcement are left to the discretion of the individual nation. This explains why drug laws often exhibit significant variations from country to country.

Since the beginning of the 1960s, when the UN replaced the League of Nations as the main body with responsibility for the international control of drugs, there have been three key UN treaties that have had a direct and significant impact on British drug laws. The first was the Single Convention on Narcotic Drugs 1961. This convention attempts to standardize the control of narcotics across nations so that certain drugs are only used for scientific, medical and, in some cases, industrial purposes. The 1961 Convention arranges drugs into schedules that determine the nature of the controls over any given drug. Any activity that contravenes the convention must be a punishable offence, with a custodial term for serious breaches. Crucially, such a requirement almost invariably makes certain aspects of drug use a criminal offence within signatory states.

The second key international convention is the UN Convention on Psychotropic Drugs 1971. This is concerned with, among other drugs, hallucinogens, stimulants and sedatives. Again, the aim here is to limit drug use to scientific or medical purposes. The important point of this convention is that it severely restricts the use of certain drugs to the extent that many cannot be used at all, even on prescription. This accounts for the fact that some cannabis type drugs (for example, cannabinol) cannot, at the time of writing, be prescribed freely in Britain. In line with the 1961 Convention, actions that contravene the 1971 Treaty must be punishable up to, and including, prison sentences for serious breaches.

Somewhat problematically, it appears that the wording of both the 1961 and 1971 UN Conventions lacked clarity in relation to the offences of possession, purchase and cultivation in relation to personal use, thereby creating a loophole in the law. The UN recognized this and used the United Nations Convention against Illicit Traffic in Narcotic Drugs and Psychotropic Substances 1988 (known as the Vienna Convention) to close this gap. The 1988 Vienna Convention specifies that breaches in the conventions must be seen as criminal offences under each signatory state's domestic law. Greater care in wording the Vienna Convention was taken in an effort to ensure that there is greater clarification of 'criminal' activity, in a concerted effort to create a loophole-free document. Both illuminating and recognizing the evolving nature of the illicit drug industry, the convention includes sections on the control of precursor chemicals, used in the manufacture of illicit substances, and money laundering by drug dealers. As with the previous two conventions, detailed implementation is left to the discretion of the signatory state.

British drug law, including the MDA, must therefore be seen in this wider international context. In many respects, the UN conventions set the broad parameters of drug legislation, but the details are left to the individual states to interpret within their own political, social and cultural frameworks. Thus, it could be argued that the best way to view the legal side of British drug policy (as with many other nation states' legal response to drug use) is as a hybrid of international law and uniquely domestic concerns and worries. With those thoughts in mind, the chapter now reviews the content of the 1971 MDA.

The 1971 Misuse of Drugs Act

This section outlines some of the main sections of the 1971 MDA so the reader is able better to understand the main points of British law relating to substances controlled under the MDA. The intention here is to provide a broad-brush overview of the law and not to enter into a discussion of the fine details of the legislation (for a fuller résumé of the 1971 MDA, see Runciman 1999, Chapters 1 and 3).

The MDA 1971 replaced the three principal drug control acts of the 1960s: the Drugs (Prevention of Misuse) Act 1964, and the Dangerous Drugs Acts of 1965 and 1967. In this way, the British state was able to bring together all the hitherto disparate controls and use the 1971 MDA to act as the statutory framework in the control of drugs. That framework included: a system of licensing of doctors to prescribe heroin and cocaine; the requirement of all doctors to notify addicts to the Home Office; the introduction of national stop and search powers for the police; the introduction of regulations on the safe custody of drugs. The MDA was also responsible for establishing Britain's first statutory advisory group on illicit drugs, the Advisory Council on the Misuse of Drugs (ACMD). Significantly, as far as the law is concerned, the MDA introduced a number of new approaches that are clearly important today.

Firstly, it instigated a strict classification of drugs. Following the passing of the MDA, drugs were placed in one of three categories, A, B or C. The category into which each particular drug is placed is determined by the extent of harm its misuse inflicts. It must be noted that this classification was based on medical knowledge that was as limited then as, arguably, now. For example, heroin and cocaine are defined as Class A drugs, recognizing the serious effects of prolonged misuse, whereas cannabis is a Class B drug, and substances such as benzodiazepines (tranquillizers) are Class C drugs. The penalties issued by the courts for any contravention of the MDA are directly related to the class of drug involved in the cases, with Class A drugs attracting the most severe legal responses. Equally important is the dichotomy inherent in the offence of unlawful possession, with a distinction being made between possession and possession with intent to supply, the latter being seen as more serious.

Running briefly through the sections of the MDA, section 1 established the ACMD and codified its duty as the standing body charged to advise the government on the prevention of the misuse of drugs, and how to deal with the social problems linked to drug misuse. This is still the case some thirty years later. Section 2 identified those drugs which were to be controlled by the MDA, and ordered them into their respective classes. Sections 3 to 6 identified those activities that became criminal offences under the MDA. These offences include: import and export, possession, supply, possession with intent to supply and the cultivation of the cannabis plant. Sections 8 and 9 made it an offence for the occupier or manager of any premises knowingly to allow those premises to be used for the smoking of opium or cannabis, the production or supply of controlled drugs, and the preparing and taking of controlled drugs. Section 9 concentrates specifically on the supply of materials or articles that can be used in the unlawful administration of drugs.

Vital for the medical profession's ability to treat and prescribe to drug users who experience problems, section 7 lists exemptions from the MDA, thus allowing the medical profession, including dentists, pharmacists and scientific researchers, the ability to carry on their work free from the fear of prosecution. Sections 10 and 11 of the MDA empower the Secretary of State to make regulations governing most aspects of drug management and administration, including transport, storing, destruction, labelling, record keeping and prescribing. Section 11 concentrates on providing directions to the occupier of any premises where controlled drugs are to be kept. Sections 12 to 16 empower the Secretary of State to withdraw the ability to prescribe, administer or manufacture controlled drugs from any member of the medical, pharmaceutical or veterinary profession.

Sections 23 and 24 outline police powers of stop and search, the searching of premises and arrest. These stipulations have subsequently been superseded in England and Wales by the 1984 Police and Criminal Evidence Act, but still apply in Scotland. Sections 25 and 26 provide for maximum penalties, and it is important to note that following the Crime (Sentences) Act 1997, a third consecutive trafficking offence involving a Class A drug receives a minimum seven-year prison sentence. Section 28 is an interesting addition to the MDA as it allows for any defendant to prove lack of knowledge as to the nature of the substance they are charged with misusing and thus be acquitted. However, Runciman (1999) notes that in reality, as a defence, section 28 'is a high hurdle for a defendant to overcome'.

It is important to reiterate the point made earlier that the above is merely a brief overview of the MDA. It is equally important to be aware that over time certain parts of the MDA have been replaced by other legislation, as in the case of police stop and search powers with the Police and Criminal Evidence Act 1984 or mandatory sentences under the 1997 Crime (Sentences) Act. It is also necessary to be aware of other related legislation such as the Criminal

Justice (International Co-operation) Act 1990, which enabled the UK to comply with parts of the Vienna Convention 1988 and is primarily concerned with the supply of precursor drugs used in the manufacture of many illicit substances. Other important Acts for consideration would include the Drug Trafficking Act 1994, which created offences in relation to money laundering and handling the proceeds of drug trafficking. It also introduced measures to confiscate the proceeds of drug trafficking.

Given the benefit of hindsight, the 1971 MDA can be seen to be a product of its time, and was drafted as a response to the situation during that period. The ever-changing nature of the illicit drug 'industry' has required the implementation of various other Acts over time. For example, when the MDA was drafted there was very little importation of heroin: as Chapter 2 notes, HM Customs and Excise only made their first major seizure of heroin in 1971. The contemporary growth and constantly changing nature of international drug trafficking have subsequently required a review of policy responses, both domestically and internationally. Worldwide, this gave rise to the Vienna Convention in 1988. As a result, Britain responded to the Vienna Convention by passing the Drug Trafficking Act 1994, demonstrating the impact changes in both international law and domestic events have had upon British law in relation to drugs.

Essentially, what the MDA tried to achieve was a codification of, and organizing framework for, the British state's legal response to the use and supply of certain drugs. Simplistically, this involves the prohibition and proscription of all aspects of use and supply of substances controlled under the auspices of the MDA. Only in extremely limited scenarios is the general public allowed to use drugs controlled under the MDA without medical approval, and, for example, as with the case of section 28, once knowledge has been confirmed, use must cease. The state's legally based reaction to drug use, as enshrined in the MDA, can be seen to be draconian with little or no leeway given. In short, the strict letter of the law prohibits the use and supply of certain substances and any transgressions that are detected will result in punishment.

Quite clearly, the MDA provides a framework within which the law enforcement agencies are able to undertake the policing of drug use. There is ample scope within the MDA for surveillance operations by criminal justice agencies and there is an ever-present danger for those illicit users, identified and arrested by the criminal justice agencies, of attracting legal sanctions. For the British legal system, the MDA is both a codification of the state's legal response to illicit drug use and the social control tool with which to promote and ensure conformity with a drug-free lifestyle. The next section moves away from the British state's legal response to examine the approach to drug use championed and directed by the DoH to the other 'police officers' of drug use: the (broadly defined) medical profession.

The medical profession: policing via prevention and prescription

The response of the state's criminal justice arm has been to control and define the type of legally acceptable drugs via prohibition and proscription. The ultimate response of the medical arm has been to attempt to control the type and amount of drugs used by the power of treatment and prescription, via the use of doctors. Before going on to review the key role played by doctors in policing drug users, it is important to point out that many other statutory and voluntary bodies, which come under the broad rubric of socio-medical agencies, also work with drug users and the wider population in preventing, reducing or altering drug taking behaviour. They represent an important part of the overall strategy and it is to these that the next section turns.

As McDermott (1998: 93) confirms, 'there have been two primary strategies . . . to deal with the drug problem . . . interdiction and demand reduction'. Essentially, interdiction is within the realm of the law enforcement agencies, and has been covered above, whereas aspects of demand reduction fall into the remit of socio-medical agencies. In itself, this type of demand reduction can take two forms: (i) general messages aimed at preventing people from starting to take drugs and/or to encourage those taking drugs to either cease, or reduce the harm they are doing or (ii) to use drugs issued on prescription by doctors, often supplemented by counselling or other treatments, to control the demand for illicit drugs. As already noted, the control of problematic drug users by prescription will be explored later in this chapter. The immediate concern is to review those general preventative techniques which are aimed at reducing demand for drugs among the wider population.

Policing via prevention

Ham (1992) informs that health promotion has had a long-term impact on improving the quality of health in Britain, but only relatively recently has it become a specialism in its own right. He points to the 1976 DHSS document *Prevention and Health: Everybody's Business* as a watershed, in as much as it gave recognition to the importance of health promotion via preventative campaigns. In the world of drug use, the importance of prevention messages was writ large during the AIDS scare of the 1980s, which ran alongside other campaigns aimed at reducing AIDS related drug use, such as the *Heroin Screws You Up* promotions of the mid-to-late 1980s.

The rationale behind the majority of most health promotion campaigns is to prevent the general population from damaging their health due to the manner in which they live their lives, whether in relation to heart disease, tooth decay or illicit drug use. Prevention campaigns generally operate on one of three levels, primary, secondary and tertiary. Primary campaigns are usually highly generalized and quite often the message is simplistic, mainly because it is aimed at the widest possible audience. This type of prevention was, for a long time, at the forefront of British drug prevention initiatives (McDermott 1998). However, the effectiveness of such a strategy has been questioned because it does

> . . . little more than confirm the beliefs of those people who were never at risk of using in the first place, while having little or no impact whatsoever on those people who were going to use drugs.
>
> (McDermott 1998: 93)

Thus, the *Just Say No* or *Heroin Screws You Up* prevention campaigns ran counter to the experiences of many young users, but at the same time perhaps reinforced some of their elders' views on drug use. The effect was to devalue information in the eyes of those sections of society perhaps most 'at risk' of drug related problems, while at the same time cementing stereotypical, uni-dimensional views of a complex social phenomenon in social groups which had little first-hand knowledge or experience of drug use.

A gradual realization of the futility of this situation led to an increase in secondary prevention campaigns. Promotions of this kind are far more specific and are aimed at groups thought to be at risk of currently using, on the verge of using or being exposed to controlled drugs. The driving principle of this approach is that of harm reduction or harm minimization, itself a primary influence in both contemporary and historical British medical drug policy. The overall impact of harm reduction on British drug policy will be explored further in Chapters 8 and 9; for now however, it is important to grasp the three guiding principles of modern harm reduction approaches in order better to understand the nature of secondary and tertiary prevention campaigns. These are:

1 Excessive behaviours occur along a continuum of risk ranging from minimal to extreme.
2 Changing addictive behaviour is a stepwise process, complete abstinence being the final step.
3 Sobriety simply isn't for everybody.

(Westermeyer 1998: 1)

Secondary prevention campaigns can take several guises and differing elements of these are often used in their support. For example, there are a number of school-based initiatives aimed at both pupils and their parents (Barton 2001), where teachers and outside specialists make their audiences aware of the dangers of drug use, as well as the importance of safer use once the decision to take illicit drugs has been taken. Likewise the Health Education Authority (HEA) publishes a number of guides. These are often magazine style booklets that promote a zero-use approach but contain sections on safe use and first aid, as well as detailing the properties and effects of different drugs. In a similar vein, again with the intent of targeting a highly specific audience, drug projects such as Lifeline in Manchester have published a series of cartoon-based pamphlets. From a completely personal perspective, my favourites are those serializing the drug-related misfortunes and adventures of characters such as *Peanut Pete* and *Claire and Jose*, which are aimed at ensuring safe use while highlighting the possible dangers associated with drug taking.

Secondary prevention in Britain is therefore moving towards a more realistic approach to drug prevention information, in as much as it recognizes that for some young people drug use is part of their cultural and social experiences. Moreover, and of special importance to the success of any prevention campaign, the tone and content of the prevention message correspond to, and resonate with, the target audiences' lived experience. The result is the beginning of a secondary prevention regime that has credibility and thus commands the respect of its intended audience by virtue of promoting a realistic and non-patronizing message. However, the central elements of policing are still visible. Surveillance of the drug taking behaviour of the population takes the form of general household surveys that, despite being imprecise, nevertheless provide tangible target populations. In this example, sanctions refer to the implications that excessive drug taking will lead to ill health and/or criminal convictions. Primary and secondary prevention campaigns thus attempt to promote and ensure conformity to the drug-free lifestyle.

The final form of prevention is tertiary. This is also targeted, being aimed directly at those whose drug use has moved towards the problematic area of the continuum of risk. It is here that the full weight of the 'hard-end' of medical policing enters the 'fight against drugs', along with its 'ultimate weapon', the right to prescribe.

Policing via prescription: a brief contextual note

As Chapter 2 noted, for many years following the findings of the Rolleston Committee in 1926, British doctors could prescribe all manner of substances to those addicted to drugs with virtual impunity. Indeed, the first controls on the prescribing behaviour of doctors only came into force during the 1960s due, in the main, to the over-prescription of heroin, leading to large quantities of licit drugs being diverted into the illicit drug market. While this legislation may have curbed the autonomy of some doctors, it was not a serious problem for the majority, due to the fact that during the 1960s and into the early 1970s the numbers of problematic drug users were relatively small, and those being treated were often referred to specialist services. This meant that the vast majority of doctors, especially general practitioners (GPs), rarely, if ever, saw a drug addict. The outcome of this scenario was that the issues of how, when and why to prescribe for drug addicts never became a pressing question for the majority of doctors.

However, as has been documented (Gerada and Farrell 1998: 330–1), the number of problematic drug users 'surged' during the late 1970s and into the 1980s, leading to the then DHSS encouraging GPs to become more involved with problematic drug users. Clearly, this placed GPs in a predicament, as many of them had never been asked to deal with a group that some see as 'problem patients' and, perhaps crucially, at that time too few medical undergraduates had received even basic education in treating problematic drug users (BMA 1997: 121). As a result, many GPs were left isolated and lacking advice or direction. Those who would accept drug addicts as patients were sometimes inundated with addicts, all demanding treatment. Some GPs quickly became disillusioned; many made injudicious prescribing policies; many more simply retreated behind long-held prejudices (Hutchinson 2001).

Given the rise in recreational drug culture and a concomitant growth in problematic use, this situation could not be allowed to continue. This was recognized in the DHSS (1982) report *Treatment and Rehabilitation*. In turn, two years later the DHSS published *Guidelines of Good Clinical Practice in the Treatment of Drug Misuse* (DHSS 1984). These were updated and re-named in 1991, appearing as *Drug Misuse and Dependence: Guidelines on Clinical Management* (DoH 1991) and were again up-dated in 1999. It is to the 1999 document that attention now turns.

The DoH guidelines

Robertson (2000: 325) emphasizes the importance of the 1999 revisions and notes their timeliness, claiming that there was a real and pressing need for the 1999 review owing to the fact that with

> [t]he demise of the British Addict Index and the revocation of the statutory requirement for British doctors to notify the Chief Medical Officer of cases of addiction, many national and international events seem to threaten and confuse clinicians and policy makers. . . . These Guidelines, therefore, are opportune and bear a considerable responsibility. . . . There should be no doubt, therefore, that they are . . . heavy weight . . . and are likely to give rise to substantial changes in clinical practice in the UK.

At a very basic level, the importance vested in the 1999 document can be seen in its size in comparison to that of its predecessors: it runs to some 138 pages compared to the 57 the 1991 guidelines contained. Obviously, the authors intended it to be a comprehensive and authoritative tome, able to be used a source of reference for all manner of drug-related information.

Running through its content, the 1999 document begins with an overview of the current situation, including the growth of illicit drug use as well as an outline of the rights and responsibilities of doctors towards the drug user, highlighting the fact that doctors who refuse to treat patients because they have a moral objection to that patient's lifestyle are in danger of adopting unethical practices (DoH 1999: 2). It then goes on to note government policy changes. Importantly, the document then makes a clear distinction between three types of doctor, the generalist, the specialized generalist and the specialist.

In turn, generalists are defined as 'medical practitioners who may be involved in the treatment of drug misuse, although this is not their main area of work . . . service to be provided would be expected to include the assessment of drug misusers and, where appropriate, the prescribing of substitute medication' (DoH 1999: 5). Further, the DoH notes an expectation that generalist doctors would undergo regular training and keep updated on issues such as the development of dependence, policy issues and the management of drug treatment.

The specialized generalist is defined as 'a practitioner whose work is essentially generic or, if a specialist, is not primarily concerned with drug misuse treatment, but who has a special interest in treating drug misusers. Such practitioners would have expertise and competence to provide assessment of most cases with complex needs' (DoH 1999: 5). The DoH offers examples of such doctors, citing a prison medical officer or GP who has a large number of users registered as patients. These doctors are also seen as potential sources of 'expert' help for other professionals and/or generalist doctors.

The specialist is seen as 'a practitioner who provides expertise, training and competence in drug misuse treatment as their main clinical activity. Such a practitioner works in a specialist multi-disciplinary team, can carry out assessment of any case with complex needs and provide a full range of treatments and access to rehabilitation options' (DoH 1999: 6). The DoH envisages that the specialist doctors be psychiatrists (continuing a trend: it will be recalled that Chapter 2 noted one of the first attempts by the medical profession to control drug users was via their inclusion into the provisions of the Lunacy Act 1890). These doctors would be able to prescribe in a manner requiring a Home Office Licence and are seen as 'the expert's expert' with an appropriate commitment to continued training and education in substance misuse.

Arguably, the DoH guidelines encourage doctors to police problematic drug use by employing a combination of four approaches: managing and treating withdrawal; agreeing to and servicing a maintenance regime; cultivating and maintaining the compliance of the patient; retaining the power to prescribe. As with the MDA, the DoH document is a large and complex volume and what follows is merely a broad summary, designed to provide a sense of the general direction in which the work moves. Bearing that caveat in mind, the essential elements of these four policing strategies will now be reviewed.

Patients with problematic drug use can present to the doctor for a broad range of reasons, but generally share the common desire for treatment designed to improve their health. This is recognized by the DoH (1999: 9), which categorically states that the primary aims of treatment are to 'assist the patient to remain healthy' until they can live a drug-free life, and to 'reduce the use of illicit or non-prescribed drugs'. The first task for the doctor is to assess the nature and extent of drug related problems, to establish patterns of use, determine the patient's motivation to change and then to determine the need for substitute medication. The DoH also stresses the need to assess the patient's expectation of treatment.

For the patient, once the decision has been made to cease or reduce drug use, one of the first effects will be the onset of withdrawal symptoms, the nature, intensity and speed at which these symptoms occur being heavily dependent upon the type of drug being used. Although some addicts can withdraw without substitute drugs (Robins 1973), the vast majority of addicts will require some help with detoxification and the withdrawal symptoms associated with this process. In order to relieve these symptoms, doctors can dispense 'temporary prescription[s] of other drugs to reduce withdrawal symptoms' (DoH 1999: 36). The guidelines offer suggestions for a number of substitute drugs for the various types of addiction problems.

Once the decision to prescribe has been taken, the next question is 'how much?' Clearly, the patient's health will be paramount, so the dose has to be one that will not place the patient in jeopardy of overdosing, especially with methadone, a drug commonly prescribed to opiate addicts. The DoH guidelines suggest doses based on the severity of the withdrawal symptoms, with overall aim of minimizing the suffering endured by the withdrawing addict. Once the initial withdrawal period is over, the doctor, following consultation with the patient, must then decide on the next step in the policing of problematic drug use.

The DoH (1999: 52) notes that for some addicts abstinence will be achieved relatively quickly, with the patient and doctor agreeing to a reduction regimen, whereby the patient will receive prescriptions of substitute drugs that gradually reduce in amount until the point is reached where the patient becomes drug-free. For the majority, however, it is usually necessary to establish a maintenance programme. This is a long-term approach to problematic drug use that can, in some cases, continue for a number of years before the patient is ready to reduce their prescription drug intake. The patient will receive a regular supply of a prescription drug that is of an appropriate dose. The amount of drug will be enough to stave off withdrawal symptoms, provide a measure of stability, yet not be sufficient to induce 'signs of intoxication' (DoH 1999: 60).

However, despite the DoH's recognition of the benefits of this strategy (DoH 1999: 47), they also warn doctors against using this approach as a 'treatment of first choice for the patient presenting for the first time' (DoH 1999: 52). Thus, obtaining a maintenance prescription requires the addict to have at least undergone one other form of drug treatment regime prior to being considered for the maintenance option. In this manner, doctors are able to 'police' those who obtain access to a long-term and regular supply of drugs. This restriction of access to maintenance regimes can be seen as one way to ensure patient compliance.

Compliance is a very important aspect of the medical profession's approach to treating this client group. The DoH guidelines contain a section on the consequences of non-compliance and on improving compliance. For example, the DoH guidelines offer a number of points of advice concerning the manner in which the doctor can build the trust and confidence of the addicted patient, thus aiding compliance. These include building a relationship via weekly appointments in the initial stages, turning into fortnightly or monthly appointments once stability has been achieved. However, the DoH also advises doctors to employ other tactics that can be seen to be more controlling.

Thus, more controlling tactics might include random urine tests designed to ascertain if the patient is still using illicit drugs, daily pick ups of the substitute drug, and supervised consumption of the substitute drug, the latter constraints only being relaxed when 'the doctor can be satisfied that compliance can be maintained' (DoH 1999: 61). In defence of the medical profession's insistence upon compliance, there are very good reasons as to it being at the centre of treating addicts. As the DoH notes (1999: 60), non-compliance can lead to overdose and death, as well as the diversion of licit drugs on to the illicit market.

Overarching all of the above is the ability of the doctor to prescribe substitute drugs. Clearly, this power is an important part of the medical profession's identity and forms a substantial part of their professional power base, at the same time carrying with it an enormous responsibility, the latter point being made forcibly by the DoH guidelines. However, it also ensures that the doctors exercise extensive control over their patients, especially those patients who are dependent upon drugs: in itself, the threat of a loss of prescription becomes an encouragement for the patient to comply. In fact, the DoH urges doctors only to begin to prescribe where 'the doctor is satisfied that the patient will co-operate and demonstrate adequate compliance with the prescribing regime' (DoH 1999: 30). Nevertheless, doctors can, and do, end treatment programmes due to the non-compliance of the patient. While this is understandable, it also provides the doctor with a considerable ability to police the lifestyle of the addict patient, due largely to the fact that non-compliance will lead, ultimately, to a withdrawal of legal, substitute drugs. When this happens, the addict will almost always be forced to return to using illicit drugs, and the concomitant risks associated with that lifestyle.

Arguably, the power to prescribe is at the heart of the medical profession's 'policing policy' in relation to problematic drug users. Without retention of the right to withdraw prescriptions, doctors quickly lose their professional identity, as well as the all-important ability to control their patient's behaviour. As Whitaker and McLeod (1998: 366) point out, 'the line between "substitute prescribing" and simply giving drug users legal drugs, thus decriminalizing that part of their drug use is indistinct'. Building upon the paradox that the possession of medically approved and supervised drug use automatically decriminalizes drug users, Self (1992) has colourfully pointed out that doctors can become '[drug] dealers by appointment to H.M. Government'. This point is taken up more forcibly by Strang *et al*. (1994: 202) who suggest that there is some concern that doctors could become 'over-paid grocers', if they are forced merely to act as signatories on prescriptions.

Although prescriptions are usually part of an overall care package, for many addicts the prescription is seen as 'the whole treatment' (Read 1995), thus allowing the power to prescribe to be employed as a form of 'carrot and stick' in the policing of problematic drug users. It is a carrot in as much that if the addict is able to convince the doctor that their problem is sufficient, their attitude is correct, and that they are able to comply with the agreed treatment plan, they will be rewarded with a prescription. On the other hand, it becomes a stick, because failure to comply will almost certainly lead to a withdrawal of the prescription, which for many will cause a return to illicit drug use.

From this perspective, it can be seen that the work of doctors in dealing with problematic, heavy-end drug users becomes a form of policing. There are clear elements of surveillance: the weekly appointments, supervised consumption and random urine tests being the most obvious. There is also the element of sanction: reviews of the treatment plan, a revocation of home consumption and a cessation of treatment and prescription. Using a combination of these approaches allows doctors to control drug addicts. It also forces addicts to conform, if not to society's mores of a drug-free life, then certainly to the medical profession's conception of a 'good' patient.

Conclusion

This chapter has tried to alert the reader to the fact that the British state (alongside almost every other western democracy) makes a significant effort to police the use of controlled drugs. In Britain's case, the state employs two different sectors – medicine and the law – to carry out this task, thereby running the risk of deploying a number of differences and similarities in the manner in which the state polices drug use. In terms of similarities, both sectors use the tactics of surveillance and sanction in an effort to ensure conformity. However, the difference lies in the effect of the sanctions each sector employs. These are dramatically different, with one, the law, treating the drug user as a criminal, and therefore by implication as 'bad', while the other, medicine, treats the drug user as a patient, and therefore as 'ill'.

In this way, contact with either arm of the British system is framed within competing discourses of knowledge, and brings dramatically different social consequences: at the same time a drug user can be defined as a criminal and as a patient, and receive the concomitant actions and responses both roles carry with them. At one level there is very little wrong with this. Indeed, it could be argued that policing drug use this way both upholds the law, thus supporting the consensual view of right and wrong, as well as fulfilling the social expectation that sick people will be treated and, if possible, cured. However, that perspective ignores three points: firstly, as we have seen, a substantial minority of the population does not share the consensus that the use and possession of every substance controlled under the MDA should be pro-scribed; secondly, not every addict patient receives the appropriate treatment as a matter of course, and thirdly, which discourse should take precedence in instances where both sectors lay claim to the same person?

There are other, deeper, critiques of the British state's response to illicit drugs, revolving around issues of organizational needs. For party political reasons, legal policing is often presented as being wholly domestic-led, con-veniently ignoring the fact that international law very often acts to set the parameters of domestic drug policies, thereby limiting the nature of the domestic response. Equally, medical policing is nearly always presented as being wholly concerned with treatment, prevention and cure, ignoring the fact that at the same time it is promoting the relatively recent moral per-spective that 'luxurious' use of certain substances is wrong. As well as this, medical control of drug addiction further cements the doctor's ownership of deciding who is eligible to receive certain drugs. The result is that referral to the general direction of British drug policy often obscures highly relevant points, thus limiting the extent and nature of debate.

These are points to which we will return in Chapters 8 and 9, both of which examine these and other issues inherent in contemporary British drug policy. The next chapter moves the book in a different direction, abandoning its somewhat parochial concerns with all things British, and widening the debate to examine illicit drug production in a global context.

5 Growth and production of illicit drugs

Introduction

This chapter marks a watershed in the book. Up to this point, illicit drug use has been discussed in a narrow and somewhat parochial manner. The purpose of this chapter is to move the debate away from a British focus and alert the reader to the fact that the British 'drug problem' is only a small part of a global phenomenon. Moreover, this chapter also marks the beginnings of a change of direction in the manner in which drugs will be conceived. Here, illicit drugs will be stripped of any moral connotations and be viewed solely as an economic commodity, better to understand the impact illicit drugs have on both the global and domestic economic and political situation.

This chapter necessarily covers much ground. It begins by illustrating the size of the global illicit drug production industry. From there, the three main plant-based illicit drugs and their primary countries of origin are identified. The next section examines the impact illicit drug production has on the developing nations by focusing on the economic, political and social situation of one nation, Bolivia. Following this, the chapter moves away from plant-based substances to examine the production of synthetic drugs in Europe. The chapter ends with a section on the problems the global nature of illicit drug production pose in relation to the local disruption of supply.

The inclusion of this material serves two purposes. Firstly, it alerts the reader to the size and nature of the illicit drug industry in order to demonstrate the complexity of the situation and the sheer size of the task faced by individual nations in attempting to combat their domestic drug problem. As the last chapter noted, most nation states have their own methods of banning importation and use: this chapter provides an indication of the scale of the business they are trying to proscribe. Secondly, and related to the former point, the chapter serves partially to answer one of the most often asked questions in the drug debate: 'Why not stop the product at source?' This seemingly straightforward idea is, as will be demonstrated, fraught with major difficulties and holds the potential to unleash drastic unforeseen consequences within the producing nations, as well as holding the potential for international repercussions.

Drug production as a global phenomenon

There is a danger that illegal drugs and the problems they bring in their wake can be seen as a purely domestic concern. This perspective is wrong, and adopting such a view of the illegal drug industry simply ensures a very partial view and restricted understanding of the illegal drug phenomenon. Illegal drugs are nothing if they are not the product of a burgeoning international industry of huge proportions. Just as in any attempt to gauge the exact nature of domestic consumption, providing definitive figures that relate to the international illicit drug industry is difficult, due to the clandestine nature of the business. This becomes clear in the literature where, for example, the United Nations International Drug Control Programme (UNDCP) (2001) notes that estimates of the annual turnover for the illicit drug industry vary from $100 billion to $1000 billion per annum. Despite the high levels of vagueness, there is a consensus that the illicit drug industry is of formidable stature, with the following quotation being representative of most of the literature:

> The international [illicit] drug trade is now worth an estimated $400 billion annually. Only the arms industry has a bigger turnover than this. Like car making, pharmaceuticals or even banking, the drug trade has become a truly global industry: it knows no frontiers and has no particular national identity.
>
> (Williams and Milani 1999: 4)

Building on this, and providing a scale by which to judge the size of the illicit drug industry, the UNDCP (2001) posits that illicit drugs account for 8 per cent of all global trade, thus outranking the worldwide trade in iron and steel and motor vehicles, and running roughly parallel to the global trade in textiles, oil and gas and world tourism. Perhaps the best indication of the size of the illicit drug industry is a comparison of the global illicit drug trade with global licit drug trade: the UNDCP estimates that the illicit trade is at least double that of its legal counterpart. This level of growth, coupled to the size of the turnover of the illicit drug industry, becomes all the more amazing when it is remembered that British Customs and Excise only made its first major heroin seizure thirty years ago. Broadening this to provide a European dimension, the United Nations Educational, Scientific and Cultural Organization (UNESCO) (1999: 3) notes that in 1970, 54 kilos of heroin and 1.1 kilos of cocaine were seized by European authorities: less than three decades later (1997), this had reached 10 tonnes and 39 tonnes respectively.

There are a number of economic and political reasons for this expansion. Firstly, as with any number of global industries, the changing nature of the world economic and political situation is a significant factor. The world-wide impact of free market economics has meant that there are fewer controls placed on the movement and import and export of goods across and between countries. There has also occurred the restructuring of the political situation in Europe, with the demise of the communist blocs in Eastern Europe, and their concomitant restrictions on trade and movements, leading to an overall freeing-up of the global market place. The cost of air travel and airfreight has fallen dramatically allowing much greater movement of people and goods across the globe, opening up more routes for the smuggler. Banking and commerce have seen a lifting of restrictions, and the introduction of new technology, allowing the movement of money on an unprecedented scale, both in terms of volume and speed.

Of equal importance is the volatile nature of the political situation in many of the drug-producing countries, which allows all manner of non-governmental factions to control various drug-producing regions, often becoming de-facto governments in themselves. In short, changes in global communication and technology, aided by uncertainty in the world political order, have created conditions where the movement of goods and money around the globe is far easier than ever before. Among those whose businesses benefit from this are the illicit drug traffickers.

The global nature of the illicit drug industry poses considerable problems for national governments, and arguably has a greater impact on some national economies than many of the licit multinationals operating in today's economic world. At this stage, it is perhaps important to note a division between the types of product used by the illicit drug industry, as the nature and origin of the 'product' has a significant bearing on the impact the drug industry has upon a region or country. Essentially, there are three types of drug that are of concern to this book: those drugs derived from plant products or plant products that have undergone some form of semi-synthetic process; synthetic drugs that are manufactured from other chemicals; and, to a lesser degree, licit drugs that are diverted from their intended medical use. Only the first two concern us here.

Much of the attention of the remainder of the chapter focuses on the global impact of the production of plant-based drugs. The rationale for this is that these substances very often have a significant relationship with the producing country in terms of economics, politics and social conditions (Morrison 1997). Equally important is the potential that addressing drug production in these nations hold for disrupting global politics and global economics. On the other hand, the manufacture of synthetic drugs, which most often takes place within the more industrialized nations of a region, still impacts on nation states, but tends to have a less strategic, more peripheral impact on the producing countries' political and economic infrastructures, especially so in the West. With that in mind the next section provides an overview of the three main types of plant-based drugs and their countries of origin.

That said, it is important to note that production of synthetic drugs is beginning to expand in some developing nations, especially where there is a growth in demand. For example, the developing beach party scene in Goa and some of the Thai islands means the travelling dance drug users are increasing the demand for dance drugs in these areas. Increased policing in developed nations such as the Netherlands and an increase in the global availability of precursors have helped create this shift in production. Notwithstanding, production of drugs still tends to represent the dichotomy visible elsewhere in global industry with plant-based crops dominating developing nations' output and synthetic products emanating from more industrialized nations.

Types of drug and their primary countries of origins

The UNDCP (1996: 127) emphasizes the importance of plant-based drugs by stating categorically that 'The largest share of drugs consumed illicitly are plant-based products'. Of these, there are three main types of plant that feed the illicit drug industry: *Cannabis sativa*, the coca bush and the opium poppy. It is these three plants, either in their pure form or semi-synthesized, that are the main raw products for the plant-based illicit drug industry. This section provides an overview of the main areas of production and the 'best-guess' output figures.

Dealing with them in alphabetical order, the first plant product is the *Cannabis sativa*. This plant is probably the most versatile of the three, as it occurs naturally throughout the world and is readily adaptable to indoor cultivation. Indeed, the UNDCP (2001) notes that some of the most potent strains of the crop are grown indoors. The result is that cannabis production is not confined to relatively small geographical regions, as are the other two, but is produced worldwide under a variety of conditions. Nevertheless, there are some areas that specialize in large-scale cultivation of cannabis, namely the USA, the Republic of South Africa, Morocco, the Central Asian Republics of the Commonwealth of Independent States, Afghanistan, Pakistan, Colombia, Mexico and Jamaica.

Because cannabis can be grown 'at home', and thus produced almost anywhere across the globe, it is difficult to begin even to estimate the level of global production, a point noted by the UNDCP (2001: 7) which bemoans the 'absence of reliable information on global cannabis cultivation'. However, as an indicator of the scale of production they point to the figures for 1999, where there was a 35 per cent increase in the seizure of herbal cannabis, worldwide, compared to the preceding year's tally. Importantly, they note that this rise in seizures has little to do with the work of law enforcement agencies but indicates an increase in use and availability of the drug in Europe, America, Africa and Oceania, providing the implication that global cannabis production is significant and rising.

The next plant product is the coca bush, which, when semi-synthesized, is the plant base for drugs such as cocaine and crack cocaine. In terms of location of production, this plant is almost the diametric opposite of *Cannabis sativa*, inasmuch as its natural growing area is concentrated in the Andean region of South America, which allows three countries – Peru, Colombia and Bolivia – to dominate world production. This is reflected in the UNDCP's (2001) figures, which claim that over 98 per cent of all the world's coca is produced by these three nations. Other nations do contribute to the overall global output, notably Ecuador, Brazil, Venezuela, Panama and Guyana, but their output is insignificant in relation to that of the 'big three' producing nations (Williams and Milani 1999).

The coca plant itself is fairly easy to cultivate and can begin to return the farmer a yield within two years of planting. It is hardy and therefore requires little in the way of maintenance, but harvesting the leaves can be labour intensive. Production of coca leaf can be broken down by country, where, in the year ending August 2000, Bolivia produced 13,400 metric tons of coca leaf, Colombia produced 266,161 metric tons of leaf and Peru produced 54,400 metric tons of leaf. These figures are reflected in the amount of land given over to coca bush cultivation in each of the major producing nations: Bolivia had 14,600 hectares under cultivation, Colombia 163,289 hectares and Peru 34,200, making the coca bush a major crop in each country. Looking at farm gate prices, in 2000 Peruvian growers received just over $3000 per metric ton of coca leaf, compared to just under $5000 in Bolivia (UNDCP 2001: 59–73). In terms of turning that raw material into cocaine or cocaine derivatives, the UNDCP estimate that in the year ending August 2000, the potential worldwide output of cocaine was 883 metric tons.

The final plant is the opium poppy, which is the plant base for heroin and opium. Again, this is a fairly easy plant to cultivate but is labour intensive in harvesting and does need some attention during growth. There are two main regions which, when combined, are responsible for the majority of the world's opium poppy. These are the regions known as the 'Golden Crescent', incorporating Afghanistan, the Islamic Republics of Iran and Pakistan, and the 'Golden Triangle', which comprises the People's Democratic Republic of Laos, Myanmar and Thailand.

However, production has recently shifted to Colombia and the Central Asian states of the former Soviet Union. Evidence seems to suggest that these relative newcomers have the potential to become major suppliers of the opium poppy. It is important to note, however, the UNDCP (2001: 6) has identified that

> at the end of the twentieth century, illicit opium poppy cultivation became concentrated in just two countries, Afghanistan and Myanmar, which accounted for more than 90 per cent of global production.

Worldwide, the UNDCP believes somewhere in the region of 4,691 metric tons of opium poppy were produced in 2000, providing the potential for the global production of 469 metric tons of heroin. Examining in more detail the output of the two main producers, in 2000, Afghanistan produced 3,276 metric tons and Myanmar 1,087 metric tons of poppies. Again, the scale of this level of production is visible in the amount of land given over to cultivation with Afghanistan having 82,171 hectares and Myanmar 108,700 hectares; the Afghans being more productive and providing a better kilo per hectare output. The farm gate prices for opium in these two countries are $30 per kilogram in Afghanistan and $142 per kilogram in Myanmar (UNDCP 2001: 59–73). In a contemporary development, we can expect to see Afghan production rise in the near future due to American removal of the Taliban who had outlawed the growth of opium poppies on religious grounds. Several of the Afghan war lords, especially those of the Northern Alliance, had strong connections with opium production and are once again free of all controls over that aspect of their work.

By way of an introduction to the next section, it is important to draw attention to the nature of the producing nations, the manner in which these crops are produced and by whom. Almost all of the nations that produce plant-based drugs are what are known as 'developing nations', that is, nations that have not yet reached the stage of industrialization, are reliant upon a mainly agrarian-based form of production and have a low Gross National Product (GNP) (Fuller 1990: 432). The UN (2001) agrees, noting with some inevitability that the vast majority of plant-based illicit drug producing nations are always among the world's poorest, both in terms of Gross Domestic Product (GDP) and GNP. The farmers who grow the crops are almost always poor subsistence farmers who cultivate the plants safe in the knowledge that, unlike the situation with some other crops they produce, they can sell their yields and obtain enough money to sustain their families.

Morrison (1997) provides an interesting discussion of the forces driving illicit drug production, which draws on the economic, political and social situation in the producing nations. She argues that drug sources are either 'concentrated' or 'diffuse', with the former generating the bulk of global drug supplies from a small number of sources, as in the case of coca and the Andes, and the latter characterized by a wide range of sources aimed at supplying local markets, as in the case of cannabis. In the case of some of the developing nations involved in concentrated drug production Morrison (1997: 127) has noted three contributing factors, all of which enhance the potential for illicit drug production. These are: weak law enforcement caused by either corruption or insurgency, economic insecurity, especially in rural areas and isolated rural areas.

All three are visible in the chosen example, Bolivia. Bolivia has been chosen because it represents an interesting example of the impact that drug production can have on an economy and social system. Equally illuminating are the effects that recent developments in terms of intervention and pressure from another nation have had on the stability of the state. It is worth mentioning that almost any of the developing nations involved in drug production would have made an interesting case study for broadly the same reasons.

Drug production as an economic and political facet of developing nations: the case of Bolivia

Stripped of moral judgements, the growth of the plants that feed the world's illicit drug business becomes a simple economic exercise – a job of work, undertaken to provide an income, sustain life and make profits. Evidence this quotation:

> . . . an Andean farmer picks leaves off a low-growing shrub. He hauls the bales of leaves up the steep, barren slope to his shack and lays them on the hard-baked ground to dry under an equatorial sun. During the following days, he will take the leaves to a secluded site and put them in a soaking pit with water, kerosene, potassium carbonate, and later, sulphuric acid. The end product from the processing of the harvest of coca leaves will be whitish balls of coca paste, which the grower will then sell to a motorcycle-riding middleman.
>
> (Smith 1992: 1)

As Smith notes, this cycle of cultivation, harvest and sale is a part of the process of plant crop production for the farmer, with the farmer often unaware, or at the very least unconcerned, about the end destination and use of their crop. Rather, the peasant farmer is simply concerned about the price per kilo the buyer is prepared to give him, for it is on that, and often that alone, that the quality of his and his family's life depends. In simple economic terms, if the farmer can get more per kilo for coca than oranges, the farmer will almost always produce coca. Painter (1994), who describes the situation in the Chapare region of Bolivia, noting that 'the ground is full of rotting oranges, lemons and grapefruit', highlights this. Farmers in this region get so little money for these crops that, as Painter notes 'it is simply not worth a farmer even picking them up . . .'.

This section seeks to explore the impact the cultivation of plant-based drugs has on the economic and political landscape of an individual country. Bolivia has been chosen because it provides an interesting example of a society where the production of plant-based drugs has had a significant impact on the economy, but also allows us to examine the results when a country decides to pursue a policy of reducing the economic importance of plant-based drug production, and suffers some political and economic unrest as a result.

Bolivia: some economic and demographic background

Bolivia is a South American country in the Andean region of that continent. It is roughly twice the size of France, and in 1999 the population stood at 8.1 million, of which 47 per cent are adults, and some 2.5 to 3 million people are economically active (World Bank 2001a). The average size of household is 4.35 people and the average life expectancy is around sixty.

Adult literacy is somewhere in the region of 80 per cent in urban areas and as low as 60 per cent in rural areas. Economically, Bolivia has a GNP per capita of $1010, making it the poorest country in South America (World Bank 2001b). The average individual wage is $45 per calendar month, with the average household income being $122.8 per calendar month. Its national debt runs to some $4.785 billion (Minestero de Capitalizacion, Republica de Bolivia 1996).

Clearly, Bolivia has other industries beyond the cultivation of coca, including other forms of agriculture, tin mining and some embryonic industries, but nevertheless, coca production has been, and remains, a key economic factor in the country's development. In addition, the growth of coca has more than a little cultural significance for certain parts of Bolivian society, but it is as an economic factor that coca provides most interest. Again, at the risk of repeating what is becoming a mantra for this work, providing accurate information on the extent of the economic importance of coca to Bolivia is difficult. There have been some attempts, however. One of the first was the work of deFranco and Godoy (1992) who estimated that in the years 1987 and 1989 Bolivia's economy saw a cocaine generated income of $1.47 billion and $489 million respectively. Following this came the work of Nadelman (1989) and Shams (1992), both of whom estimated that Bolivia's foreign exchange proceeds were boosted by the sale of cocaine by some $600 million per annum.

Arguably, Painter (1994) has conducted one of the most comprehensive studies on the extent of the illicit drug industry in Bolivia. He used the total hectares of land planted with coca bushes to estimate the potential output of coca base. Painter noted the growth of the coca industry across the end of the 1980s and the beginnings of the 1990s. Working on those figures, Painter (1994) was able to claim that in Bolivia, the total revenue from coca base was $694 million in 1990. Moving more up to date, Alvarez (1995) estimated that the revenue from exported coca base and cocaine was the equivalent of 27 per cent of legal exports, generating an income of around $240 million. Steiner (1998: 1026) places the gross cocaine income for Bolivia slightly higher than that, at $350 million in 1995.

Bolivia is a net exporter of coca, which means that the majority of coca produced, usually in its paste form because this is less bulky and easier to transport, leaves the country. Almost inevitably, Bolivia's exports of raw and semi-refined coca are destined for its neighbour Colombia. Steiner (1998: 1014) provides some figures that show Bolivia is one of two 'main suppliers of coca base that is transformed into cocaine in Colombia'. Although it is generally acknowledged that the vast majority of the profits from the illicit drug industry are not enjoyed by the growers (UNDCP 2001), the money received from the sale of the crop is sufficient greatly to improve the lifestyle and living conditions of the farmer.

Whatever the true figure, it is clear that proceeds from the growth of coca and the production of coca base have a significant impact upon Bolivia's economy and labour market. The Bolivian government (Boliviaweb.com 2001), deFranco and Godoy (1992) and Tullis (1995) have estimated that about 16 per cent (somewhere in the region of 300,000 people) of the economically active population are involved in the coca industry. Moreover, de Franco and Godoy (1992) claim that a 10 per cent shift upwards or downwards in the production of coca and cocaine in Bolivia creates a 6 per cent fluctuation in the labour market, holding the potential for serious economic and social problems in times of downward swings, especially for a country lacking all but the most rudimentary of health and social security systems. This means that any move by the Bolivian government to reduce or cease the production of coca holds the potential for economic and political instability. This predicament is neatly summarized by the Andean Information Network (2001): 'The Bolivian government has often found itself caught between the demands of "The War on Drugs" and domestic policy'. However, growing pressure by the international community, especially the USA, has meant that recently the Bolivian government has begun to take a tougher line on coca production.

Bolivia: a brief recent history

Bolivia's history of coca production offers some clues as to the genesis of the present situation as well as highlighting the difficulties faced by a government restructuring what is an important regional industry. As noted, Bolivia is a large country with a relatively small population, leading to some underpopulated and isolated areas, especially so the further away from the capital one travels. It is also very poor, with the World Bank (2001b) comparing it to 'Sub-Saharan African countries . . . with 10 per cent of children under five malnourished . . . and 67 per cent of the population living below the country's poverty line'.

The main coca producing area in Bolivia is known as the Cochabamba tropics, much of it centring on the Chapare region. This area's population consists, in the main, of relatively recently arrived settlers, often subsistence farmers responding to government-inspired campaigns to move families from the high plateau around Lake Titicaca to the jungle region. Much of the movement took place in the 1960s under the auspices of the now defunct National Settlement Institute (NSI). Each settler prepared to move to the Chapare region received 20 hectares of land, alongside the promise of roads, schools, agricultural loans and technical assistance in the growth of cacao and rubber. The NSI never had the funds to carry out this ambitious programme and left the settlers to their fate (Davila 1992: 95–6). In the absence of state-directed growing programmes, the peasant farmers of the Chapare region turned to one crop for which there seemed to be an expanding market – coca.

Nevertheless, despite moving into coca production, life for the settlers is still particularly harsh, with high rates of infant mortality, illiteracy and poverty. Davila (1992: 97) provides this description of the average peasant farmer's home

> The family's shack is a two-storey structure built of wood and bamboo over a dirt floor. On the first level, which is shared with the chickens, they cook and store their food provisions. The six family members sleep on the second floor. There are no cots, mattresses, electricity or drinking water. The most valuable possession is a kerosene lamp.

Not all the blame for the high levels of poverty in the region can be laid at the door of the Bolivian government of the time, or the failed NSI; Bolivia was a victim of the world recession of the 1970s. Sage (1987: 9) details the collapse of the Bolivian mining industry during that period, leading to an almost total economic collapse; the extreme nature of the economic crisis is underlined by a 1985 inflation rate of 8,171 per cent. He also notes, rather prophetically, that conditions such as these produce fertile ground for 'subterranean economies', such as the production of plant-based drugs. The need to overcome poverty and perceived abandonment by the central government, plus an unemployment level of at least 20 per cent in 1985, enhanced the 'attractiveness of the only sector still expanding – coca production [and] led many former miners and otherwise unemployed Bolivians to seek their fortunes in that industry' (MacDonald 1989: 78). This was further encouraged by the Bolivian government's failure to provide any alternative form of development, or find another crop that made the switch away from producing coca a viable economic option.

One other approach the peasant farmers of the Chapare region adopted in an attempt to combat poverty, and to try to ensure a decent existence for their families, was to turn to the Trades Union Movement, which has a strong tradition in Bolivia, mainly due to the influence of the unions within the mining industry. In the Chapare region, the workers' movement is broken down into nine coca-producing *sindicatos* (unions), which are affiliated to *centrales* (central bodies), which in turn are part of regional *federaciones* (peasant federations) (Painter 1994). Workers pay a monthly fee to be part of the *sindicatos*, some of which goes into building infrastructure and some to the other parts of the workers' movement. Because of the partial abandonment by the central government, and in the absence of a fully functioning regional administration, the *sindicatos* act almost as de facto local regimes, providing much of the local infrastructure (Davila 1992). In turn this provides the *federaciones* with the economic wherewithall and support base to become 'probably the most powerful pressure group from the popular sectors of the country' (Painter 1994: 24).

Although broken down into five main groups, the *federaciones* claim to represent almost 40,000 farmers or, including families, between 120,000 to 200,000 people, in the Chapare region. Despite being divided on some issues (Painter 1994), all the *federaciones* fiercely defend the right to produce coca and the right to maintain economic production and stability. Indeed, the *federaciones* have been united on two fronts related to coca production: a total opposition to eradication of coca crops without the introduction of realistic alternatives and economic opportunities (Painter 1994: 24); and an insistence on differentiating between coca growers and those who produce coca paste, thus allowing an avoidance of association with illegal activities (Davila 1992: 102). This resistance led the unions to become increasingly militant in their protests.

Despite the resistance offered by the peasant farmers of the Chapare region, the Bolivian government, under pressure from the USA, began to move against the production of coca (Fellner and Bretts 1996). Their first major move in 1988 was to pass Law 1008. The law itself has attracted fierce criticism from human rights groups across the globe since, being contrary to the Bolivian constitution, it contravenes numerous human rights standards established in international treaties (Andean Information Network 2001). Indeed, Juan Carlos Duran, Minister of the Interior during the passage of Law 1008 commented that

> We put human rights on a balance scale to see if drug trafficking caused more harm to the country than adhering to an orthodox procedure. We broke the rules and tried to find an efficient mechanism that would really battle drug trafficking.
>
> (Juan Carlos Duran cited in Andean Information Network 2001b)

Briefly, Law 1008 presumes the guilt of the accused, creates three zones of production where coca can be grown legally for traditional uses, establishes a zone of transitional production where eradication is voluntary and will be compensated, government funds permitting, and defines an illicit zone of production where eradication is forced and without compensation.

Initially, the Bolivian government did not actively pursue eradication polices with any gusto. However, as Tullis (1995) informs, forced eradication, with no compensation to the growers, started in earnest from 1991, following renewed pressure from the USA. In response, the peasant farmers' *sindicatos* and *federaciones* began to form self-defence groups and threaten violence against eradication units. The central government backed down and there was an impasse until 1995, when, again responding to US pressure, the Bolivian government ordered two consecutive ninety-day periods of siege. This allowed them to place the leaders of the *federaciones* and *sindicatos* under detention and begin the eradication process (Fellner and Bretts 1996).

However, these measures still had little overall impact on the output of coca. Following yet more pressure from the USA, the Bolivian government drafted a five-year plan (Plan Dignity). It has four pillars:

1   alternative developments;
2   prevention and rehabilitation;

3   eradication;
4   interdiction.

The Andean Information Network (2001) claims that pillar three has been the core approach, alongside a move away from compensating individual farmers towards compensating the community. The fear among the farmers is that these funds will never reach the community, let alone filter down to individual families, thereby increasing poverty in an already impoverished area.

Attempts to implement Plan Dignity have also led to growing militancy on the part of the farmers, with armed groups now blocking highways leading into coca producing regions. There have been hunger strikes and deaths on both sides, with numerous claims of brutality, looting and rape being made against the government troops. In response to even more threats of civil unrest, the Bolivian government has drafted up to 5,000 troops into the Chapare region, heightening tensions between the peasant farmers and the central government. Perhaps the plight of the peasant farmers in Chapare is best summarized by the case of Filipa Amman. Two years ago she was shot in the leg by government forces and had to have her leg amputated. On 27 April 2001 government agencies eradicated her hectare of coca and her food crops. At the time of writing, she had received nothing by way of compensation and faced a winter of starvation (Andean Information Network 2001).

There are clear problems and dilemmas faced by the Bolivian government in their attempt to reduce the importance of coca production. On the one hand, international pressure to reduce the production of plant-based drugs, including the carrot and stick approach of using loans and debt repayments to apply pressure for change, necessitates reform. On the other hand, political resistance, economic insecurity and growing poverty, plus the potential threat of revolution make rapid change politically and economically dangerous. Nevertheless, this is the reality faced by political leaders, not just in Bolivia, but across the globe in their attempts to control the plant-based illicit drug industry. The worry for the international community is that national governments in drug producing states will lose control of what are often fragile situations and create conditions where civil wars, unacceptable levels of poverty and refugee crises are real threats.

The production of synthetic drugs in Europe

Without doubt, illicit drug production in Europe is big business, but its economic and political impact on the individual nation states is less visible and of a subtler nature than that of the developing nations. The difference between the economic and political impact of illicit drug production in the developing and the industrialized nations is graphically illustrated by Medina (Painter 1994) who commented that 'For the U.S. it's like cutting off a finger because you have gangrene. For Bolivia, it's like having a tumour in your head, which you cannot cure simply by an amputation'. Nevertheless, the production of synthetic drugs does have some consequences for those nations where it occurs. The types of drug under the spotlight in this section include amphetamine-type stimulants (ATS), ecstasy and LSD.

There are parallels between the plant-based and synthetic drug industries, especially in economic terms. For example, the production of plant-based drugs is directly related to climatic conditions, and much of the synthesizing process takes place close to the growing regions, with export of the refined product to consumer nations, thus mirroring other agrarian industries in developing nations. Likewise, the production of synthetic illicit drugs mirrors many of the factors visible in licit industries in developed nations.

For example, Morrison (1997: 125) notes that many of the synthetic drug producing factories are to be found in developed countries where there are established licit chemical and pharmaceutical industries. Morrison provides a clear economic logic behind this decision: 'By setting up alongside the licit industry, producers of synthetic drugs lowered their production costs through easy access to knowledge, equipment and chemicals . . . and had a ready made market for drugs'. She also acknowledges that this pattern seems to be repeating itself in some of the newly industrialized countries of the Pacific Rim. The UNDCP (2001: 173) also comments on the localized nature of the production of synthetic illicit drugs, stating that the business tends to be 'largely intra-regional, often geographically close to the consumer market'. This fits a recognized economic pattern.

Fuller (1990: ch. 13) provides an overview of the reasons why industries locate in particular regions; his thesis can easily be applied to the illicit synthetic drug industry globally. Fuller begins his discussion by noting that transport costs are an important determinant. There are two opposing forces here, closeness to raw materials and closeness to the market. In businesses where there is a gap between raw material and market, industry tends to locate production close to raw materials and ship the refined goods, which weigh less, thus reducing transport costs. As has been demonstrated, the majority of illicit synthetic drug factories utilize their closeness to licit chemical industries and thus are close to raw materials. Given the importance of synthetic illicit drugs in Europe and South East Asia particularly, producers are clearly close to their intended market, considerably reducing transportation costs.

The next determinant of location is the requirement for access to skilled labour. Again, proximity to licit chemical and pharmaceutical industries ensures that there are reliable and regular sources of chemists, or people with chemical knowledge, to supervise the production process. There are also what Fuller (1990) terms non-economic factors. In the synthetic illicit drug industry, this may translate as a lenient approach to the enforcement of laws; the availability of secluded or isolated areas close to centres of populations within which to locate the factory; or the proximity to an intra-regional distribution centre, such as a busy sea port or airport. This pattern is visible in the global manufacture of synthetic drugs, leading to the 'local' nature of this particular section of the illicit drug trade. It appears that in each region of the world there are one or two countries that act as main producers for that area. Unlike the plant-based illicit drugs, there are no producing nations that dominate globally.

The means by which estimates of production are calculated differ in relation to plant-based illicit drugs and their synthetic counterparts. Much of the estimation for plant-based products is deduced from satellite and aerial photographs which show the extent of cultivation, allowing 'best-guess' estimates of final harvest totals. This is obviously not possible in the case of illicit drugs produced in factories. Instead, we are forced to rely on seizure data. It is worth remembering at this point that Chapter 4 noted a 10 per cent seizure rate as the maximum any customs and excise force can reasonably claim. Based on that, it is possible to argue that these figures represent, at the very maximum, only 10 per cent of overall production.

However, one of the strong points of seizure figures, when allied to economic theory relating to the location of production, is that they enable us to 'best-guess' key areas of production. Thus, if, for example, French customs officers seize a large shipment of ATS coming from the Netherlands into France, there is a strong probability that the ATS will have been manufactured within the Netherlands, due to the economic factors identified above. Examining the seizure figures from countries across Europe highlights this. With those caveats in mind, the next section reviews the known data relating to illicit synthetic drugs in Europe. All the following statistical data are derived from the UNDCP (2001: 173–211) unless otherwise stated.

Concentrating on Europe, the UNDCP figures show that 11 per cent of the global seizures of ATS and 75 per cent of the global seizures of ecstasy were made in Europe in 1999. In actual terms, this translates to 4 metric tons of ATS and somewhere close to 15 million ecstasy doses. Of the overall European totals, 94 per cent were seized in western Europe, with two nations, the UK and the Netherlands accounting for over half the amounts seized. In terms of Eastern Europe, six countries, Bulgaria, Poland, the Russian Federation, the Czech Republic, Estonia and Hungary, accounted for 98 per cent of all Eastern European seizures.

Examining trafficking patterns across Europe provides some fascinating insights into the areas of production. The UNDCP collates seizure figures from individual states and offers a breakdown in terms of main source(s) of origin and main destinations. Before scrutinizing these figures in detail it is important to stress that they relate in the main only to *imported drugs*. The figures do not represent all drugs, and certainly do not reflect all home-produced substances. Table 5.1 provides a breakdown of the UNDCP findings. It becomes clear that as far as Europe is concerned, the Netherlands seems to be either (a) the centre through which most ATS travels, (b) the chief source of manufacture or (c) a combination of both, with (c) being the most likely option. However, the domination of European ATS production and

Table 5.1 Trafficking patterns of ATS in Europe, 1999

Country reporting	Main origin(s)	Main destination(s)
UK	Netherlands (90%), Belgium (10%)	domestic
Spain	domestic, Netherlands	domestic
Germany	Netherlands (96%), Poland (1.8%), Czech Republic (1.2%) plus domestic	domestic, Switzerland, Scandinavian countries
France	Belgium, Netherlands	other European countries
Belgium	domestic, Netherlands, UK	Spain, France, USA
Switzerland	Netherlands	domestic
Denmark	Netherlands, Poland, Czech Republic, Belgium	Norway, Sweden
Sweden	Poland and Czech Republic (60%), Netherlands and Belgium (40%)	domestic
Norway	Netherlands, other European countries	domestic
Finland	Netherlands (49%), Estonia (41%), Russian Federation (10%)	domestic
Iceland	Netherlands (98%), Poland (2%)	domestic
Estonia	Poland	Sweden, Finland
Hungary	Netherlands	domestic
Croatia	Netherlands	domestic

Source: adapted from UNDCP 2001: 175

distribution by the Netherlands appears to be under some threat from some of the Eastern European countries, notably Poland and the Czech Republic.

The same exercise can be done for ecstasy. Ecstasy use has, until relatively recently, been confined to the UK and Netherlands. However, the last five years have seen a growth in ecstasy use worldwide. Table 5.2 illustrates the situation. Again, the Netherlands seems to be either the primary distribution centre and/or the centre for production. Interestingly, and veering away from the trend established by ATS, Europe seems to be, at the moment, one of the key areas for ecstasy production, supplying most of the rest of the world. It remains to be seen if production will be carried out in user countries as use of ecstasy spreads across the world.

The level of seizures indicates that there is a burgeoning market for illicit synthetic drugs in Europe, especially bearing in mind that seizures represent only a small proportion of total output.

In turn, this level of production must represent high levels of profit and income generation. For example, the wholesale price of ecstasy tablets in the Netherlands was $2,348 per thousand (prices in USA $ at 1999 exchange

Table 5.2 Ecstasy trafficking in Europe, 1999

Country reporting	Main origin(s)	Main destination(s)
UK	Netherlands (90%) Belgium (9%), Germany (1%)	domestic
Spain	Netherlands, Belgium	domestic
Germany	Netherlands (94.6%) Belgium (1.3%), Switzerland (4%)	domestic, Switzerland, USA, Austria, Italy, Poland, Romania
France	UK (79%), Belgium (16%)	USA, Spain, UK, Ireland
Belgium	domestic, Netherlands, UK	USA, Spain, France, USA, Israel, South Africa, China
Italy	domestic, Netherlands, Belgium, Germany, France	domestic, USA
Denmark	Netherlands, Belgium	Norway, Sweden, Iceland
Sweden	Poland and Czech Republic (60%), Netherlands and Belgium (40%)	domestic
Norway	Netherlands, other European countries	domestic
Finland		
Iceland	Netherlands (98%)	domestic
Netherlands	domestic (77%)	domestic, other European, South East Asia, USA
Hungary	Netherlands	domestic
Croatia	Netherlands	domestic, Yugoslavia

Source: adapted from UNDCP 2001: 1777

rates), indicating a production cost much lower than this. Given that about 15 million tablets were seized in Europe in 1999, a figure which at best represents only 10 per cent of those produced, this provides an indication of the size of the industry.

However, although the amount of income generated by the illicit synthetic drug industry is significant, it is unlikely that it would have the same effect on an economy of a highly developed western nation such as the Netherlands, in the same way plant-based production has on developing nations, such as Bolivia. On reflection, perhaps the same cannot be said of some of the eastern European nations that are currently seeking to enter the ATS production milieu. It can be suggested that the economic, political and social impact of illicit drug production in western Europe is altogether more subtle and needs to be considered in terms of the damage it does to social consensus, increased levels of crime and political disagreements. All of these will be considered in a British context in forthcoming chapters.

Conclusion

The aim of this chapter was to impress upon the reader the sheer scale of the global illicit drug industry and to give an indication of the kind of power and influence an industry of such magnitude has on some nation states, especially those in the developing world. By highlighting this aspect of the industry, it is hoped that some recognition of the difficulties in halting production at source as a policy will be gained. Although phrases such as 'no coca no cocaine' or 'The logic is simple. The cheapest and safest way to eradicate narcotics is to destroy them at source' (Bush 1989) have a simplistic, commonsense ring to them, the economic, political and social consequences are fraught with difficulties, as the Andean experience shows, and require a more nuanced and cerebral approach than that advocated by the father of the current US president.

The problem for the producing nations lies in the fact that plant-based drug production plays a major part in their economies. Indeed, for many peasant farmers illicit drug production is their primary source of income, without which their quality of life would suffer a significant deterioration. In pure economic terms, unless the government or international community can offer a suitable replacement crop that provides a similar income, offer a long-term compensation package, or provide alternative means of employment, the peasant farmers will continue to produce plant-based drugs from economic necessity.

Forced eradication, while combating the drug-production problem for that harvest, does little more than alienate the farmers and growers from their government, creating conditions of resentment and resistance. This is dangerous enough in countries where there is a stable regime; in countries where there is a strained relationship between the centre and periphery, or where there are credible alternatives to the government, it becomes akin to a form of political Russian roulette. As we have seen, the Bolivian government has adopted an eradication policy that has seen questions being asked about human rights violations, as well as strengthening the resolve of, and support for, alternative forms of government.

The problems for the international community lie in the fact that in the event of internal strife the international community can be called in to act as a form of 'policeman', or be forced to launch humanitarian aid missions. Moreover, a policy of eradication of the sources of plant-based drugs also supposes that the international political community can defeat, or at least change the behaviour of one of the largest and fastest growing global industries. Nation states seem powerless to control the activities of licit multinationals, why should we assume they can control the behaviour of illicit multinationals?

Therein lies the problem. The global illicit drug industry, when any moral questions or viewpoints are removed, is a major economic force, wields huge economic power and is able to exert a concomitant degree of political and social pressure at all levels, be they local, national or international. It may be that in order to control and 'regulate' the illicit drug industry we need to adopt an economic perspective that allows us to view drugs as a market commodity and use the laws of the market as controlling factors. This idea is explored further in the next chapter.

6 Markets and market forces of illicit drugs

Introduction

The preceding chapter established the fact that there are economic and political dimensions to the illicit drug industry, alongside the better-known medical, moral and social aspects. It also noted that for some of the illicit drug producing nations the economic and political consequences of a too-rapid reduction of output could lead to internal destabilization. However, the use of economics and economic theory to make sense of illicit drugs provides an alternative view: one that sees illicit drugs like any other tradable commodity. As a consequence, this allows the use of economic theory as an alternative policy dynamic. This chapter builds upon that idea. Again, as in the previous chapter, illicit drugs are stripped of any moral content and seen only as a commodity to be traded, and thus subject to the laws of economics, in the same way as butter, eggs or cars.

As noted, the cultivation and production of drugs have become an important and sometimes integral part of many countries' economic development. Ruggerio and South (1995: 3) endorse this perspective and claim that illicit drugs should be seen 'simply as commodities'. If this approach is adopted, and there seem to be few good reasons why it should not be, there is a need to examine the nature of market-based relationships that surround drug users. The logical corollary of this is that the market mechanism, including the laws of supply and demand, holds the potential to control the illicit drug market.

Thus there is a need to undertake a market-based review of the illicit drug milieu in order to ascertain the ways illicit drug markets resemble legitimate markets, and the ways in which they vary. In order to achieve this there are a number of requirements to be fulfilled. First and foremost there is the need to understand the value of illicit drugs in relation to other commodities. Then there is the need for an excursion into economics and economic theory in order to understand the market mechanism and the nature of markets. Following this, the chapter will examine the work of a number of authors who have applied economic analysis to the workings of the drug markets.

Before entering into the world of markets and economics, it is perhaps important to pause to consider why there is need to study this particular aspect of the world of illicit drugs. Broadly speaking, there are two policy approaches in response to the growth of illicit drug use. The first is harm reduction, which is dealt with elsewhere. The second can be called the demand reduction approach. Essentially, this approach is aimed at reducing the use of drugs by forcing up the 'cost' of drug use to an unacceptably high level.

Here, 'cost' can refer either to the monetary value of the drug or relate to non-monetary cost such as the certainty of a prison sentence for those caught dealing in illicit drugs, or emphasize the harm drugs can do to the users' health. If this is seen as a determinant of policy, it can be argued that successful prohibition will drive the price of drugs to levels way above that which we could expect if the same drugs were legal. Moreover, if we add into the equation vigorous enforcement of measures to control the illicit drug market, which would include seizure of imports, as well as high profile policing of dealers and users, we should see the cost rise above an acceptable level. This high price, in both monetary and non-monetary terms should lead to a fall in demand, supply and, ultimately, use.

If we view illicit drugs as a commodity it allows us to compare their value to other tradable commodities. For example, looking at retail sales, Caulkins and Reuter (1998: 595) claim that illicit drugs have an 'extraordinary high per unit weight'. Using figures derived from the Office of National Drug Control Policy (ONDCP 1997: 10–11), based in Washington DC, they claim that marijuana is literally worth its weight in gold, with cocaine and heroin being 'one and two orders of magnitude more expensive per unit weight than gold'. In turn, the expensive nature of illicit drugs means that they represent a significant part of the user's income, unless the user is wealthy. Thus cost, already high, may affect demand if prices rise above a certain level. This leads us inexorably toward the economic theories of supply and demand and price elasticity of demand.

Supply and demand

While this work is not being written by an economist, it is, however, necessary that these two relatively straightforward economic theories are explained in order that the reader can make sense of their potential application to the illicit drug market. With that in mind, the following section will provide a very basic overview of the laws of supply and demand and price elasticity of demand. I make no apologies for the level at which this is pitched: it will be adequate for the purposes of the text.

Illicit drugs are commodities; that is, they are goods that can be exchanged for other goods or, as is more likely in our capitalist economy, for money. As such they will have both a value and a price. From the outset, it is important to stress that value and price are not one and the same thing. Fuller (1990) notes that values are subjective things, with some people valuing goods far higher than other people may. Harvey (1998: 27; original emphasis) explains

> . . . people always *want* something. A want is significant in economics only when a person is prepared to give up something in order to satisfy it. As the strength of the different wants varies, so will the amounts which people are willing to give up. In other words, different goods have a different *value* to them. Value is measured in terms of opportunity cost.

For our purposes we can visualize value and opportunity cost in this way. A recreational drug user may wish to purchase some amphetamine in order to attend an all night session at a club. The value of that amphetamine is calculated at what that person is prepared to give up (the opportunity cost) in order to purchase the drug. In this instance, it may be two hours worth of pay, plus the prospect of a criminal record if they are found in possession of an illicit substance.

In order to obtain that good (in this example, amphetamine) the drug user will need to exchange something with the seller. In developed western nations such as the UK, we tend to use what is in economic terms a 'medium of exchange', more usually referred to as money, to facilitate this exchange. Thus, the value of the good is expressed in terms of money. In this way, we are able to measure the market value of the good by referring to its price. Thus, for Harvey (1998: 27) a definition of price becomes 'the value of a commodity or service measured in terms of the standard monetary unit'. The buyer then decides whether the cost, that is the amount of money they are going to have to give up in order to satisfy their want, plus the possibility of a criminal record, plus possible negative effects in terms of health, is worth the value they place on the good.

These exchanges take place in what economists call 'the market'. The market is an important concept in economics for, by studying the changes in price that take place in a market, markets are able to provide signals about what people want and what they are prepared to forgo in order to satisfy their want. Again, it is important to conceive of the market in theoretical terms whereby the market is not a formal structure, such as a shop or auction ring, but '*all those buyers and sellers of a good who influence its price*' (Harvey 1998: 28; original emphasis). Harvey also notes that within markets the price of a good tends to become the same across the whole range of buyers and sellers, thus establishing a 'market price'. Markets are created as a response to demand and that demand is satisfied by the supply of a good or service.

The two concepts of demand and supply are important parts of economic theory and are, according to economists, subject to laws that determine their actions upon each other. Looking first at demand, it is important to note that economics is concerned with effective demand. This refers to the amount people are able to afford and willing to buy at each price. For

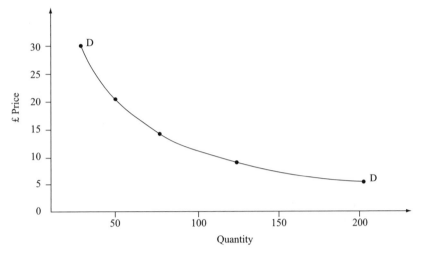

Figure 6.1 A market demand curve

example, a drug user may want to by some heroin but is unable to afford it. Therefore the want is not an effective demand as they are unable or unwilling to buy at the current price. This means that there is a relationship between demand and price, and economists often illustrate this by way of graphs.

Figure 6.1 is a graph that shows quite clearly that as price rises so demand falls. At this stage the implications for drug policy should be emerging: a rise in the price of illicit drugs should, according to economic theory at least, cause demand to fall. Turning attention to supply, this is taken to mean 'the quantity a producer is prepared to put onto the market at a particular price during a particular time period' (Fuller 1990: 38). Supply is determined by cost and, as we will see, the illicit drug market has some unusual costs attached to it, some monetary, others not. Cost tends to rise as supply is increased for several reasons, including the employment of more workers, more spent on packaging and so on. Once costs have risen to a level beyond which the producer feels is acceptable, the producer will leave the market and cease trading in that particular commodity. Thus, the economic law of supply says that more of a good will be supplied at a higher price than at a lower price (Fuller 1990: 38). Again, this can be expressed in graph form.

Figure 6.2 shows that by combining these two laws, it is possible to calculate the equilibrium price, which is the point on the graph where both lines intersect and represents the 'market price'. By the same token, it is also possible to see other aspects of the market relationship. For example, if demand remains the same but supply falls, then prices will rise, with the converse being true. Again, this has implications for the illicit drug market. For example, if a crop eradication programme reduced the supply of heroin into the UK, but demand remained the same, the price of heroin would

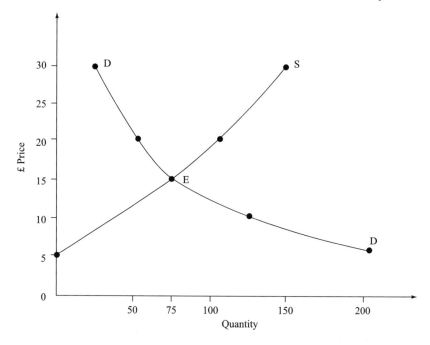

Figure 6.2 A supply and demand curve (Source: Fuller 1990: 39)

rise. However, if the state could create conditions where the price of an illicit drug rises, economic theory tells us that demand will fall as more and more would-be consumers decide that the price is higher than the value or opportunity cost. Equally, if the supplier's production costs rise above a certain level, then the supplier will leave the market.

This rise in cost for the consumer and the producer could be anything from a rise in the actual price to an increase in policing, the certainty of a prison sentence if caught, mandatory drug testing of prisoners, loss of employment and so on. Therefore, economic theory would seem to support a policy of ensuring the cost of drug use, both in terms of price and production costs, remains as high as possible. There is, however, one more economic theory that needs to be considered and that is the theory of price elasticity of demand. This refers to the susceptibility of demand to price. For some goods and for some consumers there is a strong degree of price elasticity. This is taken to mean that consumers are highly responsive to price changes and will alter their consumption pattern as soon as the price rises.

The opposite extreme is where demand is inelastic. This means that consumers will continue to demand a good irrespective of price rise. Fuller (1990: 59) provides four factors that influence price elasticity: (1) the number and closeness of substitutes, (2) the proportion of income the good accounts for, (3) whether the good is a necessity or a luxury and (4) the influence of habit. It should be clear that factors (1) and (4) have a resonance when discussing illicit drug consumption, and this is point to which we will return.

To summarize this section, it is possible to claim that there is a relationship between demand and supply. In most situations, economic theory dictates that as price rises so demand will fall. Economic theory also tells us that costs rise as production rises. However, if any or all of the above four factors of price elasticity of demand are present it may be the case that demand remains constant among some consumers despite price rises. These approaches have obvious implications for illicit drug policy and applying economic analysis to policy provides a fascinating, alternative glimpse of the illicit drug scene, and is one which will be returned to at the end of the chapter.

Market factors and their effect on prices

One of the things that economics may help us understand is the reason for the relatively high per unit price of illicit drugs. It will be recalled that most illicit drugs are at least worth their weight in gold, which begs the questions why are essentially crudely refined plant products or cheaply produced chemicals so expensive? Economic theory would point to the costs of production and it is to this the chapter's attention now turns, especially to the work of Caulkins and Reuter (1998). These two American academics have produced one of the most fascinating insights into the economics of the illicit drug market. Their work relates specifically to the situation in the USA, but it can be assumed that, broadly speaking, the same market conditions exist across the globe. Their work will now be reviewed in some detail. It is important to note that, although they base their work on 1990 prices, meaning that *actual* prices will have changed, the percentages quoted at each stage should remain broadly constant.

In essence, Caulkins and Reuter attempt to explain why illicit drug prices are relatively high, and use cocaine as their example. They begin their argument by outlining the nature of production costs that could be expected for most small businesses. Some costs that a licit business would incur are much lower, or totally absent, for the illicit drug business. For example, for cocaine, the raw material costs are very low. Chapter 5 confirms this, noting that the farm gate price for coca paste in Peru is $3000 per tonne. The illicit drug entrepreneurs do not pay taxes, neither do they pay conventional import or export duties. Conventional shipping prices are low. For example, Parcel Force can send a parcel weighing a kilo between Peru and Britain for £39.90 and guarantee its arrival within three to four days.[1] Packaging of illicit drugs tends to be minimal, accounting for as little as 0.25 to 0.5 per cent of the retail price (Caulkins *et al.* 1999). The illicit nature of the product means that promotional costs, such as advertising, are negligible. Drug dealers tend not to need shelf space, storage or specialist premises, and tend not to hold large amounts of product in stock. In short the costs of raw materials, import, packaging, marketing and supplying are negligible. Therefore, it can be seen that some of the costs faced by licit businesses are not applicable to the illicit drug businesses. Their costs are somewhat different: Caulkins and Reuter (1998) have identified four key costs that pertain to illicit drugs.

Import costs

Although conventional shipping prices are low, there is a high import cost. For example, Caulkins and Reuter remark on the fact that the wholesale price of cocaine is about $1,500 per kilogram in Colombia. This rises to $15,000 per kilo, wholesale, inside the USA, denoting a cost associated with bringing the product across the border. Clearly, this is not linked to taxes but must reflect another type of cost, most likely that associated with risk compensation (see below). Retail sales in the USA move the price up to $110, 000 per kilo. Based on this, Caulkins and Reuter (1998: 597) estimate that 12 per cent of the total retail value of cocaine is attributable to import costs.

Labour costs

Labour costs tend to be high in the illicit drug industry. There are a number of examples of this, such as the fact that packaging tends to be done by hand instead of by machine. Caulkins and Reuter point to the fact that simple machines, such as those used in the packaging of sugar, could reduce the cost dramatically. However, the clandestine nature of the business makes it risky, therefore 'costly', in terms of detection by police or competitors, to have fixed machinery. Equally, selling drugs tends to be done by crews, each of which has a specific task. In their studies, Caulkins *et al.* (1999: 233) identified crews of up to six who are paid by the hour to sell drugs from a 'spot'. Although many of these low-level employees are relatively poorly paid, their wages still represent a cost to the entrepreneur. Based on their figures for the USA cocaine market, Caulkins and Reuter (1998: 597) estimate that 13 per cent of the retail cost of cocaine comes from labour costs.

Cost of product and asset seizure

Part of the on-going 'war on drugs' are the seizures of both goods and assets of illicit drug businesses. Drug seizures and confiscation can be part of the work of the Customs and Excise agency or specialist police units of a country. Financial investigation can be undertaken by taxation squads that deal with the money laundering activities, often leading to the sequestration of assets of known and convicted traders in illicit drugs. Caulkins and Reuter (1998: 598) suggest that the cost of seizures of both kinds account for about 8 to 11 per cent of the retail price of cocaine.

Risk compensation

The illicit drug business is fraught with risks and compensation for actual or potential risks can also be considered to be a cost. As Chapter 3 noted, drug dealers get much higher sentences than those offenders charged and convicted on possession offences. Likewise, there is competition among illicit drug businesses. The very nature of the business means that inter-firm disputes are sometimes settled by resort to violence, leading to the injury or death of a participant in the illicit drug business. Caulkins and Reuter have made some calculations regarding the US situation. They suggest that the average drug dealer could expect $43,500 per annum for each year spent in prison, which, based on the number of drug dealers incarcerated in American prisons, represents about 23.6 per cent of the US retail price for cocaine in that illicit drug market. Equally, drug dealers need to be compensated for death or injury. Caulkins and Reuter (1998) argue that this needs to be higher than prison compensation and accounts for 33 per cent of the retail price of cocaine. They summarize their findings on the price determinants of cocaine and these are given here in Table 6.1.

There are, of course, slight differences between the illicit drug market in the USA and the illicit drug market in Britain. For example, up until a few years ago it would have been possible to argue that threat of physical injury was appreciably lower in Britain than in the USA, thus reducing the extent of compensation required against threat of physical injury. This is arguably still the case, although there appears to be a rising level of drug-related violence within Britain. Nevertheless, even given the differences the fact appears to remain that the highest influence on the price of illicit drugs is compensation for risk. As Caulkins and Reuter (1998: 605) argue, 'the extraordinarily high prices . . . are clearly a function of their illegality', and the need for those in the illicit drug business to be able to compensate for the costs such illegality carries in its wake. Again, this has implications for policy that will be explored in the final section of this chapter.

Table 6.1 Estimates of the magnitude of cost components for cocaine sold at retail, 1999

	%
Wholesale price in Colombia	1
Importing of drug	12
Retail Labour	13
Higher-level labour	3
Drug and asset seizures	8–11
Money laundering fees	2–4
Packaging, processing and inventory costs	2
Compensation for risk of prison	23.6
Compensation for physical risk	33

Source: Caulkins and Reuter 1998: 600

Having reviewed the factors on price within a predominantly US context, it is time to return to more domestic concerns and provide an overview of the British illicit drug business. For this, the chapter turns its attention to the work of Lewis (1994), who provides an examination of the nature of the British illicit drug market for heroin.

British drug markets: composition and key players

Lewis (1994) structured his outline of illicit heroin markets in Britain around a model for New York drug markets devised in 1969 by Preble and Casey. They offered a six-level hierarchy of the market, which, as Lewis (1994: 45) comments, 'remains relevant to European markets as a point of departure rather than a blueprint'. Rather than simply impose an alien structure on domestic events, Lewis constructed an Anglo-centric model based on his and others' observations. Again, using the terminology of economic theory it is possible to produce an overview of the characteristics and key personnel within the British illicit drug market. Before reviewing the market composition there are three key points that need to be made.

Firstly, Lewis (1994: 46) suggests that the British market in illicit heroin is more flexible than either its mainland European or North American counterpart, with fewer barriers to entry. This is partly because of the relative absence of organized criminal gangs such as the Mafia. Secondly, the British drug market is complex and multi-layered with constant exit and entry of individuals. This means that there are often three or four layers between the importers and the end-users. Thirdly, the British market tends to be characterized by small businesses. To place this in context, Fuller (1990) suggests that small businesses employ between eight and fifteen people. A review of Lewis' work illustrates the complex but interrelated nature of the British market in illicit heroin.

Importers and bulk distributors

Lewis (1994: 46) notes that the 'commercialization' of the heroin market is relatively recent, only beginning in earnest during the late 1970s/early 1980s. Prior to this, heroin users were denied reliable access to constant supplies of heroin and constructed co-operative smuggling ventures aimed at meeting the needs of the co-operative, and not for large commercial gain. However, with the expansion of production in south east Asia, and the increasing vigilance of Customs and Excise officials at major ports and airports, this type of import business became increasingly risky. As we have seen, illicit drug businesses seek compensation for risk, which, when added to the rise in heroin use, set in train the commercialization of heroin importing.

Lewis (1994: 46) argues that this process can be seen in the 'consolidation of a complex, high turnover market' that emerged at the start of the 1980s.

He suggests that this signifies a shift in the nature and motive of those involved in importing heroin. Rather than simply importing heroin as a means to ensure personal consumption and make a modest profit to allow future use, heroin importers became major investors, building sophisticated and complex smuggling empires. These businesses tend to be located in big cities, such as London, Manchester and Liverpool. Lewis notes that research and definitive information at this level of the market are perhaps the hardest to come by because the importers are far removed from the street, often tend to be professional criminals, can be linked to organized crime and are hostile and dangerous groups. However, there is need to inject a note of caution here as Ruggerio and South (1995) question the presence of 'Mr Big' in the British drug market. Certainly, thus far in the UK there is a distinct lack of a character such as the (now dead) Columbian Pablo Escobar.

Bulk wholesalers

Once the heroin has been imported into Britain (in what will be its purest form in the journey from point of entry to point of use) and has undergone the distribution process, it moves into the hands of the bulk wholesalers. Bulk wholesalers are part of a network that incorporates importers, distributors, bulk wholesalers and house dealers. Within the market, they occupy the ground between 'the large-scale importer/distributor and the low-level wholesaler and dealers' (Lewis 1994: 47). The relationship between these parts of the market is extremely fluid and often distributors will sell directly to low-level dealers. Again, while there has been little in the way of research into this part of the market, there are autobiographies such as those of Howard Marks.

Lewis informs that bulk wholesalers purchase their products from a number of sources and in a number of forms. For example, the product may be bought in a semi-refined state and converted into heroin. On the other hand, relatively undiluted heroin can be bought either from a distributor or from a place of brokerage where the wholesaler will use their existing contacts. Lewis (1994: 48) suggests that the 'average' bulk wholesaler would buy half kilo to 100 gram units that are then diluted into 100 to 30 gram units and sold to dealers.

Bulk wholesalers vary in type and can be drawn from a number of sections of society. Lewis posits that they can be

1   drug entrepreneurs, who in the past may have operated at retail level;
2   legitimate traders, who have developed sidelines as distributors or wholesalers;
3   predatory professional criminals, who have found a lucrative source of income in drugs.

(Lewis 1994: 48)

However, they appear to share a number of common characteristics. Lewis suggests that they are older than either users or retail dealers, being in their thirties and forties compared to twenties for the latter group. Bulk wholesalers also tend to have criminal records. Although distanced from street-level dealing they are vulnerable, especially when making collections or deliveries. Their presence often goes undetected, however, as the majority of police raids tend to take place at a lower level. In these situations, it is not uncommon to find empty 100 gram bags containing traces of heroin (Lewis 1994: 48), indicating the presence of a higher-level market player.

Small-scale wholesalers and apartment dealers

Lewis (1994: 48–9) identifies this group as house or apartment dealers. He notes that at this level it is likely that the market player will be a user as well. At this stage there is an overlap between the wholesale and retail ends of the market, with the small-scale wholesaler selling to both user-dealers and users. In terms of quantity, they sell lots of between 1 and 30 grams. Often, these market players are independent, not being linked to any of the professional criminals or bulk wholesalers. There is one noticeable and important difference: small-scale wholesalers and house dealers nearly always operate from fixed bases, which can be a house, flat or legitimate business. The increased risk that this entails Caulkins and Reuter (1998) identify as a cost that needs to be compensated.

Having a fixed base means that if the police or rival competitors in the market identify the permanent site, the base becomes an easy target. In terms of operation, this section of the market works from two types of base. The first, the legitimate business, is perhaps the most attractive as it allows (a) good cover in as much as prospective heroin consumers can mingle with non-heroin buying customers and (b) profits from the illicit drug trade can be diverted through licit accounts.

The second option, operating from a house or flat, is the riskier of the two. Constant streams of customers to a private dwelling can alert the attention of neighbours and the police, as well as signalling the location of the business to rival sellers. It is not uncommon for this level of market player to employ assistants who can be used to monitor telephone calls, vet existing and potential customers and perhaps supervise consumption on the premises. Interestingly enough, and dating the article, Lewis (1994: 49) comments on the centrality of the telephone to the small scale wholesalers and house dealer's business: clearly, the recent explosion of mobile phone and pager use has both enhanced business and, to an extent, reduced risk of detection. It has also raised questions as to the accuracy of information regarding fixed bases – new technology may have made such fixed bases obsolete.

Two other points that Lewis makes are worthy of inclusion here. He notes that if dealer and wholesaler also use heroin, they need to be careful to monitor their own intake. Using too much of their stock for personal consumption can leave them out of profit, in debt, and neglectful of security. Hence, for many in this position, business is conducted with the additional pressure of controlling immediate use and gratification in order to secure longer-term futures. Secondly, Lewis (1994: 49) argues that, at this level, some of the transactions resemble the market pre-commercialization, with barter and exchange taking place in lieu of cash exchanges, or the grouping together of users to buy larger amounts of the drug from bulk wholesalers.

Retail sales and user-sellers

This is the lowest end of the market, and as Lewis (1994: 50) remarks, at this level the heroin market can be characterized as 'chaotic'. Almost without exception most market players at this level are consumers as well as retailers and are drawn into the business because of the possibility of regular supplies of cheap heroin. However, the commercial world in which these 'day labourers' of the heroin trade work is equally as complex as that prevailing for the higher echelons of the market.

Lewis identifies five categories of user-dealer: appointment dealers; street dealers; network suppliers; user-sellers and social suppliers. He argues that these categories are useful in an understanding of the market because they help us differentiate between wholesale apartment dealers who enter the retail market, aid the realization that retail sales happen in places other than the street, and demonstrate that there are a number of different consumer networks within the market that are serviced in a variety of ways.

Lewis (1994: 50) also suggests that some of these user-sellers occupy a number of different roles in the heroin market, moving between a number of service roles which can encompass selling, transporting, diluting, look out duties and testing products. The common theme running through the business at this level is the high degree of risk faced by the market players: arrests at this level are more common then elsewhere in the market. For this reason, the market has developed a number of 'coping strategies' designed to reduce the likelihood of arrest by the police or aggressive competition by other sellers. These include the appointment system, the use of pagers and mobile phones to arrange meetings and the use of tightly knit networks between sellers and regular customers.

The value of works such as that of Lewis (1994) is that they serve to reinforce the message that the illicit drug industry is every bit as complex and interrelated as any licit business. Bearing this in mind, it can come as little surprise that economic analysis has been seen by some as holding the potential to act on the illicit drug market. As Caulkins *et al.* (1999: 323) point out, '. . . drug dealing organizations are . . . businesses. Furthermore, they are businesses whose operations the government seeks to regulate.' Theoretically, the employment of economic laws as a controlling mechanism, able to inform polices and shape practice in much the same way as governments use the same laws to control licit industries should offer some of the optimal methods of control. The next section explores some of the literature surrounding this approach.

Economics as a possible controlling mechanism

Based on the information supplied above, it is possible tentatively to suggest that policy makers could look towards economic theory as at least an alternative policy approach. This stance has been taken up by a variety of academics, and, in some instances, has figured in policy documents for police forces across the world. The concluding section of this chapter reviews the key arguments, and provides some thoughts as to the usefulness of economics in steering practice.

To review the situation, the economic laws of supply and demand indicate that as price rises so demand will fall, and that as costs of production rise, more and more producers will leave the market. In terms of applicability to the illicit drug market, it can be seen that actions by the authorities that raise the price of the drug to the consumer, or increase the cost of production to the supplier, should, in theory, reduce the number of consumers and suppliers. There is one exception to this 'law' and that is where price elasticity of demand is inelastic, meaning that consumers will continue to demand and buy a product irrespective of any rise in price. The implications here for drug policy is that for those users whose drug use is problematic and financed by crime, price rises will only lead to increased crime, due to the fact the user's demand remains constant and increased income is required to service that demand.

These theories have only been tested out on a number of occasions, a point noted by Warner (1993: 353), who claims that 'the state of the art is primitive'. For example, Weatherburn and Lind (1997), writing from an Australian perspective, note that economic theory dictates that in a market where the majority of the product is imported, as in the case of heroin, seizures of large quantities should cause prices to rise, leading to a fall in quantities purchased and consumed. However, they argue that, in the Australian context, there has been no hard evidence to indicate that this was the case. This led Weatherburn and Lind (1997: 557–8) to review the literature on price elasticity of demand in relation to heroin addicts. They found that opinion was mixed, with some suggesting that despite being addictive, there is a high degree of price elasticity prevalent among heroin addicts (Kaplan 1983).

Very few studies had been conducted to test this. Weatherburn and Lind (1997: 558) point to the work of Silverman and Spurill (1977) who found that demand for heroin shows little long-run price elasticity, but is price elastic in the short run. Grapendall (1992), who found that addicts tended to base their consumption on their daily income rather then vice versa, supports this view. In order further to test the applicability of economic theory to real life scenarios, Weatherburn and Lind conducted a longitudinal study of the heroin market in Cabramatta, a suburb of Sydney, NSW. Their findings shed some light on the usefulness of the application of economic theory to supply side enforcement.

In essence, Weatherburn and Lind (1997: 566–8) found no relationship between the amount of heroin seized and either street price or purity levels. They suggest the primary reason for this is that the level of seizures by customs and excise are not large enough to impact on the overall market. For example, during the two-year period from 1993 to 1995 Weatherburn and Lind (1997: 566) estimate that seizures only accounted for between 3.7 and 17.2 per cent of all heroin consumed. However, paradoxically, 67 per cent of heroin users, when asked why they were seeking treatment, cited the cost of the drug, with 30 per cent citing trouble with the police, which can also be seen as a cost. Moreover, 97 per cent of users cited being tired of the lifestyle as a reason for seeking treatment. Weatherburn and Lind suggest that this indicates an overall disaffection with both types of 'cost'.

They conclude by discussing the nature of the type of policies and the levels at which these need to operate. They suggest that in the case of Australia, seeking to raise the price of heroin by creating a shortage of the drug has failed. However, the fact that there is an agency detailed to *attempt* to do this sends signals to the importers and is factored in as a cost of production, thus having a direct impact on price, due to the need of the importers to compensate for this potential risk. Hence, even giving the impression of attaching more importance to the import and distribution end of the market can influence the street price to some degree, even if interdiction is unable significantly to reduce the amount of a drug entering a country. Weatherburn and Lind (1997: 567) conclude by stating the need for policy makers to '. . . address themselves to the question of whether the benefits of a policy designed to moderate the demand for heroin by maintaining street prices can be made to outweigh associated costs'.

In economic terms, given that there may only be a slight elasticity of demand for illicit drugs among heavy-end users, this point raises implications for the allocation of resources for supply-side enforcement policies, a point taken up by Wagstaff (1989). He notes that because of the nature of the illicit drug industry, it is difficult to map the parameters of the business, so that economic analysis is fraught with difficulties. Thus, as we have seen in Chapter 3, we have little in the way of accurate indicators of levels or patterns of consumption across the whole population, are reliant on anecdotal inforation from law enforcement agents and fieldworkers over price, and use samples taken from seizures to measure purity. Wagstaff (1989: 1174) argues that these indicators are often atypical and provide only limited information.

Similarly, Wagstaff notes that the main rationale for government intervention into illicit drug markets is that there are third party costs imposed by drug use. This is taken to mean that third parties suffer as a result of drug use in ways such as increased acquisitive crime. These costs, known in economics as external costs, need to be addressed to ensure that the community at large does not suffer the ill effects of drug use. In terms of devising policy, Wagstaff points to two problem areas. Firstly, he notes the need to balance spending on the variety of available drug reduction programmes. There is little point, he argues, in skewing resources to favour a particular approach that, in economic terms, has a lesser impact on external cost. Using economic theory as a driver of policy would demand that each type of drug reduction programme would reach a level where an extra pound spent on each programme would have exactly the same impact on external cost.

Secondly, he suggests that it makes 'little sense to spend more on reducing drug consumption than there is to be gained from the reduction in external cost' (Wagstaff 1989: 1175). In more detail, Wagstaff (1989: 1175) argues that this raises questions concerning the total level of aggregate spending on reducing illicit drug use. Put simply, economics requires us to ask the question: 'Do the gains society gets from reducing illicit drug consumption match the cost of financing them?' Again, Wagstaff (1989: 1177) returns to the point made by Weatherburn and Lind (1997) that, in terms of supply-side policies the answer to that question lies in whether demand for illicit drugs is elastic or inelastic. Given that there seems to be, at least in the short run, some price elasticity, the next policy question economics can answer is which segment of the market is the optimum area to target in terms of reducing supply.

This ties neatly into the work of Kleiman and Young (1995). They argue that the illicit drug debate is shaped by economic language, but overemphasizes the dichotomy between supply side policy and demand side policy. Instead of concentrating on these, arguably simplistic, polarities, Kleiman and Young suggest a more holistic approach that focuses on the factors of production visible in the illicit drug market. In this way, it may be possible to identify the factors of production that, in economic terms, are described as '. . . those factors that can be most readily made scarce relative to others' (Kleiman and Young 1995: 730). In lay terms this refers to the identification of the weakest link in the market operation. The difference between this perspective and the others is that it allows targeting of both demand and supply, and is therefore not reliant on the nebulous and somewhat unproven concept of price elasticity.

Conclusion

To some extent, economic theory is able to afford us a differently focused perspective on the world of illicit drugs. It does this by stripping away any connotations of morality and demands that we see illicit drugs as a commodity, subject to laws and pressures more readily associated with commonplace goods such as eggs and butter. However, for this to work to its fullest extent, we need to assume that the illicit drug market place is identical to that of licit goods. Moreover, economic theory and therefore economic analysis are centred on the availability of information – there is a need to be fully aware of all the actions of all the participants.

Just as in the case of trying to measure the extent of illicit drug use, the clandestine nature of the illicit drug market inhibits our ability to obtain accurate information. Thus, put simply, we do not have all the necessary information to use economic theory to its fullest. Nevertheless, that does not render economic theory superfluous to understanding. Its strength lies in the fact that it makes us aware of the impact of costs and benefits and, as we will see in the final chapter, can provide us with pertinent questions concerning the 'value' of pursuing particular policies. That is for the future. The immediate concerns revolve around the manner in which costs and payments affect both the users and the communities they inhabit. This, then, becomes the focus of the next chapter.

Note

1 Price quoted by telephone 27 September 2001; this relates to shipping a parcel from Lima in Peru to Plymouth, England.

7 Paying for illicit drugs and assessing the costs

Introduction

Having spent the previous two chapters examining global and economic issues inherent in the illicit drug industry, this chapter returns to more domestic concerns. In particular, it begins to focus on two related 'problem' areas often associated with illicit drug use: (a) those of the drug/crime link and (b) the damage drug use does to individuals and society. From the outset it is important to be aware of the centrality the drug/crime link holds for UK policy developments. For example, the government's Drugs Prevention Advisory Service comments that 'a significant number of crimes are committed either as a consequence of, or to help finance, drug use' (DPAS 2001: 5). This is an important point because, as noted previously, part of the rationale for the state intervening in illicit drug use lies in the damage caused to the wider community – the external costs. Crime which is linked to drug use is clearly seen as the largest and most important of these 'external costs'. In itself, this can be seen as somewhat of a paradox – as the previous chapter demonstrated, state intervention *raises* the price of drugs!

The chapter begins by exploring the link between illicit drug use and crime. From this point, it moves to offer a typology of illicit drug using offenders, identifying and discussing three distinct, but not mutually exclusive, groups. The purpose of this section is to make a distinction between the costs incurred by recreational users, offenders who use illicit drugs and 'heavy-end' or problematic drug users who are drug dependent and appear to be committing crimes to finance their drug use. It also serves to discuss the nature of the links between illicit drug use and acquisitive crime. In the final sections, the chapter examines, in detail, the notion of 'cost' and expands the previously made point regarding costs as being monetary and non-monetary, as well as individual and societal.

Just before commencing the discussion, it is important to point out that, for the purposes of this chapter, 'crime' and 'offending' will be taken to mean what Chaiken and Chaiken (1991) call 'income generating' offences, but which will be referred to here as acquisitive crime. This includes offences such as burglary, shoplifting, fraud and, unlike Chaiken and Chaiken's work,

ition and other sex crimes. It does not include crimes of violence. This
say that drug users do not commit crimes of violence – some clearly
he consequences of their actions are of concern. However, our focus
to explore the link between acquisitive property crime and illicit
drug use, for it is the link between acquisitive crime and drug use that
seems to worry the British state more than the links between crimes of
violence and illicit drug use.

The links between illicit drug use and crime

At one level, there is an obvious link between illicit drugs and crime – any
action that contravenes the parameters of the law regarding drugs becomes
criminal. Thus, for example, drug dealing, importation and possession are
all crimes, making the link between drugs and crime obvious. However,
there are other links, far more complex and requiring a much deeper analysis;
links that have taxed academics for at least the last thirty years. As evidence,
witness the manner in which the ACMD (1996: 11–12) discuss the ways
drugs and crime can be viewed:

> Every year thousands of drug misusers come into contact with the
> criminal justice system. There are three ways in which this occurs:
> - because they commit offences under the misuse of drugs legislation,
>   for example the possession or supply of controlled drugs;
> - because their misuse of drugs causes or contributes to other criminal
>   behaviour, for example committing acquisitive crime to help fund
>   their drug misuse, or crime committed under the influence of
>   drugs; or
> - because they commit offences unrelated to their drug misuse.

Although it may now be the mainstay of contemporary policy, recognizing
and establishing the link between drug use and crime has been a long process:
Sutherland and Cressey (1970: 164) stated that 'felons are over represented in
the addict population, crime rates are increased considerably by drug addiction'. However, as Chaiken and Chaiken (1991: 281) point out, at that stage
the precise links between drugs and crime were not fully thought through or
explored.

There have been a number of contemporary attempts to 'think through' the
relationship between drugs and crime, and almost without exception the
results have been strewn with ambiguity and littered with caveats. For
instance, Newburn and Elliott (1999: 6) are unequivocal in stating that 'it
is undeniably the case that crime and drugs are linked'. However, they are
more guarded in claiming causality, noting that 'the precise relationship
[between crime and drug use] is far from clear'. Chaiken and Chaiken
(1991: 282) on the other hand are certain in their conviction: they state

categorically that 'In short, no single sequential or causal relationship is now believed to relate drug use to predatory crime'.

However, for all their resolution, Chaiken and Chaiken (1991) continue by offering the caveat that there are different patterns that can be applied to different drug users, and that certain types of drug use seem to generate high frequency offending behaviour. Importantly, they note that there are a number of different types of user, and often these different types of user restrict themselves to set consumption patterns, which in turn appear to have some relationship with offending behaviour. For example, some illicit drug users may infrequently use a combination of alcohol and cannabis, but almost never add amphetamine into their consumption pattern, and show no evidence of offending. Others may frequently use heroin, cannabis and cocaine, and are persistent offenders. Thus, sweeping statements that link all drug users to acquisitive crime become unfounded and hide a complex situation. This view is not only the view of academics; witness DPAS (2001: 12; original emphasis): '*Drugs is not one issue, but several. It is not a single problem for which there is only one solution, but a range of issues that need separate but linked solutions*'.

The realities regarding crime and illicit drug use are therefore perhaps better understood if we take as a starting point Chaiken and Chaiken's (1991) assertion that there are different types of user with varying patterns of behaviour, some which includes offending, others that do not. This necessitates the creation of a simple typology of illicit drug users and offending behaviour. This task can be embarked upon by separating out those sections of the population that use illicit drugs into three broad but discrete categories:

A, the recreational/low frequency user;
B, frequent criminals who are drug users;
C, criminal, problematic drug users

Membership of each category can then be ascertained by viewing illicit drug users through four lenses:

1   the nature of drug use;
2   whether drug use is financed by crime;
3   the nature of the relationship between drug use and crime;
4   the risk posed to the community in terms of acquisitive crime.

Once this separation of users is completed, the crime/drug link debate becomes clearer and enables a sharper focus to be made. There are three important points to note here. As with all typologies these categories are 'ideal types' and therefore there will be people who do not fit into the compartmentalization inherent in typologies. Secondly, movement between categories is possible but not inevitable: a person who begins in category A may, quite quickly, end up in category C, but not necessarily so. Thirdly, recreational users are defined as 'those who take drugs fairly frequently but do not use heroin or methadone and do not describe themselves has having a problem and do not describe drug use as the dominant element in their lives' (Social Policy Association 1997: 1).

It is also important to be specific about some of the more quantifiable data such as frequency and persistence. Looking first at frequency, contrary to popular opinion, even the most habitual of criminals seldom offends on a daily basis. Using data derived from research in the USA, Chaiken and Chaiken (1991: 287) claim that most offenders commit non-violent offences at low rates. For example, Chaiken and Chaiken (1991: 293) posit that crime days per year may be as low as 11 for some non-drug using offenders, rising to 48 crime days per year for non-drug using prisoners.

However, there are small minorities of offenders who commit offences at a very high level of frequency. Coid *et al.* (2001) note that from their sample of drug using offenders who admitted to offences of theft, the number of mean crime days per six month period was 44. Equally, Bennett and Sibbitt (2000) state that some offenders who use drugs admit to at least 20 offences per month. Based on these findings it is possible to suggest that people who have more than 4 crime days per month are frequent offenders. Equally, when examining patterns of illicit drug consumption in the UK (see Chapter 3), it is clear that the vast majority of those who admit to using illicit substances do so on an infrequent basis (that is, less than once per week). For example, only 20 per cent of the highest using age group admitted to use in the last month (Ramsay and Partridge 1999). Based on those assumptions, it is possible to begin to construct a typology of illicit drug users and their relationship to crime and risk.

Category A: the low frequency/recreational user

Research findings offer no evidence to support the theory that use of an illicit drug leads inexorably to involvement in acquisitive crime. In fact, according to Chaiken and Chaiken (1991: 290), the link between acquisitive crime and illicit drug use is not even the predominant pattern for the vast majority of illicit drug users. On reflection, this finding is unsurprising. The DPAS (2001: 7) notes that, within the UK, 'more than 8 million people aged 16 to 59 admit to taking cannabis with 1.6 million still doing so each month'. There is no evidence whatsoever to support the assertion that all of those people have at one time or another committed acquisitive crime in order to purchase illicit drugs, a point endorsed by reference to the recorded crime figures. Moreover, this group's drug use is not expensive: 'Most casual drug use is inexpensive – at least in the same order of magnitude as drinking alcohol and there is no evidence that anything but a small proportion of such misuse (*sic*) is financed by crime' (Hough 1996: 10).

In terms of looking at this group through the four analytical lenses outlined above, it can be claimed that the nature of this group's drug use is recreational and mainly infrequent. It is unlikely that their drug use will be financed by crime, making the nature of the relationship between drug use and acquisitive crime low to non-existent. The risk posed to the community in terms of acquisitive crime and drug consumption is low. Thus, it appears that the majority of people who use illicit drugs do so in an experimental and relatively unproblematic fashion, failing to become involved in acquisitive crime in any significant form.

Category B: frequent drug-using criminals

While it is possible to claim that the majority of those people who have *ever* used an illicit drug have done so in an unproblematic manner, there are numbers of users for whom drug use and/or offending behaviour has a significant impact upon their life. However, that knowledge poses an interesting, chicken and egg type question for the researcher and policy maker in deciding which came first: frequent drug use or frequent offending behaviour. This conundrum has generated a wealth of literature and it is to some of this the chapter now turns.

UK-based research shows that many of those offenders who offend on a frequent basis are also frequent drug users (Wallace and Eastham 1994; Coid *et al.* 2001), giving rise to speculation as to the relationship between frequent offending and the frequency of illicit drug use. This is supported by recent Home Office research, which conducted urine analysis on arrestees and found that there are high percentages of offenders who use illicit drugs (Bennett and Sibbitt 2000). Thus, it becomes difficult to refute claims that for some offenders their offending behaviour runs at least parallel with illicit drug use. Chaiken and Chaiken (1991), in reviewing the US research, recognize this but caution that, although for some offenders use of illicit drugs may be the primary cause of onset, participation and frequency in offending, for the vast majority of offenders, illicit drug use is not the cause of offending behaviour.

Hammersley *et al.* (1989; 1990), conducting research in Scotland, echo these US-based findings. They undertook two sets of research, one on prisoners and non-prisoners with offending histories and the other on teenage users of licit and illicit drugs. In both studies Hammersley and colleagues found that illicit drug use did not cause the onset of offending behaviour, neither did frequent illicit drug use determine the frequency of criminal activity. They suggest that day-to-day criminal activity was a better explanation of drug use than daily drug use was of crime. They note that readily available income allows increased consumption of a number of goods, including illicit drugs. In turn the availability of disposable income, set in an environment where drug use is normalized, can lead to increased and, for some, ultimately problematic use. Thus, for Hammersly *et al.* (1989; 1990) being

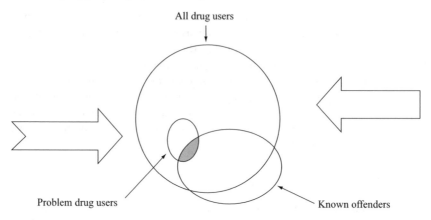

Figure 7.1 The relationship between drug use and offending (Source: adapted from Hough 1996)

involved in a criminal environment is more likely to lead to drug use than vice versa.

This is worthy of expansion, because, often, implicit in the messages of the media and politicians is the assertion that illicit drug use *causes* crime. In some cases this may be true: however, for many individuals offending behaviour pre-dates drug dependency. Searching for causality in the social sciences is very often a complex process, devoid of right answers. However, the complexity inherent in this situation can be simplified by viewing it diagrammatically. Figure 7.1, which has been adapted from Hough (1996: 11), contains three inter-locking circles. Note that the circles are not to scale and it is not intended that they map the precise overlap between each of the categories. Rather, they are intended to demonstrate the relationship between drug use and offending and highlight the different pathways into problematic drug use.

The largest circle represents all illicit drug users, and relates to category A in the typology offered here. The smaller circle relates to all those involved in acquisitive crime and the smallest circle represents those drug users whose use has become problematic. It can be seen that some offenders overlap with drug users, and these relate to category B in our typology. Finally, there is a shaded area in the smallest circle that relates to problematic drug users. Again, it will be noted that some offenders are also problematic drug users. The shaded area represents the category C drug user. The arrows at the edges of the diagram note the pathways into offending and illicit drug use.

According to researchers such as Hammersley *et al.* (1989; 1990) and Chaiken and Chaiken (1991), routes into categories B and C are more likely to come from the offending pathway than from the drug using pathway. Thus, as Hammersley and colleagues note, being involved in a social group where offending and drug taking are the norm provides a greater chance that individuals will move from offending into drug use and then sometimes, but not always, onwards into problematic drug use. Although it is possible for those who use illicit drugs and come from non-offending social groups, such as those in category A, to move into categories B and C, the likelihood is lower.

This argument is clarified and endorsed by Coid *et al.* (2001). In their research into the crime/drug link they found that some acquisitive offences such as shoplifting, theft and burglary preceded drug dependence. For example, Coid *et al.* (2001: 47) found that, among their cohort, the mean age for first burglary was 17.0 years, whereas the mean age for first opiate use among those that had committed burglary was 20.2 years. However, the phenomenon of offending predating opiate dependence only relates to certain types of offences: in the same work, Coid and colleagues note that 75 per cent of those who admitted offences of prostitution committed their first offence *after* they were drug dependent.

In many ways, Hough (1996: 5–11) further clarifies this theme. He suggests that offences where there is a drug and crime link can be viewed in one of two ways: as either *drug-related* or *drug-driven*. In detail, Hough employs the ACMD distinction between casual users and problem drug users. Problem drug users are identified as

> . . . anyone who experiences social, psychological, physical or legal problems related to intoxication and/or regular excessive consumption and/or dependence of his/her own use of drugs or other chemical substances . . . [it also] includes anyone whose drug misuse involves, or could lead to the sharing of injecting equipment.
>
> (Hough 1996: 5)

Hough qualifies this statement and warns not to take the above as an implication that 'recreational' or 'casual' drug use is unproblematic – he argues that they are not problem free and can lead to both legal and medical complications. Nevertheless, for Hough, the area of linkage between drugs and crime revolves around those users whose drug consumption has become problematic.

On this basis, Hough (1996: 10–11) offers his analytical dichotomy of offences with links to drug use. He argues for the need to examine both the motivations for committing the offence and the nature of what the proceeds from offending are spent on. He suggests that some recreational drug users who commit acquisitive crimes may use some of the proceeds of crime on drugs. However, they are equally likely to use the proceeds on a plethora of consumer goods and/or staple essentials such as food and rent. In this instance, drug purchase can be seen as an incidental item of expenditure and therefore lacking any form of causality and demonstrating only a tenuous link between drugs and crime, locating users firmly in category A, outlined above.

Moving along the continuum, Hough (1996: 11) recognizes that 'some non-dependent drug users consume a volume of drugs which would be beyond their means if it were not for the income they derive from crime'. Once again this does not constitute a causal link between drug use and crime: it does, however, begin to increase the strength of the relationship between the two variables. By way of illustration, Hough suggests that a non-dependent drug user may be motivated to burgle in order to finance a 'good time', but be indifferent as to whether that 'good time' is fuelled by alcohol or illicit drugs. Thus, the nature of the offence is *drug related*.

Bearing this in mind, it is possible to begin to create a category B drug user. For this group drug use will have become regular and relatively frequent. The nature of the relationship between drug use and crime is one where offending and drug use are frequent with drug-related crime taking place. Drug consumption will be financed at least partially by crime. Overall, this group poses a medium to high risk to their community in terms of offending behaviour.

Category C: the criminal, dependent drug-user

At the polar extreme of the continuum is the offender whose motivation to offend is directly related to drug purchase and consumption. The ACMD (1996: 12) defines this group as '. . . those individuals, some of whose offending is associated with misuse of drugs either causally or because of the influence of drugs on their behaviour.' Hough argues that this group of offenders commits crimes 'specifically to buy a preferred illegal drug'. As Hough notes (1996: 11; original emphasis), offences '. . . committed by [this group] can be regarded as *drug-driven*'. Coid *et al.* (2001: 44–5) reinforce this perspective. They note that from their sample, in the month prior to interview only 19 per cent had managed to keep their expenditure on illicit drugs within the limits of their legal income; the remaining 81 per cent had resorted to acquisitive crime in order to finance drug consumption.

Arguably, it is possible to suggest that it is in this category, for which drug use has reached problematic levels, that the link between crime and illicit drug use is at its strongest, with offending behaviour and drug consumption being frequent in the extreme. Bean (2002: 8) looking at the offending behaviour of this group, suggests that 'An out-of-control male drug user is likely to commit 80–100 crimes per year'. Coid *et al.* (2001: 67), reporting on the drug consumption patterns, note that the mean monthly total of days a heroin dependent offender uses opiates is 24.2, using on average 0.54 gram per day. When heroin is unavailable the same group will use a number of other substances.

In spite of this evidence, claiming any sort of causality for each and every type of offence remains problematic: as Bean (2002: 9) continues, 'Offenders might say they burgled because they were drug takers but they were burglars in any case'. Perhaps a better way is to study the *types* of crime this group commits and examine changes in offending *patterns* pre- and post-dependency. For example, it seems from the work of Coid *et al.* (2001) that some types of offence pre-dated problematic drug use. Equally, however, some types of offences *post-date* problematic use. It may be the case that problematic drug use causes certain offenders, whose offending pre-dated problematic use, to become engaged in offences that, hitherto, they shied away from. Possibly, then, and only then, could causality between drug use and crime be claimed.

However, such a detailed analysis is beyond the scope of this work. For our purposes we need to concentrate on fitting this group into our analytical framework. Based on this evidence, it appears that the nature of drug use for this group is problematic and extremely frequent. Drug use is, effectively, totally financed by crime. The nature of the relationship between drug use and crime is that crime is drug driven. This group poses a high risk to their community in terms of acquisitive crime. In trying to clarify and end this complex argument, it may be beneficial to the reader to view the above information in tabular form and Table 7.1 presents a typology of crime/drug relationships.

As a final thought on this matter, and as a way of introducing the next section, it is worth quoting Edmunds and colleagues:

> For the 97 per cent of people who engage in casual or recreational drug use there is little evidence of clear links between drug use and acquisitive crime. For the three per cent of problem users, the evidence of a link is overwhelming.
>
> (Edmunds *et al.* 1999: 7)

In essence, the problem population in terms of their drug use and offending behaviour could be as few as 130,000 people, probably not rising to much above 200,000. While this number may seem small, the effects of their action have huge ramifications for them as individuals and for the communities in which they live. There is a certain irony (or some may see it as poetic justice) in the fact that many of this group of offenders who cause

Table 7.1 A typology of the crime/drug relationship

Category	Drug use	Finance	Nature of crime/ drug link	Risk
A	recreational/ experimental	legal means	none	low
B	frequent/ recreational	legal/illegal mix (mostly legal)	drug related	medium
C	frequent/ problematic	virtually all illegal	drug driven	high

extensive harm and cost to society, suffer equally in terms of harm and cost in terms of their individual health and social conditions. Both the 'harm' and 'cost' of illicit drug use, in terms of crime and health and social conditions will now be reviewed.

The 'cost' of drug use and crime

This section considers the nature of 'harm' and 'cost', in individual and collective terms. It begins by continuing the theme of the previous section by concentrating on the harm which drug driven crime does to society, and, briefly, to the individual drug user. Following that, it explores the harm drug use does to individuals in terms of their health and their social conditions.

Cost, although it can be seen in purely financial terms, is perhaps better understood, and therefore will be conceived of here as being related to the concept of 'harm'. When policy makers talk of 'harm' they actually mean the cost of illicit drug use in terms of health and crime to both the individual and the community. For example, public concern over drugs has been expressed by the government in three ways:

- the link between drugs and crime;
- the health risk posed by the spread of HIV and hepatitis;
- the damage to the social fabric caused by high concentrations of 1 and 2 in some urban areas.

(Cabinet Office 1998)

Essentially, all these concerns are linked to the concept of harm (it is worth noting that 'harm reduction' is one of the key phrases used by those working within the drug field). In terms of the health risk, this is related to the harm that drug use does to the individual user, with wider concerns over public health. The concern over crime can be seen to be linked with the harm which drug driven crime does to the community, with broader worries as to the effect of criminalization on the user/offender. Taken together, the overall effect of problematic drug use is deemed to be harmful to the fabric of society.

'Cost' and 'harm' in terms of acquisitive crime

Ignoring questions of causality, there can be little doubt that illicit drug use and acquisitive crime share an affinity, especially for the small minority that composes category C users. This point has been made in a number of publications drawn from a diversity of sources. Although their arguments have been well rehearsed, it is worthwhile to cover them again, in order that the magnitude of offending behaviour may be reviewed. Edmunds *et al.* (1999) provide an official picture, estimating that, as a group, the combined annual expenditure on drugs for category C users could reach £1 billion. Given the discrepancy between licit and illicit income for this group, somewhere in the region of half of that could be raised by acquisitive crime per annum. In light of the fact that stolen property is sold for around a third of its retail value, this group could be engaged in offending that costs victims up to £1.5 billion per annum.

This perspective has been endorsed by a number of sources. For example, Wallace and Eastham (1994), conducting a piece of action research among category C clients of a street drug agency in Plymouth, found that 62 per cent of their sample (27.28 people) admitted to offending at least once a day. If that figure is rounded down and extended over a twelve-month period, those 27 people held the potential to commit somewhere in the region of 9,855 offences over the course of a year. If each crime resulted in goods to the value of £100 being taken, the yearly cost of those 27 people in terms of goods stolen equals £985,500.

Bringing this up-to-date, the work of Coid *et al.* (2001: 75), commissioned by the Home Office, found a similar picture. From their sample of category C users, they compared the weekly expenditure on illicit drugs with the weekly licit income. Their findings illustrate the nature of the problem. Coid and colleagues found that the mean weekly expenditure on illicit drugs was £312.40 compared with a mean weekly licit income of £70.45. This left a mean income deficit of £245.80. The mean six-monthly income derived from crime by this group stood at £10,984. However, high as this may appear, this sum is based on mean figures: some of the disaggregated findings of Coid *et al.* (2001: 44) are staggering. For example, some subjects claimed to be spending £280 per day on heroin. Others claimed that their maximum daily spend on opiates stood at £1,000. At the extreme, there was a claimed income deficit of £1,936 per week.

Quite clearly, this is a group comprised of prolific offenders. As a result, they will have some form of impact on their (numerous) victims. Mawby and Walklate (1994) note that this will have a number of different effects. Firstly, it will raise the fear of crime among victims, among those who live in close proximity, and within the wider community (direct and indirect victimization). Secondly, the victims themselves may suffer either some form of physical or mental trauma, as well as actual loss of property. For some, especially the poor, uninsured victim, this may have serious consequences on their ability to replace what are often essential household items. Thirdly, victims can suffer from a loss of time, due to giving statements, becoming involved in legal proceedings and so on. Finally, if the police either fail to clear up the crime, or the offender gets what the victim sees as an 'easy' sentence, the victim can suffer a form of frustration and loss of confidence in the criminal justice process.

Crime can also have a debilitating effect on community relations in terms of creating divided communities and fostering a 'them and us' mentality, where sections of the population come to be seen as 'dangerous others'.

At its worst, this can lead to the creation of a fortress mentality and the use of a 'plethora of high-tech alarm equipment' (Barton 2000: 13). This is often an indiscriminate form of community segregation and involves 'lumping together' tracts of the community, based on perceptions rather than realities. Thus, it may be the case that all young people are excluded and feared, irrespective of whether they are drug users or not.

There are two other forms of 'cost' associated with drugs and crime. The first is the cost to the government in 'dealing with' drug use. The Home Office (2001: 4, section 13) claimed that for the year 2001, the government would spend somewhere in the region of £700 million directly on 'tackling the problems of drug mis-use', a figure that is projected to rise to the £1 billion mark in the year 2003/4. While not all this figure is spent on crime-related projects, a substantial amount of that money is (around 67 per cent of the total (Mowbray 2002)), and therefore represents a hefty cost to the taxpayer. The second form of 'cost' is the cost of having a criminal record to the drug user. While in itself having a criminal record is not, in most cases, a direct block on gaining employment, the realities are that many ex-offenders find themselves victims of 'discrimination by application form' and are often unable to find much more than menial employment.

'Cost' and 'harm' in terms of health and social circumstances

This section examines the 'cost' and 'harm' that problematic drug users inflict, mostly on themselves. Ironically, many of those category C drug users who create problems for their community in terms of acquisitive crime, suffer most in terms of drug related ill health. This is perhaps best summarized by Robson (1994: 142); writing from a medical perspective he declares, 'we can only assume that for the vast majority of drug users, their drug use is occasional and spasmodic, or that drugs prove pretty well harmless to most people'. Based on that statement it would appear that, just as in the case with the criminal justice agencies, the majority of illicit drug users do not create a problem for themselves or the health service. Just to make an important point, however, that is not to say that drug use is risk free. Robson (1994: 142) notes that all drug taking involves some element of risk. However, it is equally important to remember that evidence seems to suggest that the belief that once people start using drugs there will be an inevitable spiral downwards to drug dependency appears to be based more on mythology than fact.

Nevertheless, rare as it is, some people clearly do experience serious problems with their drug use and end up becoming drug dependent (in lay terms many problematic drug users are 'addicted', although the preferred phrase among drug workers is 'drug dependent' (Gossop and Grant 1990)). For this group of users, it is the consequences of their drug dependency, in health and social terms, which hold the potential to create problematic conditions. This section concentrates upon the nature of those problems faced by drug dependent users.

According to Robson (1994: 153), definitions of drug dependency are difficult to provide, and are always open to challenge. However, he suggests that, in broad terms, being dependent upon something means being caught up in the following cycle:

> . . . a mounting desire to do something; if this is resisted or prevented, a growing anxiety or preoccupation with the act in question; carrying out the act stills the tension, satisfies the desire and briefly eliminates the need; the cycle starts all over again.

Once a person becomes locked into this cycle, their life begins to change. There is a growing preoccupation that intrudes into the person's life, skewing their priorities towards, in our case, an illicit drug. There is a sense of compulsion, which includes an element of the person feeling obliged to do something that they may not really want to do. With this compulsion come the routines which ensure a ready supply, consumption of the drug becomes less dependent on external cues and the person becomes less and less concerned about the consequences of their actions. In some instances, larger quantities of an illicit drug may be needed as tolerance develops.

Dependence may be physical and/or psychological. Physical dependence can manifest itself as withdrawal symptoms if the drug is withheld, especially where the opioids are concerned. Psychological dependence can manifest itself as a craving for the drug, often triggered by the environment. These cravings can take the shape of 'cues' and can include, among many others, a piece of music, being in the company of certain people, or the sight of injecting equipment. The exact nature of the harm which drug dependent users experience depends upon a number of factors and varies from user to user, although it is generally accepted that drug related 'harm' falls into two categories: health condition and social condition.

Health related harm

Some problematic drug users suffer from health problems prior to contracting their drug-related illnesses. For example, the research of Coid *et al.* (2001: 54) demonstrates that 39 per cent of their sample had experienced some form of depression, while small percentages had suffered from serious mental health conditions. Likewise, the same work (2001: 55) noted high percentages of those suffering personality disorders among the sample. Other work (Wallace and Eastham 1994), recognizes the presence of general health problems such as poor dental health and constipation among a similar group of drug users.

Gossop and Grant (1990: 5–6) outline the basic medical concerns of drug dependency. They claim that for the medical profession these are 'excess mortality and excess morbidity'. The former refers to the death rate among drug users when compared to a non-drug using population of the same age range, while the latter means the rates of illness among drug users when compared to a similar, non-drug using population. Gossop and Grant (1990: 6), noting that excess mortality in drug users stems mostly from overdose or, and especially in the case of intravenous drug users (IDUs), 'the direct access of disease organisms and adulterants into the bloodstream'.

In terms of mortality, comparisons of trends over the last decade demonstrate a year on year rise since 1990 (DrugScope 2000: 19). Bearing in mind methodological problems and different counting processes, statistics show that 1998 saw the total number of drug deaths in the whole of the UK stand at 3,411; this contrasts with 2,861 only four years earlier. DrugScope, looking at the demographic make up of this group, suggests that the figures demonstrate that drug-related deaths are becoming more common in men than among women. In terms of age, DrugScope notes that about 47 per cent of those who die from drug-related incidents and illnesses are located within the 20 to 34 year old age group.

Turning attention to excess morbidity, Gossop and Grant (1990: 6) claim that this is related to a complex of factors, including

> . . . the pharmacological and toxicological properties of drug(s) used, the combinations of drugs used, the accessibility of health services . . . the nutritional habits and status of drug users, the route of administration, of drugs, the quality of the social network and the social integration of the drug user. . . .

The DoH (1999: 22) provides a clear picture of how excess morbidity manifests itself in drug users. They claim that among drug users the following illnesses are more common than in similar populations:

> viral hepatitis [liver disease], bacterial endocarditis [inflammation of the heart], HIV [an attack on the body's immune system], tuberculosis [a communicable disease of the lung], septicaemia [blood poisoning], pneumonia [disease of the lung], deep vein thrombosis [blood clot in the vein], pulmonary emboli [blood clots in the lung], abscesses and dental disease.

They clarify this somewhat by noting the various component parts of drug use and the specific nature of health-related problems:

A: Drug related	Side effects (e.g. constipation, hallucinations)
	Overdose (e.g. respiratory, depression)
	Withdrawal (e.g. irritability, fits)
B: Route specific	Smoking (asthma)
	Injecting (abscesses, cellulitis)

C: Sharing needles, syringes and injection equipment	Hepatitis B and C, HIV and other blood-borne viruses
D: General	Anaemia, poor nutrition, dental caries and erosion of dentine

However, while these problems are serious for the users, it is worthwhile to examine their known prevalence among the drug using population. Be warned, however, that these figures relate to *known* cases: this work has commented more than once on the problems of painting accurate pictures of the illicit drug world.

DrugScope (2000: 20–1), employing data from the DoH (2000) reports a fall in the number of new IDU attributable HIV infections, from 447 in 1986 to 99 in 1999. There are two other blood borne viruses that are worthy of consideration, hepatitis B and hepatitis C. The prevalence of the former stands at around one in five injectors being exposed to the virus. This figure has remained stable since 1995 although 1998 showed a slight increase. It is too early to say if this represents an upward trend, however.

Hepatitis C, the more serious of the two, shows a prevalence of about 30 per cent among IDUs. However, the sensitivity of the test for hepatitis C is only about 80 per cent, meaning the true figure could be as high as 38 per cent. What is clear, however, and arguably demonstrates the value of harm reduction approaches, is the relationship between length of time injecting has been taking place and prevalence of infection. Across all the blood borne viruses, including HIV, there is a reduced prevalence of infection among those who have only been injecting for a few years, meaning that safe injecting messages and needle exchanges seem to have had a positive effect on the health of IDUs.

Socially related harm

Not only do problematic drug users run the risk of harming their health, research also demonstrates that many of this group suffer all manner of social problems, ranging from relationship difficulties, to employment problems and housing related stresses. However, it is important to point out that for many problem drug users, these problems pre-dated their drug use. Coid *et al.* (2001: 51–2) found that large minorities of their sample had suffered numerous kinds of abuse and neglect as children. For example, they found that 41 per cent came from violent households, 31 per cent grew up in poverty and 14 per cent suffered some form of sexual abuse before the age of 15.

Looking at their current situation, Wallace and Eastham (1994) found that 81 per cent of their sample declared that drug use had damaged their relationships. This figure is endorsed by the later study of Coid *et al.* (2001). Here, examining long-term relationships, the researchers found that 49 per cent of respondents claimed their drug use had as a direct consequence either divorce or the end of a relationship. Moreover, drug use seems to be a contributory factor in damaging contacts with wider family members, with 35 per cent of Coid and colleagues' study blaming drug use for causing them to break contact with their family.

Coid *et al.* (2001) and Wallace and Eastham (1994) found that problematic drug users often encounter difficulties in obtaining and/or keeping a job. Of the Wallace and Eastham sample, 75 per cent were unemployed, compared to the 77 per cent reported unemployed by Coid *et al.* Of those studied by Coid *et al.*, 34 per cent cited drug use as a reason for being sacked from a job. Arguably, a corollary of this is that many problematic drug users experience housing problems. For example, Wallace and Eastham found that only 14 per cent of their sample were owner-occupiers. Coid *et al.* found that 39 per cent of their sample were living in some form of temporary accommodation, which included squats and hostels.

On top of these concerns, problematic drug users also have other worries, related, if not caused, by their drug dependency. Most have debts to family and, in cases where they have formerly held down a job, to banks or loan companies. Equally, they are likely at some time to have sold possessions to pay for drugs, impacting on their quality of life (Coid *et al.* 2001). There are concerns over child care, with the very real risk of children being taken into care if one or both adults in a relationship are classified as drug dependent (Parker *et al.* 1998). Moreover, the very act of looking for drugs seems, for some, to be a time-consuming worry:

> It takes a lorr a time scoring and that, y'know. You've got no time for anything else. It takes up all your life really. With me working, by the time you get home at 5 o'clock, it might take you 'til 9 o'clock at night to score sometimes. You're sorta running about all the time so you don't get time for anythin' else really.
>
> (Parker *et al.* 1998: 88)

Conclusion

This chapter has examined the 'cost' of illicit drug use and, in so doing, has covered much ground. A great deal of the information reviewed above informs contemporary thinking about the 'drug problem' in the United Kingdom, both in terms of policy making and lay assumptions. It is hoped that the reader will have found it informative as well as offering a slightly clearer perspective on a number of truisms surrounding illicit drug use. Before concluding, it may be a worthwhile exercise to summarize some of the key points that have emerged from the above discussion:

- It would appear that the majority of people who take illicit drugs almost never experience health and/or legal problems.

- There is little evidence to support a 'natural' progression from recreational drug use to problematic drug use – evidence suggests that problematic drug use is infrequent and atypical of most user's experience.
- There is also little in the way of empirical data to support the assertion that drug use leads to crime, except in the minority of cases.
- There is, however, a clear link between problematic drug use and frequent offending.
- There is an equally strong link between problematic drug use and all manner of health and social problems.

What is emerging from research is the fact that there is a continuum of illicit drug use with an accompanying continuum of problems. The former continuum moves from the infrequent experimental user along to the drug dependent user, diminishing in number the closer one moves to dependent user. The latter follows a similar pattern, except that, here, problems grow the closer one moves towards the drug dependent user. What has also emerged is the fact that this is a relatively small group of people who cause a disproportionate level of harm to wider society in terms of acquisitive crime, hence the thrust of much current drug policy. Similarly, often the same people cause themselves and their immediate significant others a large degree of harm in terms of health and social problems.

Despite the fact that, however atypical it may be, some illicit drug users experience severe problems in terms of criminal justice, health, illness and social care, drug use continues to be a growing part of a significant minority of the UK population's life. This is in spite of repeated warnings; drug prevention campaigns; the statutory requirement to include drug education on the national curriculum for schools; the harmful effects of illicit drugs being part of a number of popular soap operas; and repeated exhortations from sections of the media imploring the young to resist the temptations of illicit drugs. This begs the question 'Why?' The next chapter explores some of the reasons behind the growth in the demand for illicit drugs.

8 'Forget the myth we're desperados standing on street corners. This is a demand led market'

Introduction

The previous chapter illustrated the fact that illicit drug use is far from problem free; for some it holds the potential to become life threatening. Yet, as we have seen in Chapter 3, a large minority of the population seems drawn into experimenting with some form of illicit drug at least once in their lifetime. It also appears that, as the chapter title shows (MacFarlane *et al*. 1996), the vision of an evil dealer luring unsuspecting innocents into drug use does not fit the lived realities of most illicit drug users. Rather, it would appear that the majority of those people who use illicit drugs choose freely to do so, despite the continued warnings as to the potential harm of illicit drugs. This begs the question 'Why?' For some users, the answer is simple: they are drug dependent and their consumption of, and demand for, illicit drugs revolve around dependency. However, as we have seen, that group represents a minority of drug users. The majority of illicit drug users demand drugs for reasons completely unrelated to dependency. This chapter begins to explore some of the reasons behind the continuing, and apparently unabated, demand for illicit drugs.

The demand for illicit drugs will be, in the main, youth dominated, reflecting what we know of recreational illicit drug use in the UK. That is not to suggest that drug use is only confined to the young – there is evidence to suggest that drug use, among some, continues into middle age (Patterson 2002). The latter part of the chapter will explore the growing demand for illicit drugs, particularly cannabis, by people wishing to self-medicate. The chapter begins by way of a brief review of the figures relating to illicit drug use, in order to locate recreational drug use among the young. Following this, it examines the nature of adolescence and briefly looks at British youth culture across the past five decades, identifying patterns and trends of illicit drug use across time. It then moves to explore pathways into and out of drug use among the young. The chapter then reviews the debate surrounding the contention that illicit drug use has become 'normalized' among certain sections of the British population. There follows a brief discussion of the growth of illicit drug use for self-medication purposes. In conclusion the chapter's content is reviewed as a means of entry into the following, policy-based, chapter.

Drug use in the UK: a brief review

Robson (1994) makes the point that the optimum period for using illicit drugs is between the ages of 18 to 24. This became clear in Chapter 3, which offered details of the nature of illicit drug use in the UK. Here, all that is necessary is briefly to review that information by way of offering a reminder. As noted above, lifetime use (ever having used a drug) is claimed by a large minority of the British population, with Ramsay and Partridge (1999) claiming that 32 per cent of all Britons admit to taking an illicit drug sometime in their life. However, once age has been factored into these figures, they begin to demonstrate that illicit drug use is far more widespread among the young. For example, Goddard and Higgins (1999a and b) found that around a third of all children aged 15 admit to using an illicit drug. The percentage of the population claiming use rises again in the age range 20 to 24, with 55 per cent claiming lifetime use.

Chapter 3 also demonstrated that the majority of users, be they the experimental 'one-off' user, or the more frequent 'recreational user', tend to shy away from the 'hard drugs' such as heroin and cocaine. To this needs to be added the caveat that this situation may be changing, especially where cocaine is concerned (Patterson 2002). For now, however, it is still correct that use-concentration seems to be on either cannabis, the most commonly used illicit drug, or 'lifestyle' 'dance drugs' such as ecstasy and amphetamines, with a decline in the use of LSD. Thus, in the main, illicit drug use appears to be predominantly the province of the young, and the majority of users do so experimentally, with so-called 'soft-drugs' dominating consumption patterns. For that reason the bulk of this chapter is devoted to that particular market for illicit drugs, and does not venture into the realms of drug dependency.

The nature of adolescence

Very few, if any, headlines, have screamed about the danger illicit drug use holds for those of pensionable age; most concerns seem to revolve around the effect of illicit drug use on the young. This is certainly the government's stance, with one of the four key aims of *Tackling Drugs to Build a Better Britain* (Cabinet Office 1998) being 'to help young people resist drug use in order to achieve their full potential in society'. Likewise, the Welsh Assembly (2000) stresses the importance of children and young people as targets for policy interventions. Much of this revolves around the idea that illicit drug use, as in criminal activity, is a developmental process (Sampson and Laub 1993). As Mazarolle (2000: 189) opines, 'persons rarely use cocaine before using alcohol or marijuana'. Clearly, given the developmental and progressive nature of illicit drug use, which statistically seems to run alongside the move through adolescence into adulthood (Ramsay and Partridge 1999), it makes good policy sense to target the young. This section reviews the nature of adolescence to begin the search for reasons why illicit drug taking appeals to the young, and why demand among that social group seemingly continues to rise.

Coleman (1992: 10–11), in trying to determine the key to adolescence, makes two important observations. Firstly, it is a stage of human development that can last in excess of six years, making generalizations risky. Indeed, there is evidence to suggest that 'youth' is an ever extending period that seems to be moving into people's twenties. Secondly, he notes that despite conflicting explanations, there is a general consensus that it is an important period of transition and successful emergence into adulthood is often dependent upon the contribution of adolescence:

> [adolescence] . . . results from the operation of a number of pressures. Some of these . . . are internal; while other pressures, which originate from peers, parents, teachers, and society at large are external to the young person. . . . It is the interplay of these forces which, in the final analysis, contributes more than anything to the success or failure of the transition from childhood to maturity.

Coleman identifies two traditional theoretical perspectives that deal, in turn, with these internal and external pressures. The first he calls the *psychoanalytical theory* (1992: 11). This approach begins with the presumption that there is an upsurge of instincts following the onset of puberty. As a result, the young person suffers an 'emotional upheaval' and an 'increased vulnerability of the personality'. This is further complicated by two linked factors: disengagement from childhood emotional ties to parents and the employment of psychological defence mechanisms designed to cope with the stresses and strains of maladaptive instincts and anxieties. Coleman (1992: 13) summarizes this perspective as having three core ideas. Firstly, adolescence is a period characterized by the vulnerability of the personality. Secondly, it is likely to be marked by maladaptive behaviour (non-conformity and rebellion). Thirdly, it is a period of disengagement from childhood relationships.

The second theory identified by Coleman (1992: 13–16) is *sociological theory*. He notes that this takes a different stance, despite the degree of commonality with the psychoanalytical theory in seeing adolescence as an important transitional process. Essentially, it is Coleman's contention that the sociologist, in line with the nature of the discipline, looks for external factors in contrast to the former theory's concern with internal factors. The key explanatory variables for the sociologist are the linked concepts of socialization and role. The former is defined as 'the process whereby people learn to conform to social norms, a process that makes possible an enduring society and the transmission of its culture between generations' (Abercrombie *et al.* 1988: 231).

The latter is seen as 'bundles of socially defined attributes and expectations associated with social positions' (Abercrombie *et al.* 1988: 209).

The basis of the argument revolves around the nature of role for adolescents. Briefly, Coleman (1992) suggests that in childhood, roles are more or less ascribed. However, with the onset of adolescence and the move towards adulthood and maturity, individuals are increasingly deemed capable of choosing roles for themselves, which, for the adolescent, can create confusion and ambiguity. For example, it can lead to experimentation in roles, such as moving in and out of the various youth cultures, lifestyles and sexualities. Coleman (1992) suggests that this ambiguity of role is fuelled by the confused nature of the status of the young person within wider society. He notes that in the UK, a young person can enlist in the armed forces, marry and become a parent, yet at the same time cannot vote or buy alcohol legally.

Coleman also argues that, in contrast to childhood, the socialization process is intra- rather than inter-generational. This sees the waning influence of socialization agents such as family, school and religion, and a growth in the importance of the peer group. A combination of both intra-generational socialization and confusion over roles and status offers the potential for young people to make 'mistakes' and indulge in 'experimentation', and thus, in some instances, create the situation where peer-group socialization leads to 'deviant' behaviour becoming normalized for some adolescents.

In summarizing this perspective, Coleman (1992: 15–16), points out that adolescence is viewed as a troublesome period due to external pressures and tensions. In turn, these place strain on the social roles and socialization process of young people, leading to a period of confusion, curiosity, boundary pushing and, in some cases, rebellion. Sometimes this is referred to as the 'generation-gap', implying a clear distinction between the views of the young and their elders. Among the many things that this period could lead to is experimentation with illicit substances. Just before moving on, it is worth noting that although these theories hold great credence, Coleman (1992) remarks that there is very little empirical evidence to back up their assertions.

Illicit drugs and 'youth culture'

Nevertheless, and recognizing the limitations inherent in those perspectives, there remains the fact that, for some at least, adolescence is a period characterized by experimentation and discovery, in any number of aspects of life. Equally, the latter half of the twentieth century and the beginnings of the twenty-first have seen a visible expression of this period of experimentation, which is often contained in particular, and time-specific youth cultures. Plant (1994: 55) links this to the subject matter of our text by claiming that the visibility of youth culture has bred worry and, especially that 'The use of psychoactive drugs . . . by adolescents has become firmly established as a major area of concern.'

The variety of youth cultures that has emerged over the last five decades has been marked out in a number of ways: through fashion, through music, through language, sometimes through modes of transport, and through drugs of preference. Thus, in terms of illicit drugs that match the style of any given youth culture, popular opinion has seen Mods associated with amphetamine use, Hippies linked to LSD, and Clubbers being synonymous with ecstasy (South 1997). For the student of the drug users this eclectic and ever-changing mix of drugs of choice is unsurprising: Young (1971: 41), demonstrating great foresight, noted thirty years ago that 'Groups select drugs which have psychotropic properties seemingly suitable for their problems', to which we could add, 'or their needs'.

Of course, many of those popular opinions and commonsense assertions over drug use are predicated upon media hype and aid the media's part in the creation of moral panics (Cohen 1971). This presents the opportunity for a small, but important digression within the chapter. It has been suggested that the media often amplify deviance and create moral panics around certain topics, but especially the actions of the young. As Thornton (1995: 132) informs, 'Mods, rockers, hippies, punks and New Romantics have all had their tabloid front pages'. This trait was certainly visible with the onset of the acid house movement in the late 1980s, and many of the media-fuelled moral panics of that time revolved around the use of ecstasy.

In 1989 the *Sun* ran a front page, banner headline story, with a picture showing young people dancing. The sub line was *'Night of Ecstasy . . .'*. In reality, ecstasy use was rising in the UK, but never reached the implied levels. Then, following the ecstasy-related death of Leah Betts in 1995, certain sections of the media clearly gave the impression that an ecstasy epidemic was sweeping through the UK, placing *all* young people in grave danger. Again, although this period saw a rise in ecstasy-related deaths, the actual totals were marginal in relation to, say, motor vehicle related deaths.

The effect of such media amplification is to reinforce stereotypes and raise levels of concern, which in the case of young people may already be high. Young (1971: 415) claims the result can be that

> . . . the mass media portrayal of the drug taker is not a function of random ignorance, but a coherent part of consensual mythology. . . . Although much of its world view is fantasy, its effects are real enough. For by fanning up moral panics over drug use, it contributes enormously to public hostility toward the drug taker and precludes any rational approach to the problem.

In this way, all followers of certain youth cultures are often popularly viewed as an amorphous entity, with little distinction being made between, for example, those who use drugs and those who do not. Thus, contrary to the media images, it is wrong to assume that simply because a person is an avid and regular clubber, they will automatically take illicit drugs, and if they do take illicit drugs, that they will automatically choose ecstasy and nothing else. This is clearly not the case, just as it was not the case that all Mods took amphetamine and nothing else. However, provided we recognize the weaknesses inherent in these simplistic accounts, they do contain some value. This is often based on their ability to alert us to the changes in the nature of the illicit drug market and its responses to fashion, as well as locating certain types of drug firmly within the fluid milieu that is youth culture.

This knowledge still brings us no closer to answering the question posed at the start of the chapter, why demand for illicit drugs remains high. Indeed, in all probability it has created an additional question: that of why young people take more drugs than any other section of society. Coleman (1992) has cited the move into adolescence as being central, but this is based on a highly generalized and somewhat 'commonsense' approach to a complex question. Moreover, Coleman notes, that as theories, they offer very little in the way of empirical evidence. Wincup and Bayliss (2001: 50) summarize this position

> The question 'what causes young people to take drugs?' is difficult to answer. Frequently offered explanations include: the search for enjoyment, the impact of their environment . . . curiosity, the need to manage trauma and pain linked to relationships and abuse, the natural rebellion of youth and the widespread availability of low cost illicit drugs.

The next section turns its attention to some empirical research that has attempted to ask illicit drug takers more specific questions related to understanding what motivated them to try drugs in the first place.

'Journeys and pathways'

Much of this section is drawn from the work of Parker, Measham and Aldridge (Parker *et al.* 1998; Measham *et al.* 1998; Aldridge *et al.* 1999). These constitute a group of researchers and academics from the University of Manchester who conducted a longitudinal study of adolescent drug use in the north west of England between 1996 and 1997. The sample size was 2,500, and within that sample, a number of in-depth interviews took place (Measham *et al.* 1998). One aspect of the research was to try to ascertain why young people started to take illicit drugs.

Parker *et al.* (1998: 93) found that their sample fell into three clear groups: 1 *abstainers* 2 *current drug users* and 3 *former triers/in transition*. Classification within these groups was ascertained by the responses given to the following four statements:

1   I take drugs myself. I think taking drugs is OK if you're careful and you know what you're doing.

2   I do not use drugs at the moment, but it is possible that I might in the future. I have no problem with other young people using drugs.
3   I do not use drugs and I do not expect to. I have no problem with other young people using drugs.
4   I don't use drugs and I don't expect to. I don't think people should take drugs.

(Parker *et al*. 1998: 93)

In trying to make sense of why young people take illicit drugs, Parker and colleagues use the concepts of 'journeys' and 'pathways'. They argue that some people never begin a 'journey' into illicit drug use, being abstainers, whereas others, who do choose to use illicit drugs, follow 'pathways' across time and substances (current users, former users and those in transition). In order to uncover the nature of journeys and pathways, the researchers used oral histories. As they note: 'We listen to young voices actually describing how they got their drugs, what actually happened the first time and how they assess risk before trying again' (Parker *et al*. 1998: 119). Their findings make fascinating reading.

Parker and colleagues claim that drugs are widely available to most young people by the time they reach 15 or 16 years old: seemingly illicit drugs are all around adolescents, at school, in youth clubs, as well as pubs and clubs. Interestingly, it would appear that many young people get their drugs for free, off friends, rather than through a dealer or a (demonized) 'pusher'. Other young people act as dealers for friends, but often on a not-for-profit basis. As Parker *et al*. comment, this blurs the often-made, 'commonsense' distinction between user and dealer. Parker *et al*. (1998: 125) claim that illicit drugs have penetrated the social space of adolescents to an extent where drugs, and drug use, have become routinized, and drug supply has undertaken a colonization of contemporary youth culture.

In terms of switching, that is moving from one type of substance to another, Measham *et al*. (1998) found that this is often predicated upon the idea that there is an 'image', or 'lifestyle' surrounding the use of certain types of drug, beyond being associated with a distinctive type of youth culture. For instance, Measham *et al*. (1998: 12–13), quote one respondent who saw solvent abuse as something children did, and deemed herself far too mature to be engaged in that particular activity. Another talked of 'growing out of acid' and 'preferring the mature feeling of speed'. Thus, for some young people, certain illicit drugs represent maturity, and signify to both the user and their 'audience' that an individual has 'matured' and grown-up, at least in terms of drug of preference.

Yet, even this detailed research encounters problems in defining why demand begins and remains, beyond a complex mixture of a number of factors. The authors note that

It remains very difficult to write authoritatively about why anyone
tries an illicit drug. . . . We analysed motivational accounts . . . as
why they had or hadn't ever tried a drug given almost all had had suc
'trying' opportunities or knew how to create them. *Availability, curiosity*
and the presence of *peers* and *friendship networks* who could provide the
encouragement, reassurance and know-how were seen as most important.
These factors were then mediated by each interviewee's view of themselves and their own *moral* perspective and views of *risk* for health, fitness
or vocation, and, in early to mid adolescence in particular, the views or
potential responses of their parents.

(Parker *et al*. 1998: 128–9; original emphasis)

To provide an indication of the complexity of the situation relating to pathways into illicit drug use, and the manner in which any number of factors can
be claimed as influencing choice, Francis and Mullen (1993) conducted
research into the impact of religiosity on drug taking among 13 to 15 year
olds in England. They found that religiosity is a predictor of behaviour,
with those demonstrating firm religious beliefs being most likely to view illicit substance use as wrong. Yet, paradoxically, Hyde *et al*. (2000: 188), looking at young people's perceptions of drugs in Ireland, found that no particular
value judgement was offered on drugs, and noted the fluidity and unpredict-
ability of demand for illicit drugs, commenting that, as they got older,
children's life experience could 'mediate young people's earlier perspectives
and shift toward some experimentation with drugs'.

Measham *et al*. (1998: 16–24) are, however, fairly clear as to why people
begin to stop using illicit drugs. They suggest that once a person's circumstances change, in terms of friendships, family networks, going out less,
especially to clubs, spending more time with significant others and current
or future employment prospects, so their patterns of illicit drug use alter.
Once this happens, use of an illicit drug, such as ecstasy or amphetamine,
can be confined to special occasions, such as birthdays. Equally, as drug
takers become more *drugwise*, they begin to weigh up the costs and benefits
of certain drugs, rejecting those that cause problems or give rise to anxiety
as to their effects.

There are two important points that emerge from the work of the
Manchester group. Firstly, they claim that knowledge of all aspects of illicit
drug use is a core part of adolescence, regardless of whether the young person
is a drug taker or an abstainer. They claim: 'Being *drugwise* is one of the extra
responsibilities which the 1990s' adolescents face because they must grow
up in a world where drugs are an everyday reality' (Parker *et al*. 1998: 119;
original emphasis). This entails knowledge of the effects, availability, and
the costs and benefits of drug taking. It results, they claim, in the majority
of adolescents needing to possess a quite detailed and sophisticated analysis
of the contemporary drug scene. This perspective is endorsed elsewhere: for
example, the work of Francis and Mullen (1993: 669) notes that children

of 13 and 15 'make clear distinctions in their attitudes
'ifferent substances'.

ewhat controversially, Parker and colleagues claim that
‧ use has become normalized among and within British
‧m that '. . . young Britons have become, in less than a
‧.‧ consumers of recreational drugs to the point that we
‧ about the normalization of *this* type of drug use' (Parker *et al.*
‧.‧; original emphasis). As evidence, the Manchester team cites the
‧.‧ that recreational drug use is rising, and even if and when it reaches a
plateau, which they suggest it may, recreational drug use is becoming increasingly prevalent and normalized within the lives of ordinary young people
(Aldridge *et al.* 1999: 42). This perspective has been challenged, and it is
to this debate the chapter now moves.

The 'normalization' of drug use?

On reflection, the normalization thesis, propounded by Parker and colleagues,
carries many challenges for the politician and policy maker: if illicit drug
use is endemic among the young, then whole tranches of the population
run the risk of being criminalized; the current political assertion that drug
taking is morally wrong runs counter to the belief, and lived reality, of the
next generation of voters; and any health campaigns designed to promote
totally drug-free lives are seemingly expensive wastes of time. Equally, it
is possible to claim a serious disjunction between the norms and values of
young people and their elders, perhaps requiring society to embark upon a
dramatic volte-face regarding the manner in which illicit drugs are viewed.
As Shiner and Newburn (1997: 511) argue, if the normalization thesis is
correct, 'the traditional image of drug use as a subterranean activity has been
somewhat undermined'.

However, the Manchester group's thesis has come under some critical
scrutiny. Shiner and Newburn (1997), in particular, offer a challenge to
their work. They contest that the normalization thesis is guilty of placing
too much emphasis on lifetime illicit drug use. By so doing, illicit drug use
among young people becomes generalized and thus fails to pick up the reality
of the situation. To expand, Shiner and Newburn (1997: 514–15) remark that
proponents of the normalization theory display a tendency to 'concentrate on
measures of lifetime use' which have a limited ability to 'illuminate young
people's drug using habits . . .'. They argue that evidence which focuses on
shorter time frames (last month/last week, for example) provides 'a more
conservative picture' of drug usage. This is borne out somewhat by existing
self-report data. As Chapter 3 demonstrated, there is an appreciable decline
in illicit drug use when short time frames are used.

This same critique is applicable to types of illicit drugs used. Shiner and
Newburn (1997: 518) agree that cannabis is the most widely used drug,
with dance drugs, such as ecstasy, amphetamines and LSD being the second

most popular illicit drugs of preference. Impressionistically, it thus appears that most young people who admit to being illicit drug users are polydrug users. This distorts reality: detailed examination of available figures reveals that only small percentages of respondents are, in fact, polydrug users. In addition, popular, media fuelled mythology posits that 'dance drug' use is endemic, widespread and frequent within contemporary youth culture. Shiner and Newburn question this, pointing to the fact that when shorter time frames (in the last year) are employed, it appears that recent use of 'dance drugs' hovers around one in twenty young people. Even with cannabis, the most widely used illicit drug, only one in four 16 to 25 year olds claimed use in the last year (Shiner and Newburn 1997).

Based on that information, and on qualitative data they collected for other research (Shiner and Newburn 1996), Shiner and Newburn (1997) offer a detailed critical appraisal of the normalization thesis. They argue that there is some confusion between normalcy and frequency. By this, they mean that while it may be true that increasing numbers of young people are using illicit drugs, raising the frequency of illicit drug use, the norms regarding drugs that are prevalent in wider society still apply to most adolescents. Moreover, they contest the assertion that soon 'non-drug using adolescents will be in the minority' (Parker et al. 1995: 26). Instead, Shiner and Newburn (1997: 521) point to the work of Dowds and Redfern (1994) who demonstrated that two thirds of 12 to 15 year olds saw taking cannabis as a very serious offence.

Even among those from their own sample who had used illicit drugs, Shiner and Newburn found that, far from rejecting the norm that illicit drug use is bad, wrong or dangerous, many young people still adhere to the view that using illicit drugs is wrong. They note that, even among illicit drug takers, there was a strong attachment to the general, wider population's consensus on drug use. The young drug takers overcome this apparent contradiction of adhering to wider norms, while breaking them, by employing 'techniques of neutralization which temporarily render relevant social controls inoperative and allow them to engage in delinquent activities without feeling guilty' (Shiner and Newburn 1997: 523). The ability to do this, Shiner and Newburn conclude, becomes the main difference between youthful drug takers and abstainers.

The same authors conclude that the normalization thesis overgeneralizes drug use and exaggerates its prevalence among the young. Shiner and Newburn (1997) do acknowledge, however, that this is, to an extent, a product of the measurement techniques inherent within the illicit drug field. Nevertheless, they claim that over-reliance on the extrapolated figures for lifetime use of illicit drugs among young people provides a skewed picture which fails to give cognisance to the fact that the majority of young people have a highly sophisticated approach to illicit drug use, and often make decisions about drug taking based on complex analytical issues such as harm, audience acceptance and future life-prospects. Because of this, Shiner and Newburn (1997) conclude that making blanket statements about drugs hides the nuanced and sophisticated reality of adolescent demand for illicit drugs.

It must be noted that many of the criticisms levelled at the work of Parker and colleagues in the work of Shiner and Newburn relate to the work of Parker *et al.* which was published prior to1998. In their subsequent work, Parker *et al.* freely acknowledge the complex nature of the drug-taking decision making process of young people, and give recognition to the fact that adolescents often view different types of illicit drugs through different lenses. Also, as we have seen, the latest self-report research reports, notably the BCS (Ramsay and Partridge 1999), have begun to examine illicit drug use across a shorter time frame than lifetime use. Much of these recent findings point to the fact that there is a marked difference between lifetime illicit drug use and recent illicit drug use.

As a concluding comment to this debate, it is worth noting that the pathways thesis is seen as one of the most sophisticated methods of measuring drug use and, importantly, attitudes to drug use, hence its use by the DPAS. Moreover, it may be that the critical voices raised against the normalization thesis have been overtaken by events. For example, the 2000 BCS (Simmons 2002) demonstrated that non-drug-trying adolescents are now in a minority. It may be the case that the work of the Manchester group identified the beginnings of a social change, and one that seems to be gathering pace at a rapid rate: witness the change in law regarding cannabis and the (tentative and disrupted) openings of cannabis cafés in places such as Stockport.

Illicit drugs as self-medication: a return to the 1800s?

There is another group of illicit drug users whose rationale for demanding illicit drugs differs from the mainly hedonistic reasons of the young: those who have found some form of respite from illness via the use of illicit drugs. Again, just as with recreational users, it appears that among this group the most-used illicit substance is cannabis. This brief section explores the growth of this apparent return to the 1800s, the (re-)birth of self-medication and its influence on current policy.

Under the Misuse of Drugs Act 1971 cannabis is listed as a drug with no discernible medical use and therefore doctors are proscribed from supplying it on prescription. However, anecdotal evidence, followed latterly by medical research, over the last three decades has begun to show that, for some types of illness, there appear to be medical benefits from cannabis use. (It is worth noting that while it may be easy at this stage, given the 20:20 vision hindsight supplies, to be critical of the Misuse of Drugs Act 1971, it is important to note that the 1971 Act reflects the climate and knowledge base of its time.) One of those illnesses is multiple sclerosis (MS) and, in order to demonstrate how illness creates a demand for illicit drugs, this chapter now turns its attention to the use of cannabis to relieve some of the symptoms of MS. It is worth noting that people use all types of drugs to self-medicate against all types of illness. MS has been chosen as an example because of its recent media coverage.

MS, according to Watson (1984: 850), is a 'degenerative disease . . . [that affects] nerve fibres within the spinal chord and brain'. It is a condition that is characterized by remission and relapse, making the course of the disease unpredictable and variable from patient to patient. Its symptoms are equally varied but, in its early stages, can include tingling, numbness and muscular weakness. As the disease progresses the symptoms can become more serious and can include paralysis, motor disability, impaired speech and vision, personality changes, respiratory problems and spasms, known as spasticity. MS has no known cure and is often treated by the medical profession using prescription drugs such as beta-interferon, which, like many others, carries unpleasant side-effects.

Some MS sufferers, disillusioned with or unable and unwilling to tolerate the negative side-effects of prescription drugs, have taken to using cannabis to alleviate some of the symptoms of their disease, with seemingly high rates of success. For example, the BBC (BBC 2001) recently ran a story concerning Biz Ivol, an MS sufferer from the Orkneys. Ms Ivol was diagnosed with MS and, after trying a number of different prescription drugs, each with unpleasant and varying side effects, was allegedly advised by her doctor to 'try cannabis'. This she did, and almost overnight she noticed marked improvements in her condition. In 1997, she was taken to court for cultivat-ing cannabis plants and, although only receiving 'a slap on the wrist' (BBC 2001), because of her court appearance she notes that she 'became a criminal'. However, unabashed by this, Ms Ivol continues to both use and cultivate cannabis.

She claims that each time her case is publicized she receives a number of telephone calls and letters from fellow MS sufferers: 'The last time . . . I received about 104 calls, mostly from middle-aged women with MS and most have been told to try [cannabis] by their doctors'. Clearly, given the fact that there appears to be a ground swell of MS sufferers turning to cannabis for relief from their symptoms, the government faces two dilemmas: the need to reassess the medical position of cannabis and the inherent dangers of 'criminalizing' otherwise law-abiding citizens who are self-medicating. Such pressures often lead to change, or at least an investigation of the possi-bility of change. The medical demand for cannabis has been no exception to that rule.

Following consultation with user groups and the medical profession, including the Institute of Neurology at University College London, in 1997, the government decided to fund a series of clinical trials investigating the medical potential of cannabis-based medicine. This was made necessary by a growing volume of studies that emphasized the medical potential the drug holds. For example, Consroe *et al.* (1997) noted that between 30 and 97 per cent of MS sufferers claimed significant benefits from cannabis, mostly in controlling spasticity and chronic pain in the body's extremities.

In the UK, some of this government-sponsored research is being undertaken by GW Pharmaceuticals, which was formed in 1997 for the express purpose of testing cannabis for its medical properties. Thus far, they have entered 'phase three' trials, which are the final stage of an extensive series of tests. The results have, apparently, been successful, to the extent that the company's press release talks about applying for a Product Licence Approval. If such a licence is granted, it would enable GW Pharmaceuticals to begin producing cannabis-based medicine some time in 2003 (GW Pharmaceuticals 2001).

In this instance, demand for illicit drugs by those suffering from some form of illness is markedly different from that of the recreational drug user. Here, often via word of mouth or web sites, sufferers from a number of different conditions, including MS, are demanding (mostly) cannabis in order to self-medicate. In this example, illicit drugs are removed from any hedonistic attachments and are being used by sections of the general public in a manner unseen for over a century. It is in some ways ironic that the dawning of a new millennium, which seems certain to witness ever more scientific advances in medicine, technology and communications, is heralded by advances in medicine shepherded into being by a practice which one of those very professions in the vanguard of progress has sought to eradicate: that of self-medication.

Conclusion

Demand for illicit drugs that are used as a form of medication has a clear and easily identified reason. Trying to answer questions as to why people continue to demand illicit drugs for hedonistic purposes is, as this chapter has demonstrated, fraught with problems. We can identify trends, such as that demand for illicit drugs seems to be higher in certain age groups and then wanes as age increases. We can also make generalizations revolving around theories that link youth with rebellion, experimentation and peer pressure. Equally, we can conclude that the young have high levels of disposable income, leisure time and curiosity making drug use just another facet of consumption. What we cannot do is to say for certain why *individuals* choose to try illicit drugs. That said, we can, however, begin to explore the nature of demand and the manner in which decisions to take drugs are formed. In turn, any knowledge we gather can help inform policy, making the whole exercise worthwhile.

It appears that most of those who embark on the illicit drug journey do so of their own volition: the idea of 'pushers luring unsuspecting innocents' into drug use seems unfounded. Rather, it seems that the majority of hedonistic users make logical decisions based on a sophisticated analysis of a number of factors. For example, the Manchester University research team found that the majority of their respondents obtained drugs from their friends, or at the very most, friends of friends. Very few reported buying drugs from complete unknowns. This reinforces much of the findings on street-level dealers outlined in Chapter 6. Equally, most illicit drug users have clear boundaries as to the drugs they see as 'safe', in contrast to the 'hard' drugs of cocaine and heroin. There appears to still be a taboo, although perhaps waning in the case of cocaine, as far as those particular drugs are concerned.

The findings that have emerged appear to suggest a demand-led market in which consumers make sophisticated choices based on personal preference, cost-benefit analysis and changing trends. It is also clear that there may be an age-related element to certain illicit substances with some being perceived as less adult than others. This raises two immediate questions: is the normalization theory correct, and what ramifications do these findings have for policy?

Like many social science theories, arguing for a definitive right or wrong answer to the normalization debate is arguably dependent upon a number of factors: ideology, perspective, definition of theory, definition of normalcy and so on. Each side makes convincing submissions and each side makes equally valid counter points. Perhaps the best way to answer the question is to summarize the available evidence. It appears that frequency of illicit drug use is rising, especially among the young. However, that needs to be quantified. Lifetime use of cannabis is by far the most commonly claimed illicit drug using activity, followed by relatively infrequent shorter-term use of cannabis. Following that comes lifetime use of 'dance drugs', with an even more infrequent shorter-term use claim. A long way behind all of the above is the use of heroin and cocaine.

What emerges is the feeling that young people are discerning consumers who make clear distinctions between different types of drug. In terms of policy formulation this has some important implications. For example, messages that merge all drugs together clearly run counter to the present generation of consumers' experience and perspective. Equally, any policy failing to recognize that some experimentation with substances is part of about 50 per cent of young people's life will not accurately reflect the current situation. Thus, in terms of normalization, we may be able to make the tentative claim that moderate use of certain illicit drugs, if not normalized, is certainly accepted as part and parcel of early twenty-first century life.

What we can say with certainty is that young people over the last two decades have had to become far more *drugwise*. Illicit drugs are a part of the world of the young: indeed, illicit drugs are part of all of our worlds and it appears that the general public has a more nuanced, and certainly more complex, view of drugs than does current policy. Demand for certain drugs is certainly on the rise and it is clearly a demand-led market; paradoxically, there appears to be solid support for the continued prohibition and control of other types of illicit drugs. It may be that contemporary British drug policy is out of step with public opinion and lived realities, and needs an over-haul in order to prevent it from becoming irrelevant to real world events. Perhaps the first example of this is the recent down-grading of cannabis to a Class C drug. The next chapter turns its attention to these issues and reviews contemporary illicit drug policy in the UK.

9 'Let's Get Real'

Contemporary directions in UK drug policy

Introduction

One of the intentions of this work has been to alert the reader to the complex nature of the illicit drug scene. At one and the same time illicit drug use in the UK is seen as morally wrong, and thus subject to legal sanctions, as well as being pharmaceutically dangerous, making it in need of control by the medical profession. Yet despite this formidable level of official sanction and concern, a significant minority of the British population claims some form of illicit drug use. Equally, while having to contend with its own drug problem, the UK is subject to the pressure and influence of a huge global illicit drug industry that grows, manufactures and distributes a product for which there is a seemingly inexorable demand. In some producing countries, the illicit drug industry has a major impact on economic well-being, making it difficult to impose meaningful sanctions. In an effort to control this global problem the UK, with a host of other nations, has become a signatory to international anti-drug treaties, alongside which it has developed its own, domestic policies.

It is the development of these domestic policies that informs this penultimate chapter. As we shall see, the last two decades have seen a rise in activity in the drug policy area, which has become increasingly frenetic in the very recent past. Without doubt, at the time of writing (January 2002), the UK seems to be entering a watershed period in regard to drug policy. This can be seen in the chapter title *'Let's Get Real'*, being the title of a recent DPAS document (DPAS 2001) that exhorts government agencies to make sure that communications to the public regarding illicit drugs are presented in a manner that reflects current best-practice and lived realities. Essentially, what this chapter aims to do is to chart the development of British policy from the 'Just say no' approach of the early 1980s to the current move towards the reclassification of cannabis.

The chapter begins with a brief excursion into some of the literature that describes the policy-making processes, the impact of policy communities, and the problems of joint working. It then looks at the claims for a 'British system' and identifies two distinct policy communities. This is a necessary diversion, as it alerts the reader to the difficulties and tensions inherent in policy formation, as well as providing a theoretical framework through which to view policy. From there, the chapter identifies policy options and trawls through the various policy documents, noting how the government's approach changes over time. In so doing, it searches for factors that influence change. It concludes with some thoughts on the possible future direction of policy.

Policy making, policy communities and joint working

This brief section is included for the benefit of those readers who may not have a background in policy studies. Often, when made aware of a 'social problem' such as illicit drug use, the response of the public and some sections of the media is to call for 'something to be done'. Sometimes, public and media opinion champions the 'commonsense' approach to making new policy, calling for the 'obvious' solution – ergo '100,000 Reasons Why We Must Rid Plymouth Of Drugs' (*Plymouth Evening Herald* 2001). The reality is that policy making and implementation are seldom that simple. Policy making and ensuring that new policy is delivered in an efficient and effective manner is a complex process and requires a strange and unpredictable amalgam of inputs.

There are two important points to recognize. Firstly, policy is not determined in a vacuum. By that is meant that policy often reflects contemporary social events and socially accepted norms. Changes in social behaviour or norms often lead to changes in policy. Secondly, and linked to the former point, policy makers, both nationally and locally, almost never operate with a *tabula rasa* or clean sheet. This means new proposals for policy are constrained by a mixture of present and previous policies for dealing with any particular problem. In our example, contemporary policy makers need to contend with a number of givens: the Home Office control over policy, international treaties, local policing arrangements and so on. This means that any construction of policy needs to recognize that, whatever the desired aims may be, new policy must, in the short term at least, fit into any existing frameworks. This also brings into play the next constraint on policy makers: existing organizational structures and working practices. In the field of illicit drugs this would include the division between health and law as well as the myriad of non-governmental organizations supplying policy and practice to drug users.

Policy making also suffers from something called the 'implementation gap' (Colebatch 1998). This is due to the fact that those who make national policy almost never implement their decisions: that is left to any number of organizations spread across the country. This can create differences between the aims of policy as devised by policy makers at a national level and the manner in which that policy is delivered by organizations at a local level. For example, until very recently there was no official indication from central government that policy relating to cannabis should be changed. However, as Kaal (1998) notes, the use of cautions by English police forces for cannabis, both in terms of possession and supply, rose by more than 50 per cent during the period 1987 to 1995. This would suggest that long before David Blunkett's recommendations police forces had 'downgraded' cannabis use.

The makers of policy need also to contend with the standard operating procedures of the different organizations that implement policy. These standard operating procedures relate to the manner in which organizations go about their day-to-day work and can be both formal (written rules and procedures) and informal ('that's the way we've always done things here'). Informal standard operating procedures have an enormous impact on the manner in which individuals see themselves and their work. One only needs to read the work of Reiner (2000: 85–107) on the manner in which 'cop culture' affects new police recruits to understand its power. In turn, such entrenched and self-perpetuating world views impact on the manner in which organizations and workers view the general public, other organizations and their employees, and social problems and problematic groups. This in turn impacts on another important aspect of policy making and implementation – joint working.

Joint working is less of a problem where organizations share ideologies and can form policy communities. For example, health, social services and most voluntary sector street drug agencies all share an ideology that can be broadly defined as 'welfarist', meaning that they seek to provide a caring, harm reduction-based approach to illicit drug use. This allows them to view illicit drug use and illicit drug users in broadly the same way, as well as being able to concentrate on the problems drug use poses for the *individual* drug user. However, the police, the courts, and latterly the probation service, are, by virtue of their organizational remit, almost forced to take a law and order stance to illicit drug use. This often means that these organizations view drug use first and foremost in terms of the risk and damage it does to *society*.

As a result, joint working – the coming together of a number of agencies to address a social problem – can take place more easily between like minded organizations and individuals who share a similar ideology. Historically, in terms of illicit drug policy, the gap between the law and order policy community and the welfarist policy community has not been a problem, as each section seemingly worked in isolation from the other. However, the last 20 years have seen an explosion in the requirement for agencies from all policy communities to end sectoral isolationism and devise strategies designed to promote and cement joint working. This has reached a point where it is almost impossible to launch a new policy that does not require some form of joint working. In some instances, joint working has occurred voluntarily and in others it has been reliant upon government policy.

Joint working: a brief theoretical background

As noted, in certain situations, organizations will opt to work together, yet on other occasions organizations are reluctant to join forces with other agencies to provide services. It is this reluctance, especially in a climate that recognizes the need to overcome organizational boundaries in order to provide a 'joined-up' response to social problems, which has led to increasing government pressure to form, and work within, partnerships. However, as noted by Weiss (1981: 29), 'organizations are unlikely to take up co-operation . . . simply because someone says it would be a good idea'. Therefore, some organizations, required by the demands of public policy to form partnerships, exhibit a tendency to attempt to limit the degree to which joined-up working impacts on their organizational independence.

This notion forms the bedrock of the work of Crawford and Jones (1996). Briefly, their work hinges on the idea that one of the key problems for joint working is the fact that all agencies strive to retain some form of autonomy and to retain their own standard operating procedures (Hudson 1987; Hallett and Birchall 1992; Crawford and Jones 1996). Thus, any sharing of work with other organizations has at least the potential to threaten organizational independence, making joint working a latent danger.

The presence of such a 'danger' explains why some agencies become reluctant and cautious about entering into joint working situations. This reluctance is strengthened in situations where joint working is forced, or where potential partners pose threats due to differently structured ideological bases or standard operating procedures (Hudson 1987). Crawford and Jones (1996) recognize this and note that organizations create coping strategies, developing varying degrees of partnership working along a continuum ranging from a pole which offers little threat to organizational independence to its opposite which compromises organizational identity.

Crawford and Jones (1996) use two ideal types in order to make a conceptual distinction between the polar extremes of their continuum. They suggest that the least threatening form of partnership working is multi-agency working. In this case agencies come together in order to address a problem but any joint working that takes place fails significantly to affect the work each partner agency does, nor does it affect any organizational structures. Crawford and Jones suggest that the roles of each agency remain distinct, with each participant retaining control and autonomy over their core organizational task as well as their standard operating procedures. In this instance, key officers join together to share their collective expertise, and multi-agency work is grafted on to existing practices, organizationally speaking making joint working as non-threatening as possible.

The opposite polar extreme is the concept and practice of inter-agency working. This is where the danger to agency independence and identity becomes most acute. Here, organizations enter into a form of interpenetration that affects the internal working relations of the participating organizations, often melding working practices to create a distinct pattern of work, which fails to resemble that of the host organizations. In turn, new structures, working conditions and allegiances are formed between partner organizations and their agents. These threaten a number of important organizational factors including standard operating procedures, organizational loyalty, work-place culture and identity (Hill 1997).

Crawford and Jones (1996) point to the fact that, in the real world of organizational work, partnerships lie somewhere between these two ends of the continuum. Importantly, they note that the closer partnership forums move towards inter-agency working the greater the rewards in collaborative activity, yet, at the same time inter-agency working presents increased opportunities for conflict between agencies. On the other hand, multi-agency working, which some have seen as mere public relations exercises (Gilling 1994), allows partners to appear to be working together and at the same time reduces the potential for conflict and the threat to organizational independence. Thus, for any partnership forum, one key area is the decision where on the continuum to place their particular form of joint working. In this respect, Halpert's (1982: 55) insight pre-empts Crawford and Jones's thesis, claiming as he does that

> [a]gencies have been found to deal with this problem [of a threat to organizational independence] by interpreting the command to co-ordinate in such a manner that the parameters of the constraints are as broad as possible enabling them to maintain a certain level of organizational autonomy within a minimum amount of internal disorganization.

According to Whetten (1981), the question of where on the continuum to locate partnerships is answered by referring to two key factors: assessment of the compatibility of linkages and the capacity to sustain co-ordination. However, such a stance assumes that agencies have retained some vestige of control and choice about the nature of their partnerships, and, as detailed below, this is no longer always the case. Having looked, very briefly, at some of the issues surrounding the formulation and application of policy, this chapter turns its attention to contemporary developments in British drug policy.

A 'British system'?

Before moving on to explore and examine the changing face of British drug policy, it is important, given the above discussion, to make one thing very clear: that is, the exact nature of the illicit drug policy community – particularly its dominant discourse and constituent parts. Chapter 2 noted that some commentators have identified a 'British system' in terms of drug policy, where it is claimed that there is a degree of medicalization, which allows a less punitive and more treatment-based approach to illicit drug use. That chapter was purposefully ambiguous as to the veracity of such claims. This is due to the fact that, in common with writers such as Strang and Gossop (1994), it is believed here that no such system exists, especially in the form claimed by some North American writers who contrast the 'criminalization' stance of the USA to the (supposed) 'medicalization' approach of the UK (e.g. Trebach 1982).

At most, what we have in Britain is a dual approach to the 'drug problem', with the criminal justice system and the medical profession having significant inputs, and thus making claims to domains of expertise over that area. As a result, Britain has cultivated a situation where creating drug policy has bred an ongoing power struggle between, on the one hand, the Home Office, which seeks to maintain the dominance of criminal law and punishment, and on the other hand, the Department of Health (or one of its other guises over the years), which seeks to pursue medical dominance over illicit drugs. Witness the words of the former British deputy drug 'tsar', Mike Trace, who claims that British drug policy has been weakened by the 'constant battles between criminal justice agencies and the Department of Health over policy aims' (Trace quoted in Travis 2001: 3).

This dual approach allows two different professional discourses entry into the drug policy field: treatment and punishment. It also allows professionals from entirely different ideological, professional and practice backgrounds liberty to contest for the ownership of the 'problem'. Taking a Focauldian perspective, this ensures that the 'problem' will become defined by each side in a manner calculated to emphasize their own discourse and preferred 'solution', and at the same time each discourse will be attempting to weaken the claim of the competing discourse and its solution. On top of this, politics, and the needs of politicians, has to be added to any policy equation: the 'drug problem' is an emotive issue and being seen to be 'soft' on it can lose as many votes as it gains. Moreover, it is highly newsworthy and today's political classes are acutely aware of the dangers of upsetting the moralistic tabloid press, which continues to view illicit drug use through uni-dimensional lenses. All of these factors have some influence upon the shape of British drug policy.

As we will see below, the 'British system' of drug policy, far from being led by the health lobby, has, both historically and contemporaneously, been the domain of the criminal justice agencies: our first instinct has been to punish, then, depending on the drug, treat. As an example, Dorn and South (1994: 294) refer to the policy surrounding the use of amphetamine:

> . . . social concern over the use of this drug [amphetamine] in particular by working class youth . . . led to its criminalization in the 1960s and, subsequently, more attention from the police than from the health sector. Indeed, the manner in which Britain responds to amphetamine may be seen as symptomatic of its general drug policy; here is a drug that can certainly be associated with a range of social and health

problems. . . . Yet the typical British response is to process the user as an offender. British System?

Thus, it is possible to claim that the dominant policy community in British drug policy is law and order, hence the domination of the criminal justice discourse. This is borne out by the fact that the key government department has always been the Home Office, a locus of control that shows no imminent sign of change.

However, it would be mistaken to believe that this makes drug policy the domain solely of the criminal justice agencies. Thanks largely to the continued efforts of the medical profession to 'own', or at the very least have some direct input into, policies designed to address the drug problem, the British illicit drug policy community is large and diverse. In policy terms the dual approach to dealing with illicit drug use, set in train by Rolleston in 1926, has continued to the present day, and, due to the extension of the welfare state and the concomitant growth of welfarist agencies (Kemshall 2002), has expanded in the last two decades. In policy terms this means that there is an in-built requirement for some form of joint working within any policy moves. Moreover, change in wider social policy, which has led to 'joined-up working' becoming central to government policy (Barton and Quinn 2001) has simply increased the joint working imperative.

What this entails is the creation of two possible policy directions. Firstly, policy can be aimed at reducing and controlling the degree to which illicit drugs are supplied and/or used. There are a number of possible ways in which such a policy could be implemented – vigorous enforcing of the law, strong border controls and high levels of customs and excise activity as well as a proactive education campaign. Secondly, policy could take the direction that significantly reducing supply and use is beyond the remit of the government (especially in light of the normalization thesis) and that policy should move in the direction of reducing demand and impacting upon the harm illicit drug use does to individuals and communities. In many respects it is possible to view the first option as a 'hard' law and order-based approach and to view the second as more welfare and medicine oriented.

The above points provide this chapter with an analytical framework through which to view contemporary British drug policy. It enables the chapter to review contemporary policy developments through three related but separate lenses. Firstly, policy will be examined for signs of the domination of the criminal justice discourse and the manner in which this has been achieved. Secondly, illicit drug policy will be viewed in terms of the extent to which joint working has been championed, and the manner in which the 'joined-up' approach has been embraced by policy makers and practitioners alike. Thirdly, we can search for evidence of policy moving either towards reducing drug supply or reducing demand.

The 1980s: policy formulation in a time of a rising tide of illicit drug use

Chapter 2 outlined policy developments up to the end of the 1970s, noting along the way the duality of the approach to dealing with illicit drugs. However, despite there being at least two policy sectors working within the illicit drug policy area, there was little evidence of joint working. As one commentator notes, 'Until recently, both approaches worked largely in isolation from each other . . .' (Barton 1999: 145). Indeed, questions could be asked of this period as to whether Britain had a 'drugs policy' *per se*. Strang and Gossop (1994: 343–4) suggest that 'It has not been the way of things in the U.K. to construct formal drugs policy. Policy changes are often seen to have occurred only with the benefit of hindsight'. However, the same authors suggest that, paradoxically, this may be the strength of the British approach as it enables a 'particular capacity for evolution'.

To summarize briefly, the situation as Britain entered the 1980s was one of reliance on specialist clinics to offer substitute drugs in order to manage dependence or withdrawal and reduce demand for 'street drugs'. In many of these clinics there was an air of pessimism pervading drug workers, caused by a realization that 'nothing works', and at best the interventions of the drug workers may have been little more than the social control of addiction (Strang and Gossop 1994). Outside of that, the police were still prosecuting those found in possession. Indeed, the criminal justice domination of drug policy was an outstanding feature. As Dorn and South (1994: 296) comment, 'heroin/methadone prescribing . . . constitute islands of exception within the framework of historically hegemonic criminal law responses'.

It is possible to claim that as Britain entered the 1980s the 'masterly inactivity' (Downes 1977: 89) that had characterized British drug policy up to that date was exposed as wanting in the wake of a rising tide of drug use. In turn, the growing political interest in, and politicization of, the 'drug problem' paved the way for a number of policy developments. Equally, in line with broader social policy, the 1980s began a period of change in the drug field where sectoral isolationism came under increasing pressure and there was a broadening of policy approaches. To a degree, this upsurge of government interest in illicit drug use was fuelled by a series of moral panics over 'the new heroin users' (Matthews 1995: 3).

In the vanguard of this era of change was the Advisory Council on the Misuse of Drugs (ACMD). It will be recalled that the ACMD was established as part of the Misuse of Drugs Act 1971, with a remit to be a standing committee reporting back to the government on drug-related issues. In 1982, the ACMD published *Treatment and Rehabilitation*, a document that gave recognition to the fact that oral methadone was fast becoming the preferred treatment option and that specialist clinics were increasingly being seen to offer only a partial solution to a burgeoning drug problem. The ACMD (1982) recommended that there should be a change in policy and a widening of the policy community. Among other things they suggested that there should be greater emphasis on local provision of prescription drugs and care for the addict, the locus of which should be the GP. The era of the specialist seemed to be doomed.

What the 1982 ACMD document also marked was the beginnings of official recognition that 'drug misuse requires collaboration between a wide range of public services and the specialist voluntary and independent sectors who work with drug misusers' (Howard *et al*. 1993: ix). However, despite the publication of further advisory documents in 1984, 1988 and 1989 (ACMD 1984; 1988; 1989), as well as the setting up of collaborative guidelines by the Department of Health and Social Security in 1985 and 1986 all of which called for greater collaboration between agencies, actual joint working on the ground was 'never . . . adequately fulfilled' (Howard *et al*. 1993: ix).

Arguably, this failure to implement successful joint working was due to a growing disparity between the government's hard line 'just say no/heroin screws you up' approach to the problem when contrasted with some of the independent drug agencies' more realistic, harm reduction-based approaches. Moreover, given the cross-sectoral nature of interventions, it is not surprising that joint working was never fully embraced. If we are to use our analytical lenses to view this period, it is obvious that the law and order discourse dominates. Moreover, there is a clear indication that the aim of government policy was to attempt to control and reduce supply, with demand reduction and harm reduction becoming more visible, but wrapped up in wider concerns over the transmission of HIV.

The criminal justice-led, use reduction approach is evidenced in the government's policy document of the time, *Tackling Drug Misuse* (Home Office 1985). This document was first launched in 1985 and proposed five areas of policy action:

1 reducing supplies from abroad;
2 making enforcement even more effective;
3 maintaining effective deterrents and tight domestic controls;
4 developing prevention;
5 improving treatment and rehabilitation.

The first three are all obviously enforcement led and even the fourth could be seen to refer to increased law enforcement efforts instead of a greater medical involvement. There was very little evidence of any form of co-ordinated or collaborative approach: the police and customs and excise continued to enforce the law while the medical profession continued to treat those users who came to their attention. Very little was done to reduce harm to communities or, especially in the case of recreational users, the harm drug users do to themselves. It must be noted that the Department of Health was beginning to embrace and endorse harm reduction, with harm minimization policies being launched in drug agencies as well as the development of needle and syringe exchanges around the country (South 1995: 31). However, much of such initiatives had their roots in specific concerns over the transmission of HIV rather than in wider concerns over the health and well-being of recreational drug users.

Other measures included the introduction of the Drug Trafficking Offences Act (1986) which provided the police with a substantial increase in power as well as skewing the onus of proof away from the accused person in respect of the origins of their assets. As a response to the rise in use and dealing in heroin and cocaine, the government also introduced the Controlled Drugs (Penalties) Act (1985). As South (1995: 31) comments, 'all of this placed the police, customs, courts and prisons at the forefront of control policy and practice'.

Into the 1990s: the rise of harm reduction and joint working?

Two events occurred during the late 1980s and early 1990s each, in its own way, making a significant impact on British illicit drug policy. The first is cultural. It revolves around the dawning of the acid house phenomenon and the emergence of clubbing as a significant development in youth culture. As Chapter 8 has pointed out, illicit drug use has always been a part of various youth cultures, but the club movement has been particularly synonymous with the use of drugs, even spawning the term 'dance drugs' in reference to ecstasy, amphetamine and LSD, and a multi-million pound industry. This fuelled the normalization thesis and has seen a growth in recreational and experimental drug use among young people. Moreover, clubbers and experimental drug users have been drawn from all sections of society, as evidenced by Prince Harry's rather public ticking off following tabloid revelations that he had used cannabis. This rise in use, coupled with some highly publicized drug-related deaths led to a rethinking of drug policy.

Secondly, there has been a growing realization in the UK that unilateral approaches to social problems by various organizations leads to inefficient and ineffective service delivery, creating in its wake a rise in demand for joint working (Leathard 1994). Indeed, this pressure has increased since 1997 and the election of a New Labour government that has consistently championed the 'joined-up' approach to policy making (Micheal 1998). This section reviews the impact of these two forces on our three analytical lenses of law and order dominance, degree of joint working and the balance between use and harm reduction.

The key to the developments in the 1990s was the publication of *Across the Divide* (Howard *et al.* 1994). This was an independent report commissioned by the Department of Health. It followed a 1991 report (DoH 1991a) that highlighted the problems faced by drug workers in the context of joint working, and the Conservative government's 1992 election promise that action against drug misuse would be effectively co-coordinated (Conservative Party 1992). In a nutshell, the report was justified by the changing social and organizational circumstances outlined above and called for greater levels of co-operation across all agencies involved with illicit drug policy and practice.

By way of response, and in order to fulfil its election promise, the Conservative government set up a new unit in 1994, the Central Drugs Co-ordination Unit (CDCU), charged with producing a Green Paper which examined illicit drug policy. The result was the White Paper, *Tackling Drugs Together* (DoH 1995). Interestingly, and the source of some criticism, Scotland and Wales had their own documents produced at roughly the same time, but varying in degrees from their English counterpart (for an overview, see Ashton 1994). Space precludes a discussion of the regional documents, thus this work will concentrate on the English document.

Tackling Drugs Together: a review

Arguably, despite its shortcomings, this document represents a significant shift in policy approach, yet still manages to retain the traditional domination of the law and order, supply reduction discourse. This can be seen in the opening statement where the government promises to 'fully maintain[ing] the emphasis on law enforcement and reducing supply'. However, the changing nature of drug policy is visible in the end of the sentence where it identifies the need to recognize 'stronger action on reducing the demand for illegal drugs' (DoH 1995: 1). In many respects, this marks the first central government recognition that drug use among the young is endemic and that law and order/supply reduction alone will not 'solve the problem'.

What the document also does is to increase the importance, and broaden the concept of, harm reduction. Witness the following statement of purpose:

> To take effective action via law enforcement, accessible treatment and a new emphasis on education and prevention to:
> - increase the safety of communities from drug-related crime;
> - reduce the acceptability and availability of drugs to young people; and
> - reduce the health risks and other damage related to drug misuse.
>
> (DoH 1995: 1)

Implicit in that statement is some recognition that drug misuse has the potential to harm communities as well as the individual. It allows the government space in which to develop two distinct, but linked, approaches to the drug problem and problematic drug users:

1   treatment of the individual by welfarist agencies for medical and social problems;
2   treatment of the individual by law and order agencies to relieve the harm drug misusers may do to communities in terms of acquisitive crime.

Three specific policy areas were singled out for special attention: crime, young people and public health. The new policy was to be delivered by 'multi-agency co-ordination, both at local and national levels . . .' (DoH 1995: 1). In terms of structures and resources, the government retained the ACMD, noting the respect with which it was held. The government established a Ministerial Sub-Committee of the Cabinet on the Misuse of Drugs, comprising ministers from interested departments (DoH 1995: 4). Locally, in 1995 the government also set up Drug Action Teams (DATs) which are multi-agency forums consisting of 'senior representatives from the police, probation and prison services, local authorities (including education and social services) and health authorities' (DoH 1995: 5). As an acknowledgement of the mixed economy approach to service delivery, the document also encouraged the recruitment of representatives from voluntary sector agencies. The remit of the DATs is to tackle local drug-related issues and problems.

In terms of law and order and supply reduction, the document required all police forces, probation areas and prisons to develop their own drug misuse strategies. Prisons were forced to introduce mandatory testing of prisoners and, from 1996, HM Inspectorate of Constabularies reviewed police force drug strategies. There was a categorical commitment to oppose the legalization of any controlled drugs.

Young people were the target of efforts designed to provide education and advice, and to promote abstinence and resistance. The Home Office Drug Prevention Initiative was expanded in 1995 in order to develop work with young people and their communities. In an effort to demonstrate the importance of education and young people the government provided an extra £5.9 million for training programmes for teachers and support for new and innovative drug education programmes. It also made drug education a part of the National Curriculum, although, strangely, under the science and technology heading (SCODA 1998; 1999).

In health terms, the government established a National Drug Help-Line from April 1995 and made a promise to ensure drug misusers had 'easy access' to services. However, the government fell short of an acceptance that illicit drug use may be normalized and an integral part of sections of British society by couching harm reduction in the somewhat unrealistic terms of 'drug free states' and declaring that 'abstinence remain[s] the ultimate aim' (DoH 1995: 3).

Tackling Drugs Together raises a number of issues worthy of note. Firstly, it moved the centre of the government's drug policy away from the Home Office and located it within the Cabinet Office. Secondly, it acted as a catalyst for our current policy explosion in the field of illicit drug policy and practice by identifying and defining illicit drug use as a 'major problem'. Thirdly, it began to create a climate where the law and order and medical approaches could be merged, in order to fall in line with the newly expanded concept of harm reduction. Fourthly, it placed joint working at the forefront of policy, coercing hitherto isolated agencies into some (at first, tentative) collaboration. Fifthly, it gave a tacit and seemingly grudging recognition to the fact that law and order and supply reduction policies were failing and hence there needed to be space for education-based demand reduction approaches to tackling illicit drug use.

Reaction to *Tackling Drugs Together* has been mixed. In general terms, one of the criticisms has been that, in contrast to its Scottish and Welsh counterparts, the English document relegates protecting individual users from harm to second place, below protecting communities from crime (Ashcroft 1994), thus maintaining the domination of the law and order discourse. More specifically, Roger Howard of SCODA provides a detailed review of the document (Howard 1997: 8–13), giving both positive and negative views.

On the plus side, Howard argues that there are six positive factors. Firstly, it provides national leadership and co-ordination. Howard notes that the leader of the ministerial sub-committee was the Lord President of the Council, thus negating the powerful influence of departmental needs and influence on policy. Secondly, the formation of DATs served to cement joint working in areas where it was already established and serves as a good practice model elsewhere. Thirdly, it gave recognition to the work and strengths of specialist drug service providers; Howard cites examples of good practice in prisons and youth education. Fourthly, it marks a recognition of the value of a demand reduction paradigm in an hitherto supply reduction dominated area. Howard also comments that an acceptance of the value of demand reduction carries with it a de facto support of harm minimization, fostering a more realistic approach to drug use in England. Penultimately, the provision of additional resources was seen, unsurprisingly, as a positive move. Finally, a more realistic approach to the drug scene was viewed as being positive for public perceptions about the way forward in drug policy, and as a good counter-balance to the more reactionary outpourings of some sections of the press.

On a more negative note, Howard laments the imbalance of resource allocation between, on the one hand, law and supply policies and, on the other, treatment and prevention. He notes that in the year 1993/4 two thirds of government expenditure went on the former, despite evidence from the USA that treatment is effective in reducing criminal behaviour and thus becomes a possible policy tool in reducing drug-related crime. He also takes issue with the manner in which deprivation, dependent drug use and crime are dealt with. He is critical of the manner in which multiple social problems that may have contributed to dependent drug use are ignored by the government. He notes with disapproval that *Tackling Drugs Together* does little to address the inherent problems in community care. Finally, he notes that the new direction in domestic policy is not matched by a rethinking of international policy.

Arguably, the best light in which to view *Tackling Drugs Together* is as laying the foundations and framework for a new approach to drug policy in

England. It recognized the lack of a coherent drug policy, or for that matter, direction, beyond a simplistic reliance on interdiction and prohibition, tactics that were clearly found wanting. In response, the document sets out to make concrete a philosophy and approach that correspond with illicit drug use in the late twentieth century, and this meant an overhaul of a failing system. As Bean (2002: 55) comments, 'The emphasis in *Tackling Drugs Together* was on reorganizing local services . . .'. What the document also did was to provide a green light for innovative and different means of addressing the problems of illicit drug use. In many respects, this view is endorsed by one of the White Paper's architects, Stephen Rimmer. Rimmer (1997: 5) states, 'The White Paper is deliberately focused on specific tasks . . . [it sets out] an overall statement of purpose and then develop[s] tasks within that framework'.

In terms of our three analytical lenses *Tackling Drugs Together* still enables the law and order discourse to retain priority, albeit with some challenge. Key here is the moving of control away from the Home Office and into the Cabinet Office. Nevertheless, law and order and supply reduction remain dominant. There is evidence of recognition of the work that can be done by welfarist interventions in terms of harm reduction on an individual and societal level, with concomitant space being given to demand reduction. Joined-up working was given priority in the policy document. However, referring back to the implementation gap mentioned above, the reality was somewhat different:

> There is a lot spoken about joint commissioning: clearly some agencies . . . are used to doing this. . . . But there doesn't seem to be a particular momentum generated in a lot of DATs to look at pooling resources. . . . Having worked in a multi-agency forum myself, I know that some of those difficulties require time and patience. . . .
>
> (Rimmer 1997: 7)

It would appear, therefore, that the majority of joint working taking place fell into Crawford and Jones' (1996) multi-agency definition, which some have seen as 'mere public relations exercises' (Gilling 1994).

Enter New Labour: policy from 1998 to the present

New Labour came to power in 1997 on a wave of public optimism that its election would see major changes in the UK, a belief fuelled in no small part by New Labour's own rhetoric. Many policy advisors, viz. Frank Field and welfare reform, were given the mandate to 'think the unthinkable' (Toynbee and Walker 2001: 17). However, when it came to illicit drug policy, publicly New Labour demonstrated no signs of newness at all: as Toynbee and Walker (2001: 173) point out, its stance, in public at least, was unequivocal, 'all "drugs" were harmful'. Indeed, MPs Mo Mowlam and Clare Short were made to make hasty and embarrassing retractions of statements following their innocuous comments regarding cannabis use.

This inability to publicly and overtly tailor policy designed to confront the reality of the situation regarding the use of illicit drugs by large tracts of the population is reflected in New Labour's flagship drug policy document *Tackling Drugs to Build a Better Britain* (Cabinet Office 1998). Broadly speaking, it resembles the previous government's 1995 White Paper. Bean (2002: 56) concurs, stating that the document 'largely reiterated the themes of the 1995 document whilst adding performance indicators for drug reduction in the next decade'. Of course, this can be seen as a blanket, general comment regarding New Labour's drug policy. There were clearly differences in the detail, and it is to those this section now turns.

Tackling Drugs to Build a Better Britain begins with New Labour's 'vision'. This proclaims that the aim is to create a 'healthy and confident society, increasingly free from the harm caused by the misuse of drugs'. This is to be achieved by combining enforcement with prevention. In terms of strategy, four specific policy areas are identified. These are:

1 **YOUNG PEOPLE** – to help young people resist drug misuse in order to achieve their full potential in society;
2 **COMMUNITIES** – to protect our communities from drug-related anti-social and criminal behaviour;
3 **TREATMENT** – to enable people with drug problems to overcome them and live healthy and crime free lives;
4 **AVAILABILITY** – to stifle the availability of illegal drugs on our streets.

(Cabinet Office 1998; original emphasis)

This vision was to be achieved within the following structure. Nationally, the government appointed a new anti-drugs co-ordinator, dubbed the 'drug tsar' by sections of the media. This was Keith Hellawell, a former chief constable of West Yorkshire. (This was generally considered a positive move, fulfilling New Labour's promise to 'think outside the box' – both Hellawell and his deputy, Mike Trace, were seen as people prepared to think radically about drug policy.) Hellawell's remit was to head up a new body named the UK Anti-Drugs Strategic Steering Group. This group was comprised of senior government officials, local government representatives, and representatives of independent bodies and voluntary sector agencies.

At government level, the ministerial body responsible for ensuring success was the Ministerial sub-Committee on Drug Misuse. This was to ensure those individual departments with an interest in illicit drug use contributed to the overall vision and strategy, and, presumably, kept each other informed on developments and best practice. At a local level, DATs remained, being seen as 'the critical link in the chain'. Thus, apart from cosmetic tinkering, it might be suggested that, in policy terms, little had changed from 1995 to 1998.

However, critically, the important point about the 1998 Labour approach lies in its similarity to the Conservative's policy: the groundwork and frameworks put in place by the Conservatives were allowed to come to fruition under New Labour. The result has been some interesting developments in both the scope and direction of policy, nationally and locally. Moreover, New Labour appears to have noted some of the weaknesses inherent in the 1995 document – lack of meaningful multi-agency working, lack of concrete projects – and has moved drug policy into a more active, some would argue proactive, realm, one that begins to address the realities of drug use in the twenty-first century. This is best explained and demonstrated by examining two specific policies.

Drug Treatment and Testing Orders (DTTOs) as an example of current UK drug policy

As has been made clear above, there is plenty of evidence regarding the relationship between certain acquisitive crimes and dependent drug use. As such, for at least the last eleven years there has been recognition that treatment for drug dependency can lead to reductions in criminal behaviour. The result of this interest in drug users and drug-related crime is the realization that the provision of an efficient system which addresses the needs of the user and the needs of their community depends on some form of union between the health (treatment) and criminal justice (enforcement) approaches. This policy recognition has subsequently found outlets in a variety of (criminal justice-based) Acts of Parliament.

To an extent, both the Labour and Conservative policy documents referred to above were pre-dated by the 1991 Criminal Justice Act (CJA). This set in train a (mandated) union between treatment and enforcement. The 1991 CJA included Schedule 1A(6) of the Powers of Criminal Courts Act (1973) which gave courts the power to impose treatment as part of a sentence. There was, however, a clear reluctance by the courts to use it. For instance, Hough (1996) notes, following the 1991 CJA, only 1 per cent of probation orders contained explicit conditions concerning drug treatment. This reluctance to employ coerced treatment seemingly ignored the evidence from the USA, which revealed little difference in success rates between those who are sentenced to drug programmes and those who enter voluntarily (Anglin and Hser 1990).

The unwillingness to employ drug treatment orders was noted in the Home Office consultation document *Drug Treatment and Testing Orders: Background and Issues for Consultation* (Home Office 1997). It cites a number of reasons why coerced treatment has been slow to take off, including: (i) a lack of Home Office guidelines to sentencers, plus doubts over the effectiveness of coerced treatment by probation officers, (ii) lack of information for sentencers concerning the availability and content of treatment, (iii) a perception of lack of enthusiasm by treatment providers to operate mandatory programmes and (iv) resourcing problems. The 1997 consultation document gave an indication of the faith of the government in the use of coerced treatment, a faith which manifested itself in the 1998 Crime and Disorder Act (CDA) in particular Part IV, sections 61–4.

At the heart of this part of the 1998 CDA is an awareness of the link between acquisitive crime and drug use. Sections 61–4 of the 1998 Act use legal processes to ensure that treatment is given to offenders who are 'dependent on or ha[ve] a propensity to misuse drugs and that [such] dependency or propensity is such as requires and may be susceptible to treatment' (s 61: 5(a) and (b)). It is important to note that the Drug Treatment and Testing Orders in the 1998 CDA are not forced treatment, rather offenders are coerced into treatment programmes. This is made clear in s 61: 6 where it states that 'the court shall not make such an order unless the offender expresses his (*sic*) willingness to comply with its requirements'. Offenders are thus given an element of choice, although, as some empirical data demonstrate, this is often a stark choice between a custodial sentence or treatment (Barton 1999). The treatment attached to an order will be carried out by 'a specified person having the necessary qualifications or experience ("the treatment provider") with a view to the reduction or elimination of the offender's dependency on or propensity to misuse drugs' (s 62: 1). Adherence to, and the outcomes of, the treatment will be monitored via a series of tests designed to 'ascertain whether [the offender] has any drugs in his body'. The 1998 CDA states that the offender will be required to produce a specified number of samples as and when required by the 'testing requirement' (s 62: 4).

Both the 'treatment provider' and the criminal justice system will then share information relating to the results of those tests. This is outlined in s 62: 7(c). It provides for test results to be made available to the probation officer supervising the offender as well as the courts, the latter as part of the proposed periodic case reviews (s 63: 1(a), (e)). The implementation of the new treatment and testing orders is reliant on a number of autonomous agencies, from different policy sectors, working together to provide a service for the user, the court and, ultimately, the safety of the community. Those agencies include the police, who are responsible for catching the offender, a drug worker who can be responsible for identifying the level of drug dependency and supplying treatment, the probation officer, who becomes responsible for ensuring adherence to the order, and the court for monitoring progress through treatment via review hearings. The multi-agency nature of the orders is unsurprising given the current ascendancy of partnership working in social policy, as well as the overall tone of the 1998 Crime and Disorder Act, with its focus on community safety via partnerships (Leng *et al.* 1998).

In this way, the government can claim to be adhering both to its election manifesto promise of being 'Tough on crime, tough on the causes of crime' (Toynbee and Walker 2001: 153), as well as to be making at least two aspects of their 'vision' (to protect our communities from drug-related anti-social and criminal behaviour and to enable people with drug problems to overcome them and live healthy and crime free lives) come to life.

The reclassification of cannabis as an example of current UK drug policy

The reclassification of cannabis is quite clearly a major step, and for the previous Home Secretary, Jack Straw, clearly a step too far. Throughout his tenure at the Home Office, Straw was adamant that there would be no move to decriminalize cannabis. However, while the government took a firm stance, elsewhere within the drug policy communities cannabis was being downgraded in terms of its perceived 'problem' status, by a policy community not readily associated with radical thinking: the police. As noted above, Kaal (1998) provided evidence to suggest that many police forces have had in place a policy of tacit decriminalization for some time. This is evidenced by the growing use of cautions for cannabis possession.

Indeed, by the end of the 1990s, some were prepared to take this further and publicly question the logic of criminalizing all drugs. For example, the Cleveland Police had this to say:

> It can be argued that there is no logic to the current pattern of illegality . . . the illogicality of this approach (which seems to be based on no more than historical accident) leads many young people in particular to level charges of hypocrisy at the 'establishment'. This is a very difficult argument to counter.
>
> (Cleveland Police 2000: 5.2)

They went on to suggest that: 'the most obvious alternative approach [to this problem] is the legalization and subsequent regulation of some or all drugs' (Cleveland Police 2000: 10.1).

This reinforces the message emanating from the Police Federation report chaired by Viscountess Runciman (Runciman 1999), which recommended a total rethink of the manner in which cannabis was viewed by the law. It offered eight recommendations, including:

i)   Cannabis should be transferred from Class B to Class C. . . .

ii) Possession of cannabis should not be an imprisonable offence. As a consequence, it will no longer be an arrestable offence in England and Wales. . . .

iii) Prosecution of offences of cannabis possession should be the exception . . . an informal warning, a formal caution, a reprimand or warning in the case of those aged 17 or under, or a fixed out of court fine should be the normal range of sanctions.

(Runciman 1999: Ch. 7, 77(i) (ii) (iii))

In the wake of this report, police forces have been more open about their hitherto clandestine 'liberal' approaches to cannabis possession. For example, the Metropolitan Police have been running a 'softly-softly' pilot scheme on cannabis possession in Lambeth since June 2001 (Hopkins 2001: 1). Here, people caught in possession are given on the spot warnings rather than being arrested and possibly charged. Clearly, for reasons that will be discussed below, the police's traditional law and order response to cannabis has been under an internal challenge for some time, creating a gap between the law and the primary agency charged with upholding the law.

Moreover, this radical approach to drug policy seemingly does not stop with 'soft' drugs. In November 2001, Commander Paddick of Lambeth Police told an all-party committee of MPs that recreational use of drugs including ecstasy and cocaine was 'low' on his operational priorities as a police officer. This stance later earned the commander a rebuke from the Commissioner of the Metropolitan Police (Travis 2001: 1). A few weeks later, ACPO announced that it was rethinking its policy on heroin, calling for mass prescriptions and the setting up of official 'shooting galleries' where heroin could be injected under medically supervised conditions (Bright 2001).

Although Jack Straw dismissed these recommendations out of hand, his successor, David Blunkett, clearly saw the value in this radical approach. In May 2001 Blunkett announced a proposed change in cannabis laws. The proposal included the downgrading of cannabis from a Class B to a Class C drug, thus removing the police's power to arrest for possession offences. Downgrading is not decriminalization, meaning that possession and supply remain illegal, but the maximum penalties, two years for possession and five for intent to supply, will be lower than the current five and fourteen years respectively. There were also indications of the intent to license cannabis for medical purposes.

Current directions in UK drug policy

These two examples arguably encapsulate the current direction of British drug policy. On the one hand, there is the recognition that dependent heavy end users, who are committing drug driven crime, represent a serious problem both to themselves and their communities. In order to address this problem the government, via DTTOs, has mandated joint working between health and law enforcement and coerced this problematic group of users into treatment (some would argue the same government has coerced reluctant partners into joint working!), in order to tackle both use and offending behaviour. On the other, there is an admission that recreational use of drugs is both widespread and not overly problematic for the majority of recreational users.

As such, the reclassification of cannabis marks recognition by the government that not all drug use is 'problematic' and that, in truth, there is very little the government can do to control use or supply. It also signals official recognition of the distinction between what in Chapter 7 we classed as category A and possibly B users and the more problematic category C user. How, then, does contemporary drug policy look when examined through our three analytical lenses?

Firstly, we could argue that in terms of domination by the criminal justice discourse not much has changed. Looking at the key policy initiative, the DTTOs, it is clear that they are criminal justice led and dominated by the needs and requirements of the law and order discourse. Indeed, some have argued that all those workers, be they health or justice based, become de facto officers of the court as soon as they begin to work within the DTTO framework (Barton and Quinn 2001). The same authors posit that there is a strong chance that the DTTOs serve to undermine the standard operating procedures and ideological base of the health workers involved in their implementation, citing the work of Blagg *et al.* (1988) who warned of the 'criminalisation of social policy'.

Equally, it could be suggested that the liberal stance being adopted on cannabis is a facet of the police's suggestions and unofficial 'street-level' policy of downgrading cannabis, bearing in mind that welfarist agencies have been calling for the same move for some time. Police reasoning revolves around the time and cost of processing cannabis offences when compared with the sentence the offenders are likely to receive should the case go to court. The rationale for downgrading cannabis seems to centre around the needs of the police, with the argument that it frees up officers to concentrate on 'real' crime. In many respects, this adds further weight to Garland's 1996 thesis that the state has realized that it cannot control all crime, neither should it be expected to do so. In the same work Garland (1996: 450) also suggests that, as a response to the demands of new public management and budgetary restrictions, the police are in the process of 'defining deviance down' thus justifying absent or slow responses to certain crimes.

In terms of joined-up working, contemporary policy seems to be faring better, with both health and justice being involved in a number of schemes across the country, accompanied by official recognition that treatment for problematic drug users is at least as effective in the long term as punishment. However, on a note of caution, it is worthwhile reminding ourselves that joint working in the *inter-agency* sense of the term has had to be mandated in order to become effective, and then only on terms acceptable to the hegemonic discourse of law and order. Nevertheless, there are a number of other joined-up health and education-based schemes operating successfully throughout England and Wales (Barton 2001).

Finally, has policy moved away from a law and order, supply reduction approach? This is difficult to answer with any certainty. At one and the same time it is possible to argue that the government has acknowledged that it can do little to stem the tide of drugs entering the country. As demonstrated in Chapter 3, it is seemingly prepared to let some smugglers free in order to concentrate on those who smuggle 'hard drugs' (Miller 2001). Equally, there is greater weight attached to harm reduction, safe use message in schools and youth groups around the country. Nevertheless, *Tackling Drugs to Build a Better Britain* contains, as part of its vision, a commitment to stifle the availability of drugs on the streets. Perhaps the best way to answer the question, and summarize our current approach, is to suggest that the government seek to control the supply of hard drugs such as heroin and cocaine, while downgrading efforts to control the supply of the soft drugs.

Conclusion: a more 'liberal' future?

If there is a second edition to this book, in, say, ten years time, what changes will need to be made to the above section? How will UK drug policy look in 2012? Of course, being an academic and not a fortune-teller, that is impossible for me to answer with certainty. However, it is possible to make some tentative suggestions. Firstly, it is possible to suggest that the current (embryonic) policy dichotomy between recreational use of soft drugs and problematic use of hard drugs will continue and perhaps expand. If that is the case then the influence of harm reduction will increase, especially if the recreational use of some drugs continues at its present rate. It is conceivable, for example, that drugs such as ecstasy and LSD could be downgraded, allowing a greater degree of control of the substance and its use. Should that occur, there seems little reason to oppose innovations such as testing units outside clubs.

Equally, at the problematic end, there seems little chance that the current thrust of the merger of treatment and punishment will falter. Indeed, if DTTOs prove to be successful then we could see the expansion of schemes that merge treatment and punishment. Already, there exists at least one project that sees the police referring targeted offenders, not yet arrested, but under suspicion and part of on-going investigations, to drug workers – a nascent pre-arrest referral crime prevention/reduction initiative.

There is one certainty: drug policy will need to change too as a response to two factors. Firstly, social and cultural change, and simple demographics mean that more and more of the adult population of the future will have experimented to some degree with drugs. From their and their peers' experiences comes the recognition that not all drugs and not all drug use is problematic and that currently the law does not reflect the reality of the situation. As Cleveland Police (Cleveland Police 2000) pointed out, the present situation is not logical and not easily defended. Secondly, the UK's drug policy cannot stand still in the face of changes in policy elsewhere in Europe. As the EMCDDA (Drugscope 2001) notes, there are the beginnings of a discernible move to decriminalize certain drugs across the EU. As in other areas of social and legal policy, the UK will have to move in broadly the same direction as its European neighbours. It is to Europe that this work now turns.

10 British drug policy in a European context

Introduction

This concluding chapter once again moves us away from purely Anglo-centric concerns by turning attention to two of our European neighbours' drug policies. The rationale for this lies in the fact that internationally, just as in domestic policy, there is a recognition that it is impossible to 'go it alone' in dealing with illicit drugs, thus creating a need for international joint working to address the problems caused by an international industry. For example, Chapter 5 stated that 90 per cent of the ecstasy that is consumed in the UK originates in the Netherlands. If this situation is occurring as a direct result of the drug policy of the Netherlands then it is clear that Britain has some interest in the manner in which the Dutch 'police' their own drug problem.

Another reason is that as social scientists we need to expand our horizons and challenge our own ethnocentricity. Giddens (1986: 19) powerfully warns us of the perils of '[t]he tendency to use our own society and culture as a measure to judge all others'. Arguably, Britain is still a long way from winning its own 'war on drugs' yet some British policy makers seem all too quick to dismiss the actions of others. Equally, it is important not to overlook the growing influence the European Union has on British policy. In several areas there are strong moves towards harmonization and integration of policies. Leibfried (1993: 133) comments that Europe seems to be moving towards a 'steadily increasing pool of shared sovereignties. . . . [T]his process has been steadily gaining momentum . . .'. This is given further weight in documents such as *Decriminalization in Europe?* (European Legal Database on Drugs 2001) which examines the possibility of a Europe-wide relaxation of drug laws. That being the case, it is imperative that policy makers, practitioners and academics become aware of developments elsewhere.

The chapter begins by exploring the usefulness of comparative research, noting the need for some form of comparative framework. Following on from that point, the next two sections explore drug policy in the Netherlands and Sweden respectively. The chapter, and indeed the book, concludes with a comparison of the factors that influenced drug policy in Britain, the Netherlands and Sweden, concentrating particularly on the impact society, politics and economics have had on the nature and construction of British illicit drug policy.

The usefulness of comparative research

Comparative research is now an established and important aspect of social science: nearly a decade ago Cochrane (1993: 1) argued that 'it is perhaps no longer necessary to make the case for the comparative approach . . . on the contrary, it may be single-country studies that need to be justified'. However, the establishment of comparative research as a central approach to study does not automatically justify its use: undertaking something simply because it is fashionable is often self-defeating. As the same author notes, comparative analysis only becomes really useful if it allows us to examine supranational trends and identify policy specific to individual countries. In that way, we can compare the manner in which different countries deal with similar problems; in our case, policy formulation in relation to the use of illicit substances.

What can happen in comparative research is that the researcher, when examining approaches to a social problem elsewhere, begins to look beyond the obvious and delves into a critical examination of history, politics and culture. As a result, these factors are included within the final explanations. However, because of the tendency towards ethnocentricity, researchers often fail to give full recognition to a critical examination of their own nation's development, leading to an acceptance of 'traditional' explanations of the state of affairs.

For example, as the previous chapter noted, the feature that is claimed as distinguishing the British approach to illicit drugs from the approach of other punitive regimes, such as that prevailing in the USA, is the so-called 'British model'. This claims that British drug policy has an equal space for treatment and law and order. However, as we have seen, the hegemonic discourse in British drug policy has been, and remains, law and order – Britain has had a tendency to punish first and treat later.

Traditionally, the reason for the development of this approach, as spelt out in Chapter 2, is mainly historical and stems from the early Home Office domination of drug policy. This is then added to Britain's ratification of the first, US-led, international treaties that mirrored the emphasis the USA placed on prohibition and interdiction over treatment. Seeing this as an encroachment on medical practice, the British medical establishment carved its own niche in drug policy and practice by establishing the right of doctors to treat drug use. Latterly, the adherence to a law and order dominated approach has been explained in terms of the need to reduce supply in order to control use, with equal space given to treat those whose drug use has become problematic.

However, this traditional account ignores several key points. Firstly, the lack of reference to global issues disguises the extent to which the USA has sought to influence and dominate a world approach to illicit drugs. The simplistic and moralistic stance that 'luxurious' drug use is wrong, the mantra 'just say no', and the certainty of severe punishment for drug offences have been key themes of US drug policy. All have been translated into the fabric of international treaties, to be embraced to a greater or lesser degree by other nations.

Secondly, the genesis of the British model reflected a period during which there was a distinct lack of a 'drug problem' either for the criminal justice agencies or the health sector. The subsequent rise of recreational drug use among the young has not been confined to Britain. Other countries across the globe have witnessed similar trends. The British law and order dominated approach has meant that large numbers of young recreational drug users, whose lives are otherwise law-abiding, have become 'criminals', and many users that do not fit the medical definitions of 'problematic' have been denied treatment and suffered all manners of social exclusion. Yet this does not have to be the case: other European nations have effectively decriminalized use of some illicit drugs and relied on education and prevention to halt use and demand, viewing drug use as essentially a socio-medical problem. As we shall see, others have restricted space in drug policy for medical interventions.

Thirdly, the traditional approach fails to recognize the influence of class, race and gender factors in British drug policy. When Rolleston reported in 1926, the majority of problematic users came from the medical profession, a trend that continued up until the 1950s. Thus, it could be suggested the liberal policies advocated by Rolleston were designed to keep problematic drug use confined to the professional middle classes 'in-house', thereby ensuring that the middle-class professional drug user did not suffer the ignominy of being dealt with by the criminal justice system. As drug use increased among the (young) working class in the late 1950s and 1960s the medical profession's claim of ownership of the problem was conspicuous by its absence. Indeed, one could argue that the recent liberalization of drug policy in Britain has more to do with the needs of the police than the desire of the medical profession to ensure treatment and education for the masses.

The value of comparative research becomes clear: it allows us to look beyond 'traditional' explanations of events and equips us with the tools to make a critical appraisal of our approach to any number of social problems. In this way, we avoid Giddens' (1986) trap of becoming ethnocentric and can begin to perceive British approaches in a wider context. Paradoxically, comparative research enables us to examine specific policy in more detail. For example, supply reduction techniques which rely on interdiction have been found wanting across all western nations. Britain has continued with this stance while some other European states have seemingly become resigned to the fact that interdiction alone cannot stem either the supply of, or the demand for, illicit drugs. Comparative research may enable us better to understand why this is the case, and what, often hidden, forces lie behind it.

With this in mind, the chapter now turns its attention to the Netherlands. What follows is a concise account of the development of Dutch drug policy. The reader is urged to keep in mind some of the material outlined in Chapter 2, which examined the development of British drug policy, and to note some of the degree of similarity that exists between the two nations' 'drug problems'.

The development of drug policy in the Netherlands

As was the case in Britain during the nineteenth century, the use of what are now illicit substances for self-medication purposes was the norm rather than the exception in Holland. De Kort (1996: 4) informs that by the end of the 1800s, 'a large part of the [Dutch] population had never even visited a physician'. Many of those who self-medicated used opium – or cocaine-based quack remedies, freely available from a variety of outlets. As in Britain, the growing professionalization of medicine in the 1800s meant that there was a sustained attack on the quacks and their patent medicines. This mirrored developments elsewhere in Europe and America, and was justified by the growing science of addiction, particularly related to opium, morphine and cocaine. Unlike the situation in Britain, however, de Kort (1996) fails to mention any great moral crusade against the 'luxurious' use of substances for recreational purposes.

As de Kort (1996: 6) notes, the result of this was that by the end of the nineteenth century drug use which, just as in Britain, had hitherto not been seen as a problem, was redefined by the medical profession as 'problematic' and in need of specialized control for largely the same reasons as in the British experience. However, the parallels with the development of British drug policy do not stop there: like the British, the Dutch had a vested interest in the trade in opium, which had a clear and obvious impact on the manner in which the Dutch state viewed the drug trade.

Again, in a remarkable mirror image of the British experience, concern as to the 'luxurious' use of drugs at home was not matched by a like concern about the luxurious use of drugs in the colonies by the indigenous populations. De Kort (1996: 7) views this situation as a direct consequence of the fact that '. . . the smoking of opium by the local population [of the colonies] had resulted in huge profits for the Dutch for centuries'. To place this in context, de Kort (1996: 7) claims that between 1816 and 1915 profits from opium accounted for 10 per cent of the total income from the Dutch colonies. Moreover, the same author notes that as cocaine grew in popularity, the Dutch traders imported coca bushes from Peru, Columbia and Bolivia and created new coca plantations in Java. These were successful to the point that by 1920 the Dutch had ranked as the world's largest cocaine producer for the previous ten years.

This is seen as a key contributory factor in the reluctance of the Dutch to be any more than unwilling partners in the first series of international treaties signed in Shanghai in 1909. Given the scale of economic benefits that accrued from the drug trade, this degree of reluctance on the part of the Dutch is somewhat understandable. De Kort (1996: 10–11) notes that, much to the chagrin of the Americans, the Dutch, Germans and British all failed to see domestic use of drugs as a problem and gave the impression that there was no pressing need to arrange a further international conference. Notwithstanding, pressure from the USA led the Dutch to arrange the world's first international conference on illicit substances, the Hague Opium Convention of 1912. Those who attended spent most of their time drawing up guidelines for the production and trade in opium and cocaine. In the Netherlands this eventually laid the foundation for the 1919 Opium Act.

Interestingly, Dutch public opinion on drugs in the domestic sphere showed remarkable foresight, given the problems that are now faced by western nations. De Kort (1996:11) claims that by the 1920s, '. . . the majority opinion was that the "war on drugs" . . . could not be won . . .' using law and international treaties. Moreover, the Dutch demonstrated that they were sceptical both about joining the American anti-drug crusade and about the efficacy of the Americans' tactics:

> Several Dutch sources from that period suggest that the illegal drug trade would be difficult to control due to the importance of the financial and economic interests involved in the highly priced, easily concealed drugs. . . . The notion that is was impossible to eliminate international illegal drug smuggling was referred to as the 'American position' – a position which is '(virtually) unenforceable'.
> (de Kort 1996: 11; and Tan Tong Joe 1929: 13–14 in de Kort 1996: 11)

Thus, while the Netherlands were signatories of the 1912 Hague Convention, and had their own legislation based on the treaty, enforcing the law was given low priority. The period between the two world wars saw some prosecution of drug offences, mostly among the Chinese community whose method of using opium – smoking – was different from the European norm and very obviously devoid of any 'medical' connection. Even in those cases however, it appears that the fine was cursory, with mild sentences being the standard. De Kort (1996), drawing on the work of Parssinen (1983), likens the illicit drug situation in the Netherlands to that of Britain at the same time: very few addicts, little in the way of a problem and a system policed by both the Justice and Health Departments.

However, mirroring the situation in Britain, the drug scene altered following the Second World War. Initially, there was little in the way of a drug problem, although Amsterdam did create a Narcotics Division, following the example of Rotterdam (de Kort 1996). In the latter half of the twentieth century, developments paralleled Britain: recreational drug use increased among the young during the very late 1950s and 1960s. As the drug culture developed, the Dutch Opium Act expanded its remit to keep pace with changes: for example, LSD was included in the Act in 1966. During this period, the Dutch Police and Justice Departments were keen to use the power of the law to clamp down on users and dealers alike. However, despite increasingly severe penalties, 'this repressive approach could not prevent the fast increase in the use of marihuana . . .' (de Kort 1996: 16). Alongside the use of marijuana there was a rise in the use of heroin, especially among the young Dutch population. This led to a more repressive policy that, hitherto (arguably because opium use was more or less restricted to Chinese), had been relatively tolerant to drug use and drug users.

By the end of the 1960s, Dutch drug policy was still closely aligned to that of Britain. However, the 1970s saw a major change in direction for the Dutch and a departure from the rest of Europe: the de facto decriminalization of marijuana. The foundation for this was twofold. Firstly, the Hulsman Committee issued its report *Options in Drug Policy* (1971). Hulsman, a law professor with strong abolitionist views, was appointed by the state sponsored Institution for Mental Health (Leuw 1996: 28) to review drug policy. The committee took a radical view of illegal drug use, based on the concept of relative risk analysis. Its findings concluded that opiates, barbiturates and amphetamine held potential dangers, but cannabis, relative to other drugs, including tobacco, posed little risk of creating dependency. Moreover, Hulsman disregarded the gateway thesis, and held that it was the criminalization of cannabis that caused a stepping stone effect, not the properties of the drug itself (Leuw 1996: 29).

In sociological terms Hulsman found that cannabis was a sub-cultural phenomenon. The committee noted that, in a pluriform society such as the Netherlands, space needed to be made for 'alternative' lifestyles, and that not all lifestyles needed to conform to the norms of the so-called respectable citizen. Indeed, Hulsman argued that moral rejection, when added to reactionary and repressive control mechanisms, would only serve to marginalize sub-cultures. Hulsman was particularly specific about overt use of state power in dealing with alternative lifestyles and sub-cultures: 'The Government should not take a censuring position based on the fact that a certain behaviour does not fit into the life concept of those holding state power' (Hulsman Report 1971, in Leuw 1996: 29).

Hulsman used the argument of John Stuart Mill's essay 'On Liberty' to defend the philosophical position of minimum state interference in instances where behaviour only had consequences for the individual. His report also noted the lack of logic in outlawing one drug (cannabis) when other, legal drugs, caused as much or more harm. Finally, echoing the sentiments of Tan Tong Joe (1929) more than forty years previously, Hulsman observed that fear of legal consequences was unlikely to prevent people using drugs. Moreover, when the law was invoked, it was important that the state recognized and calculated the costs and benefits. As an example Hulsman claimed that over-reliance on implementing the law could lead to the cost of police resources outweighing any benefits accrued in terms of sentences, deviance being amplified, sub-cultures marginalized and excluded, civil liberties eroded, and respect for the law undermined.

What Hulsman reflected was the moral climate of the Netherlands (and, many would argue, of some sections of most western societies) at the start of the 1970s. Sagel-Grande (1997: 87) claims that these were, and still are, '. . . sobriety, pragmatism, search for a happy medium, humanity and tolerance of the freely chosen life-style of others'. Hulsman's lacked the luxury of being a committee directly appointed by the government; however, the Baan Commission, appointed in 1968, was. Its remit was to re-evaluate the Dutch government's drug policy. Clearly guided by the work of Hulsman, Baan established the philosophical base for contemporary Dutch drug policy. This is:

- a distinction between soft drugs and hard drugs;
- differention between major and minor offences, with possession of soft drugs made a minor offence;
- differention between roles in the drug milieu: between dealers and consumers; between hard drug dealers and soft drug dealers; between national and international dealers;
- a two track approach: medical approach to addicts and users and a law and order, repressive approach to large-scale dealers of hard drugs;
- a central aim of prevention or alleviation of social and individual risks caused by drug use;
- a recognition of the inadequacy of the criminal law with regard to any aspect of the drug problem except trafficking.

(Adapted from Leuw 1996, Sabel-Grande 1997 and Boekhout van Solinge 1999)

These resolutions were incorporated into law in 1976 when the Dutch government revised the Opium Act (Boekhout van Solinge 1999: 2). It is important to stress, however, that the Dutch have not legalized cannabis: 'According to the Opium Act, possession of marijuana for personal use is a crime' (European Legal Database on Drugs 2001: 5). The revised Act established a number of guiding principles. Firstly, it allowed that drug use should be located firmly in the socio-medical field. Drug problems were to be seen as one of a number of normal social problems, rather than as a specific set of problems requiring special treatment. In this way, all forms of drug use and all types of drug users become 'normalized' and not marginalized. This is evidenced by the fact that for drug users punishment is routinely not an option. For example, even possession of small quantities of harder drugs carries with it a low prosecution priority. Moreover, there is an extensive care system with methadone and needle exchanges widely available. As a result, there is a good level of contact between problematic drug users and health agencies, allowing the Dutch to be able to claim that 65 to 85 per cent of addicts are in regular contact with the authorities.

Secondly, there is a recognition in the Netherlands that recourse to criminal law should be as infrequent as possible for addressing drug problems. Thus, using the police to deal with drug use becomes as unusual as using the police to deal with, for example, unemployment. The policy distinction between soft and hard drugs means that a strategy of 'market separation' can be embraced, allowing soft drugs to be bought and used in a market place devoid of harder drugs and free from 'criminal elements'. In line with this approach, the Dutch government made possession of up to 30 grams of cannabis a misdemeanour, thereby 'allowing' possession. It also made space for 'house dealers' in youth clubs; a phenomenon that quickly turned into the coffee shops (Boekhout van Solinge 1999: 512).

This situation continued until the mid-1990s. Then, in 1995, the Dutch government released a paper entitled *Drug Policy in the Netherlands: Continuity and Change* (Ministry of Health, Welfare and Sports *et al.* 1995). This made a number of alterations to the Dutch drug policy, including the reduction of the maximum acceptable purchase of cannabis from 30 to 5 grams and a crack down on the importation of cannabis for coffee shops (Boekhout van Solinge 1999). However, while this appears to be a tightening of policy and a move away from the liberal base established in 1976, Boekhout van Solinge (1999: 516) argues that the apparent repressive nature of the post-1995 changes obscures an even greater degree of liberalization and clarification of policy.

For example, he notes that post-1995 Dutch coffee shops can carry larger stocks of the drug than previously, moving from 30 grams of cannabis to 500 grams. Equally, the crackdown on imported cannabis and large-scale domestic production is a clear indication that the Dutch now favour small-scale indigenous cultivation, made increasingly possible by the fact that the post-1995 changes allow for up to five cannabis plants to be cultivated with impunity. The idea is to encourage small-scale producers to stock the coffee shops rather than large importers or large domestic producers. Away from the large cities, the municipalities have the option of whether to allow coffee shops: most have allowed this, thus taking the pragmatic view that cannabis will be used anyway, and opening coffee shops allows safer use in a more controlled and regulated environment, free from criminal influences.

In terms of hard drugs, the post-1995 changes to the Netherlands' drug policy have moved to create a higher enforcement priority for hard drugs, especially in the trafficking and production of synthetic drugs, largely as a result of Holland becoming a major producer and exporter of such substances. As far as users of hard drugs are concerned, the focus remains on health intervention above that of the criminal justice system. There have also been experiments with the prescription of heroin, as opposed to methadone, to drug dependent users who are facing real problems in addressing their addiction.

Clearly, the Netherlands' approach to illicit drugs is different from that of Britain, and can be seen to very much experimental in comparisons with other nation states. However, comparative analysis shows that, while the Dutch system is different and some would argue unique, its uniqueness is, in fact, disappearing as more and more EU countries seek to embrace a less repressive stance in relation to cannabis. It appears that while the supranational trend in Europe is towards a rise in illicit drug use, most nation states have begun to move in a similar policy direction. The exception is Sweden. The next section illustrates this by an examination of the development of Swedish drug policy.

The development of Swedish drug policy

Sweden, it could be argued, has a diametrically opposite approach and philosophy to illicit drug use to the Netherlands. The Swedish National Institute of Public Health (1998: 1–2) notes that 'Sweden has a restrictive policy on drugs . . . the overriding aim of Swedish drug policy is a drug-free society'. This may come as something of a surprise as Sweden has built itself a reputation as a progressive and enlightened state committed to social equality by mitigating class and gender inequalities (Ginsberg 1993). However, this may not be the case for all citizens or lifestyles:

> . . . the remoteness and authoritarianism of the welfare state . . . has come to prominence around questions of the rights of social assistance claimants, *drug addicts*, and parents of children taken into care.
>
> (Ginsberg 1994: 200–1; emphasis added)

Sweden's historical experiences of illicit drugs share some similarities with its other European neighbours with one important exception: the key problem drug has been amphetamines and not heroin. Our review of Swedish drug policy begins just before the start of the Second World War and the introduction of amphetamines into Sweden in 1938. Their introduction was followed by a huge advertising campaign promoting their use as stimulants and slimming pills. Boekhout van Solinge (1997) notes that 'Newspapers, magazines and radio broadcasts recommended the "pep-pills" for all kinds of people, from students to tired housewives'. Surveys taken at this time suggested that up to 80 per cent of students had tried amphetamines. In order to stem their use, amphetamines were made available only on prescription in 1939. Nevertheless use of amphetamines continued to be widespread. By 1942/3, 3 per cent of the population were using amphetamines between one to four times a year.

Despite government concerns, manifested by increasingly repressive policy, amphetamine use in Sweden continued to rise. By the end of 1959 the total registered sale of amphetamine-based substances amounted to 33.2 million doses (Boekhout van Solinge 1999). Importantly, the bulk of that rise seems to have been located among the young, particularly those within a criminal sub-culture. This created a subtle but important shift in types of use and types of user. Olsson (1994) compares numbers and types of user across time from 1943 until 1965. The research demonstrates that in 1943 there were around 133,000 occasional users, 4,000 regular users, with 3,000 abusers (*sic*) and 200 severe abusers. However, by 1965, this figure had shifted to 40,000 to 60,000 occasional users, 12,500 to 17,500 regular users, 2,225 to 3,225 abusers and 1000 to 1,500 severe abusers.

This research indicates a trend of decreasing widespread occasional use among the general population, replaced by a more focused, increasingly problematic type of use among a younger (sometimes) criminally deviant population. In an effort to control and suppress this, amphetamine based stimulants were put under the auspices of the National Narcotic Drug Act in 1959. As is always the case, prohibition of a substance opened up and increased the size of the illicit market. In summary, it is possible to suggest that in Sweden amphetamine moved from being a socially acceptable medicine to an illicit substance in the short period from 1938 to 1959. As a result, amphetamine use almost disappeared from 'normal' society, but became an integral part of Sweden's criminal sub-culture. Concern about this led to the formation of the National Drug Committee (Boekhout van Solinge 1999). It found, in 1967, that Sweden had around nine thousand addicts, almost all dependent on amphetamines. This may have been one of the contributory factors that led to a new direction in drug policy at the end of the 1960s (Lenke and Olsson 1996: 106).

However, one of the key reasons for the shift from a socio-medical drug policy to a clear law enforcement approach was the (failed) experiment of legally prescribing drugs that took place in Stockholm between 1995 and 1997. The failure of this experiment was exacerbated by the reaction of Nils Bejerot, a Stockholm police doctor, to the experiment (Lenke and Olsson 1996). Essentially, the Stockholm experiment revolved around the prescription of amphetamine, some morphine and methadone to a small number of drug dependent patients (ten at the beginning, rising to one hundred and twenty at the project's zenith). It was led by Sven-Erik Ahstrom, an outspoken liberal doctor who believed that patients should manage their own doses and be given 'take away' drugs that were replenished if stocks ran out sooner than expected. Ahstrom also allowed a few patients to prescribe and distribute drugs to other users.

By the middle of the experiment Ahstrom was the only doctor prescribing. There were a number of problems. As with the British experience, large quantities of prescribed drugs were finding their way into street markets, there were high mortality rates among those participating, and crime failed to fall. The final straw seems to have been the death of a 17-year-old girl, not participating in the project, but caused by a project member injecting her with an overdose of amphetamine and morphine. In the two year period of the experiment 15 kilos of amphetamine and 3.3 kilos of opiates had been prescribed to just one hundred and twenty patients (Boekhout van Solinge 1999).

Such a project almost guarantees critics. One such critical voice was that of Bejerot. His main thesis revolves around the notion that drug use is contagious and that once a group of users has formed it will grow unless or until supply and availability have been restricted. Logically, therefore, those infected with the 'contagion' are in dire need of 'treatment' for their and society's well-being. Bejerot's thesis exerted a great influence on Swedish drug policy, not due to its scientific base, but in the words of Lenke and Olsson (1996: 110–11) because, 'as a police officer [he] was given massive support and promotion by a police organization that has no equivalent in western society'.

At this juncture it is vital to point out the role (or lack of it) of the medical profession and to say something about Swedish society's reaction to stimulants generally. Nycander (1998) notes that the Temperance Movement has always held great sway in Swedish political, cultural and social life. As a result, between 1909 and 1955 Sweden's policy on alcohol teetered on the brink of prohibition. As it was, alcohol sales were severely restricted and incorporated moral and social censure for 'drunks': 'Some of the system shops had lists of people who were not allowed to buy [alcohol] because of frequent offences such as public drunkenness' (Nycander 1998: 23). 'Treatment' for drunkenness was delivered not by doctors but by the social services who viewed it as a form of social disease from which the sufferer could almost be resocialized. Equally, new recruits could be avoided by limiting contact with the 'infected' drunk. It appears that the Swedes simply transferred this approach to alcohol to other, illicit, drugs.

Because of this mix of reasons, Swedish drug policy altered in the late 1960s. Medical involvement, already on an unsound footing, was even further marginalized. As a result, the medical profession abrogated degrees of control over drug use. A combination of law and order and a form of social service-led interventions filled this vacuum. Bergmark (1998: 37) describes this as

> an undermining of the position of experts as an essential characteristic, closely connected to a new type of activist, the socially committed lay person, who not only criticized the general management of the drug problem but also questioned the legitimacy of the experts.

As a result, the lack of medical input allowed a more repressive approach to drug use. For example, Bergmark continues by noting the influence that reformatory institutions for young offenders had on drug treatment. He informs that the ideology of these organizations was one of 'socialistic fosterage' which was predicated upon the need for coercion into treatment. It is important to note that this coercive and judgemental approach was mirrored by public opinion – Bergmark and Oscarrson (1988: 175) claim that drug addicts are seen as 'drug-controlled criminality machines'. Moreover as Gould (1999) notes, for a professional to be seen as a 'drug liberal' is tantamount to professional suicide.

Throughout the 1980s a pressure group, the National Association for a Drug-Free Society (RNS), was active in campaigning for a 'hard-line' approach to drug use. This was given weight by the onset of social problems caused by the economic down-turn affecting the West, including relatively high rates of unemployment. As a result the level of associated social problems rose, and with them the clamour for a tougher approach in their amelioration. This climate allowed for a more draconian line on drug policy. By the end of the 1980s the RNS had achieved, via the Swedish Parliament, its goals of an extension of the time drug and alcohol users could be taken into compulsory custody, the rejection of a national syringe exchange scheme and the criminalization of drug use. The criminalization of use was extended in 1993 to make being under the influence of a drug punishable by six months' imprisonment (Gould 1999).

This draconian influence is visible up to the present day. Swedish drug policy is arguably the most repressive in Europe. Indeed, as Gould (1999: 13) notes, the liberal drug policies operated elsewhere in Europe are seen in Sweden as a potential source of 'contamination', again reflecting Bejerot's influence. In brief, Sweden's approach to drug use is best summarized with reference to the following policy and ideological points:

- the aim of a drug free society;
- reducing the recruitment of 'new drug abusers' (*sic*);
- inducing 'more drug abusers to kick the habit';
- reducing the supply of drugs;
- a belief that limiting drug policy to harm reduction amounts to capitulation;
- a refusal to distinguish between hard and soft drugs;
- a limit of 600 patients at any one time to be allowed on the national methadone programme;
- a determination to eradicate market places for drugs;
- a mixture of prevention, education, law enforcement and coerced treatment aimed primarily at the user.

(Adapted from Swedish National Institute of Public Health 1998;
Boekhout van Solinge 1999; Gould 1999)

Clearly, this is removed from the Netherlands' approach and is different from that of Britain. Essentially, and as a direct result of Bejerot's legacy, the Swedes have focused their drug policy on the consumer rather than the supplier. As Gould (1999: 12) points out, Bejerot's thesis revolves around the notion that suppliers can always be replaced but, without consumption, there is no market in the first instance.

Aside from making interesting reading, the purpose of this section has been to alert the reader to the fact that, in supranational terms, the 'drug problem' for all western nations has been the rising numbers of people who are experimenting with illicit drugs, coupled with a rise in problematic drug use in all its forms. However, comparative research enables us to view not only the actual policies that inform the present day approach but also the background in terms of a framework which includes economics, politics and cultural and social pressures all of which have figured prominently in developing contemporary policy in Holland and Sweden. Employing this framework to assess Britain's potential move towards a reclassification of cannabis should enable us to view the changes in a more nuanced and critical manner. The task for the remaining sections of this book is just that: to attempt to make sense of this, and at the same time engage the reader with the key factors that influence and shape British drug policy in the third millennium.

British drug policy

By this stage of the book, it is hoped that the reader has acquired a clear appreciation of the complex nature of the illicit drug milieu. As we have seen, there are very few, if any, clear-cut solutions or even agreement as to reasons for the problem in this field. It seems as if every area is contested – there is disagreement as to whether cannabis is a gateway drug; there is an argument over the link, if any, between drugs and crime; there is confusion as to whether to control supply or use – and so it goes on. Additionally, in many countries there is a huge moral, and therefore political, dimension to illicit drug use. As Young (1971) noted more than thirty years ago, it is often not the illicit drug that is the problem, it is the hedonism associated with drug use that leads to moral condemnation. Clearly, finding a solution to the contemporary 'drug problem' is fraught with difficulties as well as being a product of its own history. The aim here is to attempt to navigate through some of the more confusing issues and areas. With that in mind, the first question that needs addressing is to establish whether or not there is an actual 'drug problem'.

The nature of the British 'drug problem'

Vigilant readers will have noticed the almost constant use of inverted commas around the phrase 'drug problem'. It denotes a degree of uncertainty as to the actual problematic nature of drug use. For example, as Chapter 3 noted, our measuring instruments provide, at best, 'guestimates' as to the extent of illicit drug use. Self-report data would seemingly indicate that a substantial minority of the British population tries some form of illicit drug at least once, most often in their youth. The same type of data indicate that a smaller proportion continues to use illicit drugs on a semi-regular recreational basis. Over time, such recreational use diminishes across age cohorts, but the trend has been for even greater numbers of the next generation to continue with some form of recreational (illicit) drug use. Finally, there is a small minority within all generations for whom drug use becomes problematic in both medical and social terms.

However, does this pattern really constitute a 'drug problem'? True, some of those people with problematic drug use do commit a great deal of crime (category C users outlined and described in Chapter 7) and members of the same category of user do suffer serious legal, social and medical consequences for their actions. However, it could be argued that the 'drug problem' is largely confined to somewhere in the region of 200,000 people. Moreover, is the 'problem' here a medical or legal one? For some, especially those category A users, who in the past have included the offspring of royalty and (former) Home Secretaries, the most 'problematic' aspect of their drug use is the potential for a criminal record. If this is indeed the case, the 'problem' is not a facet of the drug, but is created by social reactions to hedonistic or 'luxurious' use. That being the case, for most users 'the drug problem' could be seen to be as much a social and political construct as it is a property of the drugs themselves

That is not to suggest that drug use is unproblematic – it remains the case that use, however infrequent, of any or all illicit drugs holds the potential seriously to damage the health of the user, as well as carrying serious social and legal consequences. The point is that for the majority of users this is palpably not their experienced reality, nor that of their peers. The vast majority of drug users do not commit acquisitive crime in order to feed their drug use, nor do the majority of illicit drug users act as a significant drain on scarce health resources. Moreover, except in a small number of instances there is little evidence to suggest that recreational use of illicit drugs leads inexorably to drug dependency, any more than alcoholism automatically and consistently follows social drinking. This begs the question as to where exactly the 'drug problem' lies and what is its exact nature.

In order to begin to address this question it is necessary to revisit some of the points made in previous chapters, specifically, the impact of economics, politics and socio-cultural factors. It is the contention here that it is a combination of these three pressures that informs and shapes drug policy, not just in Britain, but elsewhere. With that in mind, the next section examines the part economic factors play in shaping British drug policy.

Economic pressures

Chapters 2, 5 and 6 established the relationship between economics and illicit drugs in both domestic and international terms. Put bluntly, the illicit drug industry is a huge global phenomenon that produces an annual turnover which makes that of most licit multinationals look insignificant. It is a major player in international trade and is based on commodities for which there is a seemingly insatiable worldwide demand. Looked at from a business perspective this is startling for a product that for the most part cannot be freely advertised, cannot be freely distributed, is relatively difficult to obtain and for which trading in the commodity can cause multiple harms to the consumer and vendor alike.

Paradoxically, as Chapter 6 outlined, it is the illicit nature of some substances that drives up the prices and levels of profitability in this market. Put simply, the act by nation states of attempting to control the supply of illicit drugs serves to interfere in the market mechanism. The drug producers see interdiction as a factor of production; in turn, this is seen as a 'cost' and factored in to the price. In economic terms, the artificial inflating of the price caused by the banning actions of the nation states allows greater profits to be made and thereby increases the economic power of the large-scale drug dealers. As Chapter 6 noted, about 50 per cent of the retail cost of illicit drugs is factored in as a direct result of countries attempting to interfere in the market by making these substances illegal. Economic theory tells us that at these levels of profit, new illicit drug entrepreneurs will always be attracted into the business and are quick to replace any dealers who do get caught.

Because of the overall profitability of the illicit drug business, coupled with the scale of consumption and production, few, if any, governments can halt or even significantly disrupt the international trade in illicit drugs. Moreover, and further complicating matters, production of illicit substances has become an integral part of the economy of some developing nations thereby limiting the range of actions open to the international community. Equally, as the war on Afghanistan has proven once again, one of the potential consequences of action by developed nations in these areas is a change in culture and control that sometimes leads to increased production of illicit drugs. Thus, in cost/benefit terms there are real questions to be answered surrounding government actions designed to control the importation of illicit drugs and the effect this has on the market.

What must never be lost sight of is the fact that those nations that are now reaping economic benefits from the production and distribution of illicit drugs could charge countries such as the Netherlands and Britain with hypocrisy. A convincing case could be made for the claim that the new drug trading nations are simply carrying on a tradition of trading in drugs pioneered and subsequently refined by these two northern European states. In many ways Britain could be seen to be Afghanistan's China.

These are the often-quoted macro-economic factors. However, there are other micro-economic calculations that can be made. According to Kraan (1996), extrapolating from an examination of the economics of Dutch drug policy, politicians and government organizations in the Netherlands are prone to making explicit cost/benefit analyses of policy implementation. Thus, in deciding the allocation of scarce resources politicians are often forced to consider the benefits of continuing with certain directions in policy, especially if the costs are outweighing the benefits. Here, costs do not always need to be monetary.

For instance, Kraan (1996) examines the costs to the Dutch criminal justice system in policing illicit drug use. He found that 7 per cent of the total budget of the Dutch police force was spent on policing drugs. Given the fact that very little of this money will be spent on policing soft drugs, it could be argued that this represents a solid investment in an attempt to control hard drugs, which the Dutch see as most problematic. However, what if a similar review was undertaken in Britain? It will be recalled that Chapter 3 noted the vast majority of 'drug crimes' processed by the British criminal justice system centred on simple possession of cannabis. In turn, most of these crimes drew relatively minor punishments of fines or community sentences. Moreover, it appears that large tracts of the British population fail to see cannabis as a major 'problem drug'. Mowbray (2002: 14) notes that Strang bemoans the fact that 65 per cent of the total drugs budget goes on law and order, with relatively little effect on drug use.

Goodchild (2002) informs that in Britain policing cannabis use alone costs around £50 million per annum, equivalent to the work of 500 full time police officers. Can this be seen as a solid investment, given that cannabis use is relatively unproblematic and draws low levels of public opprobrium? In pure economic terms this level of investment of scarce resources can be seen to be wasteful. Good managers would therefore question this and attempt to redirect resources on more profitable enterprises. This is clearly the case in the Metropolitan Police force in relation to cannabis possession. Economically, it makes more sense for the law and order wing of British drug policy to concentrate its efforts on the harder drugs that, in some instances, lead the user into committing large volumes of acquisitive crimes. It could even be suggested that the costs and benefits of a regime aimed at treatment and education would be, in the long run, more successful.

Arguably, if a British drug policy was structured in pure economic terms, little in the way of law and order-based attention would be paid to relatively unproblematic drugs such as cannabis (and possibly ecstasy and LSD). Moreover, where interventions took place with cannabis, they would be health-based, promoting safe use, harm minimization approaches. Even in terms of the *users* of hard drugs, law and order would have a restricted role, better to concentrate on the importers and large-scale dealers of these substances. At the time of writing, this is exactly what the Liberal Democrat Party is proposing, with the other main political parties all in the process of reviewing their policy options (Goodchild 2002). In the changing world of public policy, with its emphasis on value for money and measurable outputs, an uneconomic drug policy simply cannot be sustained.

However, while the political classes can make convincing arguments for a change of drug policy in economic terms, there are also other costs to be considered by politicians: the dual need to be seen to be credible by all sections of the electorate and the concomitant requirement of ensuring and maintaining respect for the law. This is an often-delicate process in areas where the law is contested, as there will almost always be conflicts of interest, with one group supporting a particular stance and others in opposition. For example, in instances where there is a clear gap between the law, public action and public opinion, the politician risks damaging the often-delicate balance that exists between themselves and opposing pressure groups.

Sometimes, a situation develops where politicians need to come off the fence and align themselves with one lobby or the other. Failure to judge the public mood correctly holds the potential to 'cost' the politician greatly in terms of credibility and respect for the law. The issue of illicit drugs at the beginning of the twenty-first century is one such area. Unfortunately, while politicians may see the economic benefits of a relaxation of drug law relating to cannabis, in moral terms many are hoist by their own petard, unable to move from the entrenched 'all drugs are evil' perspective. This has its roots in the dawn of contemporary drug policy, and it is to this attention now turns.

Moral pressures

As Chapter 2 noted, concerns about the morality of the working class were central in the formation of British drug policy. Specifically, much of the direction emanated from the Victorian era, when the bourgeois middle class became increasingly worried about the contamination of the 'respectable' poor by the residuum and undesirable elements of society, such as prostitutes. Over time, this form of morality – reflected in the emphasis on middle-class respectability mirrored (and in some instances ridiculed) in contemporary novels by authors such as Dickens and Collins – consciously distanced itself from the more permissive practices of the upper and working classes.

Such a bourgeois view of morality was given even greater credence by the eugenics and Darwinian movements of that period, which purported to prove a hierarchy of the classes, the supremacy of European races and the male gender, leading to the promotion of strict controls over the 'feeble-minded' and calls for an eradication of 'bad' character traits among the working classes (Thane 1996: 51). Moreover, this period witnessed the introduction of the age of consent for various sexual acts and a consolidation of heterosexual and homosexual identities (Haste 1993). As the middle class grew, this moral perspective came to be the defining British morality.

Concomitantly, this peculiar perspective on right and wrong imported some anomalies into the emergent moral climate. This can be witnessed elsewhere, away from illicit drugs. For example, Victorian morality is redolent with concern with all forms of intoxication, but in a quintessentially British middle-class approach, different alcoholic intoxicants were treated in different manners – beer was preferred to gin, the latter seen to be more 'evil' and 'corrupting' than the former (Tobias 1972). Much the same point can be made regarding illicit drugs. Laudanum and other opium derivatives, clearly the preference of the working classes, seem to have been singled out as in need of greater attention than cocaine, which from its introduction into Britain has been associated with creativity (viz. Conan Doyle's character Sherlock Holmes' use of cocaine as a 'mental stimulant') and as a luxurious drug of choice for the rich, the artistic and the chic urban middle classes. Indeed, this attitude persists today: the stimulant effects of cocaine and amphetamine are roughly similar, yet even Robson (1994: 57), in his otherwise excellent book, cannot resist commenting that amphetamine 'lacks the eloquent advocacy of cocaine' and that it is 'a rough and ready drug with a rough and ready clientele'.

Over time, and especially since the inception of the burgeoning drug culture of the past four decades, middle-class morality has been the dominant factor in British culture and its concerns have been fuelled every so often by moral panics (Goode and Ben-Yehuda 1994), often surrounding working class youth, violence and/or drug use. Debate about a number of social issues has come to be dominated by these views, aided and abetted by a conservative, mainly right wing popular press. This, coupled with the growing embourgeoisement of the traditional working class has seen politicians pander more and more to middle-class values and morality. In terms of illicit drugs, this has led to the polarization of views at the expense of reasoned debate. As Goode and Ben-Yehuda (1994: 28) comment, in times of moral panics politicians are most likely to align '. . . themselves against the devil and on the side of the angels . . . what count[s] [is] not the nature of the target but what side they were on and what they were against'. Clearly, over the last four decades British politicians have been against 'drugs' and have been on the side of a variety of anti-drugs 'moral entrepreneurs'.

For example, across the decades we have witnessed panics and concern over cannabis 'pep-pills', LSD, crack cocaine and heroin. Following the ecstasy related death of Leah Betts, an anti-ecstasy campaign gathered momentum in Britain. Ecstasy became the 'new heroin', the new folk devil: police were instructed to crack down on the sellers of the drug, courts were handing out draconian sentences to those caught and the media stories were such that one could be forgiven for thinking that each and every teenager in the country was taking dangerous amounts of the drug daily. Subsequent research indicates that its use is relatively rare among young drug users (Ramsay and Partridge 1999). It is also interesting to note that in the intervening seven years, the police's attitude to ecstasy is now closer to their approach to cannabis than to heroin.

This current and gradual loosening of the moral stranglehold over the tone of the debate and the direction of drug policy in Britain is an emergent feature of the early twenty-first century. One can only surmise the reasons for this. Arguably, it is part of a shift in social and cultural values that has its roots in the 'swinging sixties'. The generation that holds the power in Britain are almost all 'children of the sixties' and has lived through a culture where drug use has moved from a marginal activity to somewhere near normalized behaviour in sections of society. Across all forms of social variables – sexuality, promiscuity, marital status, pornography and others – the Victorian-based bourgeois middle-class value system is being challenged as people either reject its strictures or, more likely, are honest about their actions. Political rhetoric and action need to reflect this change in attitude in order to remain credible. Equally, with large tracts of the population breaking drug laws relating to cannabis on a regular basis, respect for the law is under threat, as it become increasingly difficult to defend what many see as an unjust or unenforceable law.

Once again, this state of affairs is evident in statements issued by a number of senior politicians and policy makers. The remarks of various police officers have been dealt with above. Goodchild (2002) notes that the Home Secretary is 'minded' to change the cannabis laws. She quotes David Blunkett as saying that '. . . it is time for an honest and common sense approach focusing on drugs that cause most harm', making Blunkett's approach diametrically opposed to that of his hard-line predecessor, Jack Straw. The same author also suggests that Tony Blair, while in the past notable for his opposition to change, denies ever having had a 'closed mind' on the subject. Arguably, the need for this sudden and dramatic volte-face reflects the fact that there has been a shift in public morality, thereby allowing politicians some leeway to adopt a more pragmatic line in drug policy.

Political pressure

As the previous two sections have highlighted, politics and politicians play a leading role in the construction of British drug policy, and also have a significant influence in defining and redefining the problematic nature of illicit drug use. This is about to happen. If, as widely predicted, David Blunkett opts to reclassify cannabis, he will also reclassify the 'problematic' nature of that particular drug, effectively lowering its 'problematic' status. Building on the points made above relating to morality, shifts in policy such as this are difficult for politicians as they demonstrate weaknesses and fallibility in previous policy directions. In the same vein, many of today's 'drug liberals' were very recently adherents of the 'war on drugs' rhetoric. The relaxation of drug laws, often made for very good reasons, can be seen as an admission of having lost the 'war' and as a last-ditch attempt to salvage a decent peace. This makes recent developments dangerous as politicians are wary of being seen as weak and unable to control a 'problem'.

Politicians are also under pressure from a variety of other sources. Above, it was noted that Europe-wide there is a trend towards a relaxation of drug laws. This in itself is an overt and obvious political pressure. However, there may be a less obvious political pressure: that of the disengagement of the young from politics. As I write, *The World At One* (BBC Radio 4) is broadcasting an interview with the producer of *Pop Idol* in relation to employing a similar format to engage the young, predominantly disaffected voter. One of the reasons for such a device is the perceived irrelevance of politics to the lifestyle of the young, and the distance between them and politicians. Showing an awareness of issues – including the (contested) normalization of illicit drugs within the culture of the young – may be one tactic in the re-engagement process.

They are also under pressure from agencies and organizations charged with implementing policies. This is clearly the case with cannabis. The medical profession is keen to use the drug for medicinal purposes. From a critical perspective, we could argue that it is a case of history repeating itself. Just as the doctors were unwilling to allow widespread self-medication with opiates in the 1800s, they are now keen to 'own', and thus stop self-medication, of cannabis in the year 2002. The willingness and desire for this to happen on the part of the medical establishment have caused the politicians to allow trials, and, it seems, prescription of cannabis.

For some time now in certain police forces there has been a de facto liberalization of cannabis with the police being unwilling to enforce the law. There have also been reports and press briefings from police-based sources that have all called, or demonstrated tacit support, for a change in the law. This also puts pressure on politicians as they need to uphold the legitimacy of the law and law making and enforcing bodies. When there is a law that will not be enforced by those charged to do so, it ceases to be a credible law.

Finally, they are also under pressure from each other. Gauging swings in public opinion is a key skill, and failure to do so can lead to accusations of 'being out of touch'. It may be that there is a big enough groundswell of opinion in favour of the reclassification of cannabis that opposition to the movement becomes politically damaging. That is a risk few politicians are prepared to take. Thus, if we are looking critically at the proposed reclassification of cannabis, it is possible to say that it is a product of its time, shaped by forces that actively promote change now. In many ways, all drug policy since DORA and before could be subjected to the same examination and, arguably, the conclusion would be the same. What is interesting is that virtually the same set of pressures – economic, moral and political – that led to the criminalization of drug use in the first instance is now leading a change in approach.

In many respects, this situation is little different from elsewhere in Europe. As demonstrated, the current drug policy of both the Dutch and the Swedes is aimed at addressing a growth in the use of illicit drugs. Each nation state has developed a policy that reflects, not just their respective cultures, but also the economic and political climate as well. What we have in Europe is the supranational trend of a surge in the use of recreational drugs. In most countries there appears to be a pragmatic move towards the liberalization of soft drugs, a division in the market between soft and hard drugs and a move towards treatment and harm reduction policies, especially in terms of the user. Recent proposed changes in Britain simply reflect a larger, pan-European development. How long Sweden can remain the 'hard man' of Europe remains to be seen.

Final thoughts

It is a happy coincidence that this work is being written at the same time as Britain seems finally to be ready to engage in an honest and open debate about our future attitude towards drugs. It has been the intention of the book to enable the reader to understand that this particular aspect of social life is a complicated, multifaceted phenomenon, devoid of clear-cut answers. It is hoped that by now it will be clear that the weekend cannabis user settling down with their spliff after work on Friday evening, or a Saturday night clubber feeling the first rush of a 'dance drug' prior to leaving home, are the final link in a process that, among many other things, has its roots in the nineteenth century; has taxed the resources of a number of nation states; is part of a global industry almost without parallel in size; and represents an on-going battle between the needs of law and order and the needs of health agencies.

The sub-title of the book, *use and control,* sums up the problem in a nutshell. Use, I believe, will always be a part of society: people have seemingly always used mind-altering substances and show no desire to stop. The problem comes in attempts to control, or at least supervise use, a necessary but incredibly difficult task. As we have seen, it requires an almost impossible combination of national and international policy, political will, a shared perspective on morality and a conducive set of economic circumstances to even begin to control the production, distribution and consumption of drugs. In an uncertain milieu there is arguably just one certainty – dealing with the use of illicit drugs will be near the forefront of developments in all aspects of social policy.

Bibliography

Abercrombie, N., Hill, S. and Turner, B.S. (1988) *The Penguin Dictionary of Sociology* (2nd edn). Harmondsworth: Penguin.

Advisory Council on the Misuse of Drugs (ACMD) (1982) *Treatment and Rehabilitation*. London: HMSO.

Advisory Council on the Misuse of Drugs (ACMD) (1984) *Prevention*. London: HMSO.

Advisory Council on the Misuse of Drugs (ACMD) (1988) *Aids and Drug Misuse* (Part One). London: HMSO.

Advisory Council on the Misuse of Drugs (ACMD) (1989) *Aids and Drug Misuse* (Part Two). London: HMSO.

Advisory Council on the Misuse of Drugs (ACMD) (1995) *Volatile Substance Abuse: Report by the Advisory Council on the Misuse of Drugs*. London: Home Office.

Aldridge, J., Parker, H. and Measham, F. (1999) *Drug Trying and Drug Use Across Adolescence: a longitudinal study of young people's drug taking in two regions of northern England*. DPAS paper 1, London: DPAS.

Alvarez, E.H. (1995) 'Economic development, restructuring and the illicit drug sector in Bolivia and Peru: current policies', *Journal of Inter-American Studies and World Affairs* 37 (3), 25–149.

Andean Information Network (2001) *Bolivia: Economic and Demographic Information; Law 1008; Human Rights and the War on Drugs*. Online HTTP http://www.scbbs-bo.com. Items accessed on 18, 21 21 August 2001.

Anglin, M. and Hser, Y. (1990) 'Legal coercion and drug abuse treatment: research findings and policy implications', in Inciardi, J., ed., *Handbook of Drug Control in the United States*. Westport, Conn.: Greenwood.

Ashton, M. (1994) 'New drug strategies for England and Scotland', *Druglink*, November/December 1994.

Ashworth, A. (1998) *The Criminal Process: An Evaluative Study* (2nd edn). Oxford: Oxford University Press.

Balding, J. (1999) *Young People in 1998*. Exeter: Schools Health Education Unit.

Barclay, G.C., Tavares, C. and Prout, A. (1995) *Information on the Criminal Justice System 3*. London: Home Office.

Barton, A. (1999a) 'Sentenced to treatment? Criminal justice orders and the health service', *Critical Social Policy*, 19 (4), 463–83.

Barton, A. (1999b) 'Breaking the crime/drugs cycle: the birth of a new approach?', *The Howard Journal*, 38 (2), 144–57.

Barton, A. (2000) 'A tale of two projects: the growth and development of two Neighbourhood Watch schemes in South Wales', *Crime Prevention and Community Safety: An International Journal*, 2 (3), 7–16.

Barton, A. (2001) 'Devising substance use education programmes for parents: a case study from Wales', *Health Education*, 101 (6), 274–82.

Barton, A. and Quinn, C. (2001) 'The supremacy of joined up working: a Pandora's box for organisational identity?', *Public Policy and Administration*, 16 (2), 49–62.

Barton, A. and Quinn, C. (2002) 'Risk management of groups or respect for individuals? Issues for information sharing and confidentiality in Drug Treatment and Testing Orders', *Drugs: Education, Prevention, Policy*, 9 (1), 35–43.

Bean, P. (1994) 'The drug takers 1920–1970', in Coomber, R., ed., *Drugs and Drug Use in Society: A Critical Reader*. Greenwich: Greenwich University Press.

Bean, P. (2002) *Drugs and Crime*. Cullumpton: Willan Publishing.

Bennett, T. and Sibbett, R. (2000) 'Drug use amongst arrestees', *Home Office Research Findings no. 19*. Home Office: London.

Bergmark, A. (1998) 'Expansion and implosion: the story of drug treatment in Sweden', in Klingemann, H. and Hunt, G., eds, *Drugs, Demons, and Delinquents*. London: Sage Publications.

Bergmark, A. and Oscarsson, L. (1988) *Drug Abuse and Treatment: A Study of Social Conditions and Contextual Strategies*. Stockholm: Almquist & Wiksell International.

Berridge, V. (1978) 'Victorian opium eating: response to opiate use in nineteenth-century England', *Victorian Studies*, Summer, 437–61.

Berridge, V. (1989) 'Historical Issues', in MacGregor, S., ed., *Drugs and British Society: Responses to a Social Problem in the Eighties*. London: Routledge.

Berridge, V. and Edwards, G. (1981) *Opium and the People*. London: Allen Lane.

Blagg, H., Sampson, A., Pearson, G., Smith, D. and Stubbs, P. (1988) 'Inter-agency co-operation: rhetoric and reality', in Hope, T. and Shaw, M., eds, *Communities and Crime Reduction*. London: HMSO.

Boekhout van Solinge, T. (1999) 'Dutch drug policy in a European context', *Journal of Drug Issues*, 29 (3), 511–28. Pre-publication version. Online HTTP http://www.cedro-uva.org/lib/boekhout.dutch.html (accessed 11 February 2002).

Boliviaweb.com (2001) *Bolivia: Economic and Demographic Information*. Online HTTP http://www.boliviaweb.com (accessed 16 August 2001).

Bright, A. (2001) 'Changes called for in approaches to drug injectors', *Plymouth Evening Herald*, 23 June, p. 2.

BBC (2001) *Pain Drove Me to Pot*. Online HTTP. http.//www.bbc.co.uk. Accessed 19 December 2001.

British Medical Association (BMA) (1997) *The Misuse of Drugs*. Amsterdam: Harwood.

Bruun, K., Pan, L. and Rexed, I. (1975) *The Gentlemen's Club: International Control of Drugs and Alcohol*. Chicago: University of Chicago Press.

Burke, R. (1996) *The History of Child Protection in Britain: A Theoretical Reformulation*. Leicester: The Scarman Centre for the Study of Public Order (Crime, Order and Policing, Occasional Paper no. 9).

Bush, G. (1989) quoted in Hoffman, D. (1998) 'Proposal is Marked Shift from Border Interdiction', *Washington Post,* 27 May 1989.

Cabinet Office (1998) *Tackling Drugs to Build a Better Britain*. London: HMSO.

Caulkins, J.P., Johnson, B., Taylor, A. and Taylor, L. (1999) 'What drug dealers tell us about their costs of doing business', *Journal of Drug Issues* 29 (2), 323–40.

Caulkins, J.P. and Reuter, P. (1998) 'What price data tell us about drug markets', *Journal of Drugs Issues* 28 (3), 593–612.

Chaiken, J. and Chaiken, M. (1991) 'Drugs and predatory crime', in Tonry, M. and Wilson. J., eds, *Drugs and Crime: Crime Justice, Volume 13*. Chicago: Chicago University Press.

Chesneaux, J., Bastid, M. and Bergere, M.-C. (1976) *China from the Opium Wars to the 1911 Revolution*. New York: Pantheon.

Cicourel, A. (1964) *Methods and Measurement in Sociology*. London: Macmillan.

Cicourel, A. and Kitsuse, J. (1963) *The Education Decision-Makers*. New York: Bobbs-Merril.

Cleveland Police (2000) *Drugs*. Paper supplied to the chairman and members of the Cleveland Police Authority, 10 December 1999. Online. Available HTTP. http://www. drugtext.org/reports/ukpol/clp1.htm (accessed 24 May 2000).

Cochrane, A. (1993) 'Comparative approaches and social policy', in Cochrane, A. and Clarke, J., eds, *Comparing Welfare States: Britain in an International Context*. London: Sage Publications.

Cohen, S. (1971) *Folk Devils and Moral Panics*. Oxford: Martin Robertson.

Coid, J., Carvell, A. Kittler, Z., Healy, A. and Henderson, J. (2001) *Opiates, Criminal Behaviour and Methadone Treatment*. London: Home Office. HTTP available. http://www.homeoffice.gov.uk/rds/pdfs/crimebehav.pdf (accessed 29 October 2001).

Colebatch, H.K. (1998) *Policy*. Buckingham: Open University Press.

Coleman, J.C. (1992) 'The nature of adolescence', in Coleman, J.C. and Warren-Adamson, C., eds, *Youth Policy in the 1990s: The Way Forward*. London: Routledge.

Coleman, V. (1985) *The Story of Medicine*. London: Jill Norman.

Conservative Party (1992) *The Best Future for Britain*. London: Conservative Central Office Election manifesto.

Consroe, P. *et al.* (1997) 'The Perceived Effects of Smoked Cannabis on Patients with MS', *European Neurology* 38, 44–8.

Corkery, J.M. (2001) *Drug Seizures and Offender Statistics, United Kingdom 1999*, Home Office Statistical Bulletin, 5/01. London: Home Office.

Crawford, A. and Jones, M. (1996) 'Kirkholt Revisited: Some reflections of the transferability of crime prevention initiatives', *Howard Journal* 35 (1), 21–39.

Davidson, N. and Sturgeon-Adams, L. (1997) 'Participatory drug profiling: Developing a police contribution to *Tackling Drugs Together*', paper presented to the British Criminology Conference, Belfast 1997.

Davila, A. (1992) *Why People Grow Drugs*. Rome: Panos Institute.

Department of Health (DoH) (1991a) *Co-ordinating Drug Services: The Role of Regional and District Drug Advisory Committees*. London: Department of Health.

Department of Health (DoH) (1991b) *Drug Misuse and Dependence: Guidelines on Clinical Management*. London: HMSO.

Department of Health (DoH) (1995) *Tackling Drugs Together*. London: Department of Health.

Department of Health (DoH) (1999) *Drug Misuse and Dependence: Guidelines on Clinical Management*. London: Department of Health.

Department of Health (DoH) (2000) *Statistics from the Regional Drug Misuse Databases for the Six Months Ending March 2000*, Bulletin 2000/31. London: HMSO.

Department of Health and Social Security (DHSS) (1976) *Prevention and Health: Everybody's Business*. London: DHSS.

Department of Health and Social Security (DHSS) (1982) *Treatment and Rehabilitation*. London: HMSO.

Department of Health and Social Security (DHSS) (1984) *Guidelines of Good Clinical Practice in the Treatment of Drug Misuse*. London: HMSO.

De Quincy, T. (1977) *Confessions of an Opium Eater*. Harmondsworth: Penguin Classics. First published 1821.

Dorn, N. and South, N. (1994) 'The power behind practice: drug control and harm minimization in inter-agency and criminal law contexts', in Strang, J. and Gossop, M., eds, *Heroin Addiction and Drug Policy: The British System*. Oxford: Oxford University Press.

Dowds, L. and Redfern, J. (1994) *Drug Education amongst Teenagers: A 1992 British Crime Survey Analysis*. London: Home Office.

Downes, D. (1977) 'The drug addict as folk devil', in Rock, P., ed., *Drugs and Politics*. New Brunswick, NJ: Transaction Books.

Doyal, L. and Pennell, I. (1979) *The Political Economy of Health*. London: Pluto Press.

Drug Prevention Advisory Service (DPAS) (2001) *Let's Get Real: Communicating with the Public about Drugs*. London: Home Office.

DrugScope (2000) *UK Drug Situation 2000: The UK Report to the European Monitoring Centre for Drugs and Drug Addiction (EMCDDA)*. London: DrugScope.

Duin, N. and Sutcliffe, J. (1992) *A History of Medicine*. London: Simon & Schuster.

Edmunds, M., Hough, M., Turnbull, P.J. and May, T. (1999) *Doing Justice to Treatment: Referring Offenders to Drug Services*. London: DPAS, paper 2.

Edmunds, M., May, T. and Hough, M. (1997) 'Drugs interventions and the criminal justice system', paper presented to Evaluating Effectiveness: Drugs Prevention Research Conference, Liverpool 1997.

Edwards, G. (1981) 'The Background', in Edwards, G. and Busch, C., eds, *Drug Problems in Britain: A Review of Ten Years*. London: Academic Press.

Fellner, J. and Bretts, S. (1996) 'Bolivia under pressure', *Human Rights Watch*, 8 (4b), 1–33.

Francis, L.J. and Mullen, K. (1993) 'Religiosity and attitudes towards drug use among 13–15 year olds in England', *Addiction*, 88 (5), 665–72.

Franco, M. de and Godoy, R. (1992) 'The economic consequences of cocaine production in Bolivia', *Journal of Latin American Studies*, 24, 357–406.

Fraser, D. (1984) *The Evolution of the Welfare State* (2nd edn). Basingstoke: Macmillan.

Fuller, N. (1990) *Fundamental Economics*. Sevenoaks: Tudor Publishing.

Gamble, A. (1981) *An Introduction to Modern Social and Political Thought*. London: Macmillan.

Gamble, A. (1986) *Britain in Decline* (2nd edn). London: Macmillan.

Garland, D. (1996) 'The Limits of the Sovereign State: Strategies of crime control in contemporary society', *British Journal of Criminology*, 36 (4), 445–71.

George, V. and Wilding, P. (1992) *Ideology and Social Welfare* (2nd edn). London: Routledge.

Gerada, C. and Farrell, M. (1998) 'Shared care', in Robertson, R., ed., *Management of Drug Users in the Community: A Practical Handbook*. London: Edward Arnold.

Giddens, A. (1986) *Sociology: A Brief but Critical Introduction*. Cambridge: Polity Press.

Gilling, D. (1994) 'Multi-agency crime prevention in Britain: the problem of combining situational and social strategies', *Crime Prevention Studies* 3, 238–48.

Gilman, M. (1999) 'Beyond opiates . . . and into the '90s', in Coomber, R., ed., *Drugs and Drug Use in Society: A Critical Reader*. Greenwich: Greenwich University Press.

Ginsberg, N. (1993) 'Sweden: the social democratic case', in Cochrane, A. and Clarke, J., eds, *Comparing Welfare States: Britain in an International Context*. London: Sage Publications.

Gladstone, D. (1995) 'The welfare state and the state of welfare', in Gladstone, D., ed., *British Social Welfare: Past, Present and Future*. London: UCL Press.

Goddard, E. and Higgins, V. (1999a) *Smoking, Drinking and Drug Use among Young Teenagers in 1998: Volume 1: England*. London: HMSO.

Goddard, E. and Higgins, V. (1999b) *Smoking, Drinking and Drug Use among Young Teenagers in 1998: Volume 2: Scotland*. London: HMSO.

Goodchild, S. (2002) 'Cannabis is now just a signature away (over to you Mr Blunkett)', *Independent on Sunday*, 10 March, p. 1.

Goode, E. and Ben-Yehuda, N. (1994) *Moral Panics: The Social Construction of Deviance*. Oxford: Blackwell.

Gossop, M. and Grant, M. (1990) *Preventing and Controlling Drug Abuse*. Geneva: World Health Organization.

Gould, A. (1999) 'A drug free Europe? Sweden on the offensive', *Druglink* 14 (2), 12–14.

Grapendall, M. (1992) 'Drugs and crime in an accommodating social context: the situation in Amsterdam', *Contemporary Drug Problems*, Summer, 303–26.

Grilly, D.M. (1998) *Drugs and Human Behaviour*. Boston: Allyn & Bacon.

GW Pharmaceuticals (2001) *Home Page and Related Links*. Online HTTP, http://www.gwpharm.com (accessed 19 December 2001).

Hallett, C. and Birchall, E. (1992) *Co-ordination and Child Protection: A Review of the Literature*. London: HMSO.

Halpert, B. (1982) 'Antecedents', in Rogers, D.L. and Whetten, D.A., eds, (1986) *Inter-organisational Co-ordination: Theory, Research and Implementation*. Iowa: Iowa State University Press.

Ham, C. (1992) *Health Policy in Britain: The Politics and Organisation of the National Health Service* (3rd edn). London: Macmillan.

Hammersley, R., Forsyth, A., Morrison, V. and Davis, J.B. (1989) 'The relationship between crime and opioid use', *British Journal of Addiction* 84 (9), 1029–43.

Hammersley R., Forsyth A. and Lavelle T. (1990) 'The criminality of new drug users in Glasgow', *British Journal of Addiction*. 85 (12), 1583–94.

Harding, G. (1998) 'Pathologising the Soul: The construction of a nineteenth-century analysis of opiate addiction', in Coomber, R., ed., *The Control of Drugs and Drug Users: Reason or Reaction?* Amsterdam: Harwood.

Hardy, T. (1981 [1880]) *The Trumpet Major*. Harmondsworth: Penguin Classics.

Harrison, P. (1985) *Inside the Inner City*. Harmondsworth: Penguin.

Harvey, J. (1998) *Intermediate Economics*. London: Blackwell.

Haste, H. (1993) *The Sexual Metaphor*. London: Harvester Wheatsheaf.

Hay, G. (1998) 'Estimating the Prevalence of Substance Misuse', in Bloor, M. and Wood, F., eds, *Addictions and Problem Drug Use: Issues in Behaviour, Policy and Practice*. Research Highlights in *Social Work* 33. London: Jessica Kingsley Publishers.

Health Education Authority (1995) *D-mag*. London: ISDD.

Heuston, J., McNeill, A., McVey, D. and McLean, D. (1996) *Drug Realities: National Drugs Campaign Survey (Summary of Key Findings)*. London: Health Education Authority.

Hill, M. (1997) *The Policy Process in the Modern State* (3rd edn). Hemel Hempstead: Prentice Hall.

HMSO (1985) *Tackling Drug Misuse*. London: HMSO.

Hobsbawm, E. (1969) *Industry and Empire*. Harmondsworth: Penguin.

Home Office (1997) *Drug Treatment and Testing Orders: Background and Issues for Consultation*. London: Home Office.

Home Office (2001) *Blunkett to Focus on the Menace of Hard Drugs*. London: Home Office. Press Release.

Hooker, P. (1996) *Chinese Cultural Studies – Opium Wars*. Online. Available HTTP: http://www.accc6.its.brooklyn.cuny.edu (accessed 21 March 2001).

Hopkins, N. (2001) 'Police extend softly-softly pilot scheme on cannabis possession', *Guardian*, 29 December.

Hough, M. (1996) *Drugs Misuse and the Criminal Justice System: A review of the literature*. London: Home Office.

Howard, R. (1997) 'The Service Provider's Perspective', in Braggins, J., ed., *Tackling Drugs Together: One Year On*. London: Institute for the Study and Treatment of Delinquency.

Howard, R., Beadle, P. and Maitland, J. (1993) *Across the Divide: Building Community Partnerships to Tackle Drug Misuse*, report to the Department of Health. London: Department of Health.

Howarth, G. (1999) 'A view from government', in Marlow, A. and Pearson, G., eds, *Young People, Drugs and Community Safety*. Lyme Regis: Russell House Publishing.

Hudson, B. (1987) 'Collaboration in social welfare: a framework for analysis', *Policy and Politics* 15 (3), 175–82.

Hutchinson, J. (2001) 'The role of doctors in treating drug dependency'. Unpublished papers. Glamorgan: University of Glamorgan.

Hyde, A., Treacy, M., Whitaker, T., Abanuaza, P.S. and Knox, B. (2000) 'Young people's perceptions of and experiences with drugs: findings from an Irish study', in *Health Education Journal* (59), 180–8.

Institute for the Study of Drug Dependency (1995) *Drug Misuse in Britain*. London: Institute for the Study of Drug Dependency.

James, A. and Raine, J. (1998) *The New Politics of Criminal Justice*. Longman: London.

Johnson, C. (1991) *The Economy Under Mrs Thatcher: 1979–1990*. Harmondsworth: Penguin.

Jones, L.J. (1994) *The Social Context of Health and Health Work*. London: Macmillan.

Kaal, H. (1998) 'Do trends in criminal justice statistics reflect changing attitudes in the English criminal justice system toward drug offences?', paper presented to the 9th International Conference on the Reduction of Drug Related Harm, São Paulo, Brazil, 15–19th March 1998.

Kahn, S. (2001) 'Mothers March To Clean Up Needle City', *Observer*, 8 April.

Kaplan, J. (1983) *The Hardest Drug: Heroin and Public Policy*. Chicago: University of Chicago Press.

Kemshall, H. (2002) *Risk, Social Policy and Welfare*. Milton Keynes: Open University Press.

Kidd, B.A. and Sykes, R.A.D. (1999) 'UK policy', in Stark, C., Kidd, B.A., and Sykes, R.A.D., eds, *Illegal Drug Use in the United Kingdom: Prevention, Treatment and Enforcement*. Aldershot: Ashgate.

Kleiman, M.A.R. and Young, R.M. (1995) 'The factors of production in retail drug dealing', *Urban Affairs Review*, 30 (5), 731–48.

Kohn, M. (1992) *Dope Girls: The Birth of the British Drug Underground*. London: Lawrence & Wishart.

Kort, M. de (1996) 'A short history of drugs in the Netherlands', in Leuw, E.and Haen Marshall, I., eds, *Between Prohibition and Legalisation: The Dutch Experiment in Drug Policy*. London: Sage Publications.

Kraan, D. J. (1996) 'An economical view on Dutch drugs policy', in Leuw, E. and Haen Marshall, I., eds, *Between Prohibition and Legalisation: The Dutch Experiment in Drug Policy*. London: Sage Publications.

Lawrence, C. (1994) *Medicine and the Making of Modern Britain 1700–1920*. London: Routledge.

Leathard, A., ed. (1994) *Going Inter-Professional: Working Together for Health and Welfare*. London: Routledge.

Leathard, A. (2000) *Health Care Provision: Past, Present and into the Twenty-first Century,* (2nd edn). Cheltenham: Stanley Thornes.

Leech, K. (1991) 'The junkies' doctors and the London drug scene in the 1960s: some remembered fragments', in Whynes, D. and Bean P., eds, *Policing and Prescribing*. London: Macmillan.

Leibfried, S. (1993) 'Toward a European Welfare State', in Jones, C., ed., *New Perspectives on the Welfare State in Europe*. London: Routledge.

Leitner, M., Shapland, J. and Wiles, P. (1993) *Drugs Use and Prevention: The Views and Habits of the General Public*. London: HMSO.

Leng, R., Taylor, R. and Wasik, M. (1998) *Blackstone's Guide to the Crime and Disorder Act 1998*. London: Blackstone Press.

Lenke, L. and Olsson, B. (1996) 'Sweden: zero tolerance wins the argument?', in Dorn, N., Jepsen, J. and Savona, E., eds, *European Drug Policies and Enforcement*. London: Macmillan.

Leuw, E. (1996) 'Initial construction and development of the official Dutch drug policy', in Leuw, E. and Haen Marshall, I., eds, *Between Prohibition and Legalisation: The Dutch Experiment in Drug Policy*. London: Sage Publications.

Lewis, R. (1994) 'Flexible hierarchies and dynamic disorder – the trading and distribution of illicit heroin in Britain and Europe 1970–1990', in Strang, J. and Gossop, M., eds, *Heroin Addiction and Drug Policy: The British System*. Oxford: Oxford University Press.

Lifeline (1993) *A Trip Around Manchester With Peanut Pete*. Manchester: Lifeline.

Lifeline (1994) *Claire and Jose Get Off Their Cake*. Manchester: Lifeline.

London, M., O'Regan, T., Aust, P. and Stockford, A. (1990) 'Poppy tea drinking in East Anglia', *British Journal of Addiction* 85 (10), 1345–47.

Lowes, P.D. (1966) *The Genesis of International Narcotics Control*. Geneva: Libraire Droz.

McDermott, P. (1998) 'Contemporary Drug Taking Problems', in Robertson, R., ed., *Management of Drug Users in the Community: A Practical Handbook*. London: Edward Arnold.

MacDonald, S.B. (1989) *Mountain High, White Avalanche: Cocaine Power in the Andean States and Panama*. Washington, DC: The Center for Strategic and International Studies.

MacFarlane, A., MacFarlane, M., and Robson, P. (1996) *The User: The Truth about Drugs*. Oxford: Oxford University Press.

Marks, P. et al (1973) 'Public attitudes to drug taking: short report on work carried out by the OPCS for the Home Office', unpublished.

Matthews, R. (1995) 'Dealing with drugs: a new philosophy?' (introduction), in Martin, C., ed., *Dealing with Drugs: A New Philosophy?* Report of a conference organized by the Institute for the Study and Treatment of Delinquency, 1 March 1995. London: Institute for the Study of Drug Dependency.

Mawby, R. and Walklate, S. (1994) *Critical Victimology*. London: Sage Publications.

May, T. (1997) *Social Research: Issues, Methods and Process* (2nd edn). Buckingham: Open University Press.

Mayhew, P. (2000) 'Research the state of crime', in King, R.D. and Wincup, E., eds, *Doing Research on Crime and Justice*. Oxford: Oxford University Press.

Mazarolle, P. (2000) 'Understanding illicit drug use: lessons from developmental theory', in Simpson, S.S., ed., *Of Crime and Criminality: The Use of Theory in Everyday Life*. Thousand Oaks, CA: Pine Forge Press.

Measham, F. and Aldridge, J. (2000) *Dancing on Drugs*. London: Free Association Books.

Measham, F., Parker, H. and Aldridge, J. (1998) *Starting, Switching, Slowing and Stopping*. A Report for the Drugs Prevention Initiative Programme, paper 21. London: DPI.

Michael, A. (1998) Keynote Speech to the Social Policy/Criminal Justice: Compatible or in Conflict Conference. Cardiff, May 1998.

Midwinter, E. (1994) *The Development of Social Welfare in Britain*. Milton Keynes: Open University Press.

Miller, I. (2001) 'Customs let cannabis smugglers walk free', *Daily Mirror*, 31 May.

Minestero de Capitalizacion, Republica de Bolivia (1996) *Bolivia: Economic and Demographic Information*. Online HTTP http://www.boliviaweb.com (accessed 16 August 2001).

MORI (1998) *Modern Britain*. Survey conducted for the *Independent on Sunday*.

Morrison, S. (1997) 'The dynamics of illicit drug production: future sources and threats', *Crime, Law and Social Change*, 27, 121–38.

Mott, J. (1994) 'Notification and the Home Office', in Strang, J. and Gossop, M., eds, *Heroin Addiction and Drug Policy: The British System*. Oxford: Oxford University Press.

Mott, J. and Bean, P. (1998) 'The development of drug control in Britain', in Coomber, R., ed., *The Control of Drugs and Drug Users: Reason or Reaction?* Amsterdam: Harwood.

Mott, J. and Mirlees-Black, C. (1993) *Self-Reported Drug Misuse in England and Wales: Main Findings from the 1992 British Crime Survey*. Home Office Research and Statistics Department, Research Findings no. 7. London: Home Office.

Nadelman, E.A. (1989) 'Drug prohibition in the United States: costs, consequences, and alternatives', *Science*, 245, September, 937–47.

Navarro, V. (1979) *Medicine under Capitalism*. London: Croom Helm.

Newburn, T. and Elliott, J. (1999) *Risk and Responses: Drug Prevention and Youth Justice*. London: DPAS, paper 3.

Nycander, S. (1998) 'Ivan Bratt: the man who saved Sweden from prohibition', *Addiction* 93 (1), 17–25.

Office of National Drug Control Policy (1997) *Pulse Check: National Trends in Drug Abuse*. Washington, DC: ONDCP.

Olsson, B. (1994) *The Background of the Drug Problem*. Swedish Council for Information on Alcohol and Other Drugs: Stockholm.

Painter, J. (1994) *Bolivia and Coca: A Study in Dependency*. London: Lynn Reiner Publishers.

Parker, H., Bakx, K. and Newcombe, R. (1988) *Living with Heroin*. Milton Keynes: Open University Press.

Parker, H., Measham, F., and Aldridge, J. (1995) *Drugs Futures: Changing Patterns of Drug Use Amongst English Youth*. London: Institute for the Study of Drug Dependency.

Parker, H., Aldridge, J. and Measham, F. (1998) *Illegal Leisure: The Normalisation of Adolescent Recreational Drug Use*. London: Routledge.

Parssinen, T.M. (1983) *Secret Passions, Secret Remedies: Narcotic Drugs in British Society 1820–1830*. Philadelphia, PA: Manchester University Press.

Patterson, S. (2002) 'Cocaine nation', *Observer*, 21 April.

Pearson, G. (1999) 'Drug policy dilemmas: partnership, social exclusion and targeting resources', in Marlow, A. and Pearson, G., eds, *Young People, Drugs and Community Safety*. Lyme Regis: Russell House Publishing.

Plant, M. (1994) 'Drugs and adolescence', in Strang, J. and Gossop, M., eds, *Heroin Addiction and Drug Policy: The British System*. Oxford: Oxford University Press.

Plymouth Evening Herald (2001) '100,000 reasons why we must rid Plymouth of drugs', 23 July.

Preeble, E. and Casey, J.J. (1969) 'Taking care of business: the heroin user's life on the streets', *International Journal of the Addictions* 4, 1–24.

Preston, A. (1992) *The Methadone Handbook*, Bournemouth: Andrew Preston in association with CADAS, West Dorset Mental Health Trust.

Quinney, R. (1970) *The Social Reality of Crime*. Boston: Little Brown.

Ramsay, M. and Partridge, S. (1999) *Drug Misuse Declared: Results of the 1998 British Crime Survey*. London: Home Office.

Ramsay, M. and Percy, A. (1996) *Drug Misuse Declared: Results of the 1994 British Crime Survey*. London: Home Office.

Ramsay, M. and Spiller, J. (1997) *Drug Misuse Declared: Results of the 1996 British Crime Survey*. London: Home Office.

Read, A. (1995) 'Why prescribe? The philosophy behind good practice', *Release*, (8), 1–3.

Reiner, R. (2000) *The Politics of the Police* (3rd edn). Oxford: Oxford University Press.

Rimmer, S. (1997) '*Tackling Drugs Together*: an overview', in Braggins, J., ed., *Tackling Drugs Together: One Year On*. London: Institute for the Study and Treatment of Delinquency.

Robertson, I. (1975) Personal communication to Berridge, V. (1978) in 'Victorian opium eating: response to opiate use in nineteenth century England', *Victorian Studies*, Summer 1978, 437–61.

Robertson, R. (2000) 'New British guidelines on the clinical management of drug misuse and dependence', *Addiction* 95 (3), 325–6.

Robins, L. (1973) *The Vietnam Drug User Returns*, Washington, DC: US Government Printing Office.

Robson, P. (1994) *Forbidden Drugs: Understanding Drugs and Why People Take Them*. Oxford: Oxford University Press.

Ruggerio, V. and South, N. (1995) *Eurodrugs: Drug Use, Markets and Trafficking in Europe*. London: UCL Press.

Runciman, B. (1999) *Drugs and the Law: Report of the Independent Inquiry into the Misuse of Drugs Act 1971*. London: Police Foundation.

Sage, C. (1987) 'The cocaine economy in Bolivia: its development and current importance', *Corruption Reform* 2, 99–109.

Sagel-Grande, I. (1997) 'Drugs policy in the Netherlands: continuity and change', in Braggins, J., ed., *Tackling Drugs Together: One Year On*. London: Institute for the Study and Treatment of Delinquency.

Sampson, R. and Laub, J. (1993) *Crime in the Making: Pathways and Turning Points Through Life*. Cambridge, MA: Harvard University Press.

Self, W. (1992) 'Drug dealer by appointment to HM Government', *Observer*, 13 September.

Shams, R. (1992) 'The drugs economy and anti-drug policy in developing countries', *Intereconomics*, May/June, 139–44.

Shapiro, H. (1999) 'Dances with drugs', in South, N., ed., *Drugs: Culture, Controls and Everyday Life*, London: Sage Publications.

Shiner, M. and Newburn, T. (1996) *The Youth Awareness Programme: An Evaluation of a Peer Education Drugs Project*. Home Office Research Study, 151. London: Home Office.

Shiner, M. and Newburn, T. (1997) 'Definitely, maybe not? The normalisation of recreational drug use amongst young people', *American Journal of Sociology* 31 (3), 511–29.

Silverman, L.P. and Spurill, N. L. (1977) 'Urban crime and the price of heroin', *Journal of Urban Economics* 4, 80–103.

Simmons, J. (2002) *Crime in England and Wales 2001/02*. London: Home Office.

Smith, M.L. (1992) *Why People Grow Drugs*. London: Panos.

Social Policy Association (1997) 'Findings: young people and drugs', *Social Policy Research* 133, November, 1–6.

South, N. (1995) 'Innovation and consolidation: new and old directions in current drug control policy', in Martin, C., ed., *Dealing with Drugs: A New Philosophy?* Report of a conference organized by the Institute for the Study and Treatment of Delinquency, 1 March. London: ISTD.

South, N. (1997) 'Drugs: use, crime and control', in Maguire, M., Morgan, R. and Reiner, R., eds, *The Oxford Handbook of Criminology* (2nd edn). Oxford: Clarendon Press.

South, N. and Teeman, D. (1999) 'Young people, drugs and community life: messages from the research', in Marlow, A. and Pearson, G., eds, *Young People, Drugs and Community Safety*. Lyme Regis: Russell House Publishing.

Standing Conference on Drug Abuse (SCODA) (1998) *The Right Choice: Guidance on Selecting Drug Education Materials for Schools*. London: SCODA.

Standing Conference on Drug Abuse (SCODA) (1999) *The Right Approach: Quality Standards in Drug Education*. London: SCODA.

Stearn, P.N. (1975) *European Society in Upheaval: Social History since 1750* (2nd edn). London: Macmillan.

Steiner, R. (1998) 'Colombia's income from the drug trade', *World Development*, 26 (6), 1013–31.

Stimson, G. (1987) 'The war on heroin', in Dorn, N. and South, N., eds, *A Land Fit for Heroin: Drug Policies, Prevention and Practice*. London: Macmillan.

Strang, J. and Gossop, M. (1994) 'The "British System": visionary anticipation or masterly inactivity?' in Strang, J. and Gossop, M., eds, *Heroin Addiction and Drug Policy: The British System*. Oxford: Oxford University Press.

Strang, J., Griffiths, P., Powis, B. and Gossop, M. (1992) 'First use of heroin: changes in the route of administration over time', *British Medical Journal* 304, 1222–3.

Strang, J., Ruben, S., Farrell, M. and Gossop, M. (1994) 'Prescribing heroin and other injectable drugs', in Strang, J. and Gossop, M., eds, *Heroin Addiction and Drug Policy: The British System*. Oxford: Oxford University Press.

Sun (1989) 'Spaced Out', 26 June.

Sutherland, E. and Cressey, D. (1970) *Principles of Criminology*. New York: Reynolds.

Sutton, S. and Maynard, A. (1993) 'Are drug policies based on "fake" statistics?', *Addiction* 88 (4), 455–8.

Swedish National Institute for Public Health (1998) *Swedish Drug Policy*. Online HTTP http://www.hnnsweden.com/strategy.htm (accessed 21 February 2002).

Taylor, A.J.P. (1992) *English History 1914–1945*. Oxford: Oxford University Press.

Thane, P. (1996) *Foundations of the Welfare State*. London: Longman.

Thornton, S. (1995) *Club Cultures: Music, Media and Subcultural Capital*. Oxford: Polity Press.

Thurlow, R. (1994) *The Secret State: British Internal Security in the Twentieth Century*. Oxford: Blackwell.

Tobias, G. (1972) *Victorian Life: The Changing Nature of City Living*. London: Edward Arnold.

Toynbee, P. and Walker, D. (2001) *Did Things Get Better? An Audit of Labour's Successes and Failures*. Harmondsworth: Penguin.

Travis, A. (2001) 'Up in smoke', *Guardian* (Society Section), 12 December.

Trebach, A. (1982) *The Heroin Solution*. New Haven, Conn.: Yale University Press.

Tullis, LM. (1995) *Unintended Consequences: Illegal Drugs and Drug Policies in Nine Countries*. Boulder, Col.: Lynn Reiner Publishers.

Turk, A.T. (1969) *Criminality and Legal Order*. London: Rand McNally.

United Nations (2000) *World Economic and Social Survey 2000*. New York: United Nations.

United Nations Educational, Scientific and Cultural Organization (UNESCO) (1999) *Source*, no. 111.

United Nations International Drug Control Programme (UNDCP) (1996) *Economic and Social Consequences of Drug Abuse and Illicit Trafficking*. Geneva: UNDCP.

United Nations International Drug Control Programme (2001) *Global Illicit Trends*. Geneva: UNDCP.

Wagstaff, A. (1989) 'Economic aspects of illicit drug markets and drug enforcement policies', *British Journal of Addiction* 84, 1173–82.

Walker, W.O. (1991) *Opium and Foreign Policy: The Anglo-American Search for Order in Asia, 1912–1954*. London: Chapel Hill.

Wallace, G. and Eastham, G. (1994) *A Survey of Drug Use and Offending in Plymouth*. Harbour Centre: Plymouth.

Warner, K.E. (1993) 'Legalizing drugs: lessons from (and about) economics', in Bayer, R. and Oppenheimer, G.M., eds, *Confronting Drugs Policy: Illicit Drugs in a Free Society*. Cambridge: Cambridge University Press.

Wasik, M., Gibbons, T. and Redmayne, M. (1999) *Criminal Justice: Text and Materials*. London: Longman.

Watson, J.E. (1984) *Medical-Surgical Nursing and Related Physiology*. London: Saunders.

Weatherburn, D. and Lind, B. (1997) 'The impact of law enforcement activity on a heroin market', *Addiction* 92 (5), 557–69.

Weber, M. (1976) *The Protestant Ethic and the Spirit of Capitalism*. London: Allen and Unwin.

Weiss, J. (1981) 'Substance vs. symbol in administrative reform: the case of human services coordination', *Policy Analysis* 7, 1, 21–45.

Welsh Assembly (2000) *Tackling Substance Misuse in Wales*. Cardiff: The Welsh Assembly.

Welsh Drug and Alcohol Unit (1998) *A Strategic Prevention Action Plan for Drugs and Alcohol in Wales*. Cardiff: Welsh Office.

Westermeyer, R.W. (1998) *Reducing Harm: A Very Good Idea*. Online. HTTP http://www.cts.com/crash/habsmrt/harm.html (accessed 17 December 1998).

Whetten, D.A. (1981) 'Interorganisational relations: a review of the field', *Journal of Higher Education* 52 (1), 1–28.

Whitaker, A. and McLeod, J. (1998) 'Care in the community', in Robertson, R., ed., *Management of Drug Users in the Community: A Practical Handbook*. London: Edward Arnold.

Wilde, O. (1986) *The Picture of Dorian Gray*. London: Marshall Cavendish.

Williams, S. and Milani, C. (1999) 'The globalization of the drug trade', *Sources*, (111), April. Paris: UNESCO.

Wincup, E. and Bayliss, R. (2001) 'Problematic substance use and the young homeless: implications for health and well being', *Youth and Policy*, (71), Spring, 44–58.

World Bank (2001a) *Bolivia at a Glance*. Online. HTTP. http://www.worldbank.org.data/countrydata/ (accessed 21 August 2001).

World Bank (2001b) *Bolivia*. HTTP online. http://www.worldbank.org

Young, J. (1971) *The Drug Takers: The Social Meaning of Drug Use*. London: Paladin.

Index